DIVINE BECOMING

DIVINE BECOMING
RETHINKING JESUS AND INCARNATION

CHARLENE P. E. BURNS

Fortress Press
Minneapolis

To my son,

Thomas Flynt Burns

WHOSE LIFE HAS PRESENTED THE GREATEST OF BLESSINGS
AND OPPORTUNITIES FOR GROWTH

∾

Book design: Sarah Anondson
Cover design: Joseph Bonyata
Cover image: "Christ Among the Children," by Emil Nolde, 1910, gift of Dr. W. R. Valentiner, The Museum of Modern Art, New York. Used by permission.

ISBN 0-8006-3278-8

Library of Congress Cataloging-in-Publication Data is available upon request.

The paper used in this publication meets the minimum requirements of American National Standard for Information Sciences — Permanence of Paper for Printed Library Materials, ANSI Z329.48-1984.

Manufactured in the U.S.A.   AF 1-3278

06   05   04   03   02   1   2   3   4   5   6   7   8   9   10

CONTENTS

PREFACE

> Therefore, following the holy fathers, we all with one accord
> teach men to acknowledge one and the same Son, our Lord
> Jesus Christ, at once complete in Godhead and complete in
> manhood, truly God and truly man.
>
> COUNCIL OF CHALCEDON, 451 C.E.

The problem of how to understand the figure of Jesus has plagued
Christianity from the outset. It is one of history's great ironies that
controversy over Jesus' identity has at times flared so intensely that the
foundations of the faith were threatened. In fact, contention over the
divinity and humanity of Jesus during the early centuries made
Christianity seem unfaithful to Jesus' message. The formative years
(especially the fourth century) were turbulent times when believers
and theologians literally took christological debate to the streets. Exile,
excommunication, imprisonment, riots, church burnings, military
maneuvers, political machinations, covert operations aimed at dis-
crediting prominent bishops, even beatings and torture: all were
employed by devout Christians campaigning over what was to become
the orthodox Christian interpretation of the incarnation, formalized at
Chalcedon in 451 C.E.[1] It is an embarrassment to the faith that so much
violence was employed in working out the doctrine of God incarnate.

Although less prone to physical violence these days, theologians in the past two centuries have again tackled the issue with great energy. In a reversal of history, this time the outcome is potentially more threatening to the faith than the process. There is a growing consensus that the christological enterprise as traditionally undertaken is bankrupt. In the words of one prominent thinker, "the dogma of Jesus' two natures, one human and the other divine, has proved to be incapable of being explicated in any satisfactory way."[2] If this is so, Christianity may well be, like the fabled emperor, doctrinally naked with delusions of being clothed in finery. In this book I hope to demonstrate that Christianity is in fact fully clad in the raiment of the divine. The problem with christology lies not so much in the claim it makes but in theology's tendency to privilege philosophy over other forms of reflection in speech about incarnation. I believe we can explicate the doctrine satisfactorily through appeal not to philosophy but to the social sciences.

The intellectual journey that led me to write this book began during Easter break, 1992, in a Tokyo book store. Browsing for something to read during the trip home, I picked up *The Dance of Life: The Other Dimension of Time* by anthropologist Edward T. Hall. Although it cost 1880 yen (almost twice what it would have cost at home), its thesis was so captivating that I rationalized the purchase. The book promised to divulge "the ways in which individuals in a culture are tied together by invisible threads of rhythm."[3] This was my introduction to the fascinating phenomenon of entrainment, the human ability to enter into what amounts to unconscious states of rhythmic physiological synchrony with others. It would be five years, however, before meditations on this intriguing human capacity for sharing in the lifeworlds of others began to bear theological fruit.

Intimations of the connection between entrainment and empathy first beckoned me when reading Max Scheler's work on sympathy. His description of sympathy as an act of self-transcendence distinct from emotional contagion, shared feelings, or identification, resonated with the concept of entrainment.[4] Just how that might be the case and what the theological implications were did not become clear until I undertook a full-scale exploration of the role of empathy and sympathy in healing, human development, and psychoanalysis. I traced the development of empathy as a concept through Sigmund Freud, D. W. Winnicott, Heinz Kohut, to Daniel Stern, and there it all fell into place. It was then a fairly straight path from that point to this book, in which I show how it is that Christianity's talk about divine and human natures in Jesus can indeed be satisfactorily explicated for believers today.

The thesis of this book has been powerfully shaped by the participation of others in my own life, personally and professionally. I must first mention Linda Corson, whose steadfast friendship and confidence have kept me going even when the future looked dark. Next, the Reverend Robert Manning, deceased, my first theological mentor. His brilliant intellect and deep faith worked together in life to show those who knew him that Christian truth is forged in the heat of faith-filled inquiry. I owe a debt of gratitude to the Reverend Joseph Way and his wife, Joanne, who gave me Easter in its deepest meaning. And thanks to those whose sustained participation in my life has shaped its outworking—my parents, Charles and Jackie Embrey; my sisters, Linda, Sharon, Vickie, Katrina, and their families. Finally, I give thanks to and for my son Thomas, to whom this book is dedicated. Motherhood, more than any other encounter, has taught me how humbling and awesomely rewarding participation in the life of another is meant to be. Had this admirable young man not been a part of my life, I doubt the thesis of this book would have come to me as it did.

There are also many in the professional realm to whom I owe thanks. I can single out only a few of those who have shaped my theological mindset: first, Sallie McFague and Peter Hodgson for their careful reading and comments. They serve as role models for my own theological aspirations. Also, Volney Gay, who understood where I wanted to go with this right from the start; Gene TeSelle, especially for his review of the patristics material; and of course, Fortress Press. Thanks to the production staff for their skill in putting together the final work; and especially to my editor, Michael West, whose humor and professionalism helped smooth the rough spots in the process and in the work itself.

1

Was Jesus God?

> The past can only be preserved in its purity by someone who
> accepts responsibility for the future, who preserves in so far as
> [s]he overcomes.
>
> KARL RAHNER, *God, Christ, Mary, and Grace*

Was Jesus God? Bookshelves today brim with texts aimed at revealing the truth about Jesus. The variety of theories about him can be overwhelming. Was Jesus a Jewish rabbi who offered nothing more than a reinterpretation of his received faith? A Jewish mystic? Was he a Cynic philosopher? Was he a political revolutionary, a Zealot intent on overthrowing Roman rule in Palestine? Was he a Jewish eschatological prophet, concerned with the end of worldly things and the inauguration of God's reign on earth? A magician? A prophet of the divine Sophia/Woman-Wisdom? An Essene Jew of the Qumran sect? Or perhaps the leader of the Qumran sect, the Teacher of Righteousness himself? As we survey the dizzying array of interpretations of this man who lived and taught two millennia ago, an important theological question begins to form: where, in all of this, is a place for the Christian tradition's historic understanding of Jesus as the messiah, the Son of God, God come to earth in human form to redeem and offer salvation to all?

The search for the historical truth behind the Gospels is a thoroughly modern problem. With roots in the Renaissance, the search gained momentum with the Enlightenment's turn to science and the growing belief that human reason could offer an explanation for all the mysteries of life. Before the Enlightenment, questions of historical truth were virtually nonexistent in theological endeavors. Since the Enlightenment, it has become virtually impossible to avoid the questions. Baruch Spinoza's (1632–1677) argument against miracles, the English Deists' denial of revelation, and David Hume's (1711–1776) empiricist skepticism, which demolished the foundations of knowing, were very influential in paving the way for the search for historical proofs of Christian claims.

The writings of Herman S. Reimarus (1694–1768), unpublished until after his death, mark the start of the first real quest for the historical Jesus and the concomitant scrutiny of Christian texts. Reimarus was the first to distinguish between what is referred to today as the Jesus of history and the Christ of faith. He argued that Jesus had been a devout Jew who had no thoughts of himself as divine and that the authors of the Gospels knew they were writing theological interpretations and had no intention of writing history. The search for the historical truth behind the religious fiction of the Gospels was on.

David Friedrich Strauss's 1835 *The Life of Jesus Critically Examined* was one of the most influential nineteenth-century works of theological reflection.[1] He argued that any text as riddled with inconsistencies and depictions of events that so obviously violate the laws of nature as the Christian testament cannot possibly be historical. He argued for an understanding of the texts as sacred myth and drew on philosopher G. W. F. Hegel's (1770–1831) ideas to explain incarnation as a stage in the evolution of world history toward union with God. Many followed Strauss's lead, and the nineteenth century saw the development of a number of variations on these themes. The ardor of the search to uncover the "real" Jesus was quelled for a time by Albert Schweitzer's devastating critique of prior efforts in 1906. His own reconstruction portrayed Jesus as a disappointed apocalyptic prophet who went to his death to deliver the Jews from oppression, expecting that he could "force" divine intervention through this act. *The Quest of the Historical Jesus: A Critical Study of Its Progress from Reimarus to Wrede* was deeply skeptical about our historical knowledge of Jesus and also raised a number of new problems for theology.[2] For example, if Jesus was God incarnate, how could he have been mistaken in his predictions of the end times?

In the early years of the twentieth century, theologians frustrated by problems like these continued to dampen enthusiasm for the search. They often argued that historical data about the man Jesus are irrelevant to faith. Rudolf Bultmann (1884–1976), for one, summarized the core issues in his *Jesus Christ and Mythology*: the Christian texts are filled with mythological and symbolic language, and the believer's task is to learn to discern the deeper meanings buried underneath this language. In "de-mythologizing" the texts, the reader is enabled to hear what the Scriptures have to say to us here and now. In this way, the Scriptures become God's word addressed to each individual believer in her present-life circumstances. What matters about the Scriptures is not the details they present of Jesus' life and death but the impact they have on each of us. This argument fit neatly into the newly developing existentialist philosophy and sufficed to end the quest for historical proofs for many believers. The great questing spirit lay dormant for a time, reviving briefly during the late 1950s and into the 1970s in response to new developments in biblical studies.

In the closing decades of the twentieth century, the pursuit underwent aggressive resuscitation, in large part due to the impact of archeological discoveries in the Middle East and attention to the history of ancient Judaism. Translation of ancient Gnostic Christian texts found at Nag Hammadi in Egypt and ancient Jewish writings at Qumran discovered between 1945 and 1947 has brought about a renewed excitement over interpretations of Christian origins. The Gospel of Thomas, uncovered at Nag Hammadi, has generated new theories about the origins of the four canonical Gospels. Release of the Dead Sea Scrolls to general scholarly examination in the early 1990s, after nearly half a century of closely guarded oversight by a small team of editors and translators, has resulted in an explosion of interest.

Implications for understanding the origins of Christianity and its
relationship to the forms of Jewish faith that predate the birth of Jesus
are exciting. This, along with the need after World War II and the
Holocaust, to reassess traditional interpretations of Jesus and
Judaism, has led to renewed interest in the historical person of Jesus.

One of the most challenging recent findings has to do with the
core Christian claim that Jesus is the messiah, long awaited by the
Jews. It has long been known that there were other Jewish men during the first century C.E. who either claimed themselves or were
proclaimed by others to be messiahs and prophets—Josephus, the
first- century Jewish historian, mentions a number of them in his
writings on the history of the Jews.[3] But the implications for
Christianity were in large part dismissed until scholarship on the
Dead Sea Scrolls began to uncover striking similarities between the
Qumran community's beliefs and the teachings of Jesus. There is so
much similarity that one scholar actually theorized that the Teacher
of Righteousness referred to in the scrolls was Jesus himself.[4]
Although it is now widely accepted that the scrolls predate
Christianity by decades, meaning that the Teacher and Jesus are
obviously two different men, the similarities in their teachings
remain an important lens into the convictions that animated
Jewish movements of the time, including the Jesus movement.

One recent book, *The First Messiah: Investigating the Savior
Before Jesus*, by Dead Sea Scrolls scholar Michael O. Wise, speculates
that the Teacher of Righteousness was the first of a number of
Jewish messiah figures, of whom Jesus and John the Baptist are
the most well known.[5] Ancient sources have named a number of
prophets and messiah figures who lived from about 100 B.C.E. to
the final expulsion of Jews from Palestine in 135 C.E., and there is
evidence that more "messiahs" died without history having recorded their names. Among those about whom we do know something
are: the Teacher of Righteousness (Qumran community leader, 76
B.C.E.); Judas the Galilean (leader of a census/taxation revolt in 6
C.E. which resulted in the crucifixion of 2,000 Jews); Athronges the
shepherd (crowned himself king of Judea, around the death of
Herod in 4 B.C.E.); Simon the Perean (also 4 B.C.E.); John the

Baptist (beheaded around 27 C.E.); Jesus of Nazareth (crucified around 30 C.E.); Theudas (led followers to the Jordan River, which he promised to part so as to lead them to freedom from Rome, captured and beheaded by the Romans, 45–46 C.E.); "The Egyptian" (led hundreds up the Mount of Olives, where he said he would command the walls of Jerusalem to collapse. Four hundred of his followers were killed and 200 taken captive, while he escaped and vanished from history, 52–60 C.E.); Jesus ben Ananus (publicly cried out in the streets of Jerusalem against the Romans for seven years after the 62 C.E. execution of James, the brother of Jesus; was arrested and beaten by authorities; died from head injury during the first revolt of the Jews against Rome, 66–73 C.E.); Menahem ben Hezekiah (a leader during the first revolt); Simon bar Giora (executed as commander of the Jews during the first revolt); and Simon bar Kosiba (132–135 C.E., executed by the Romans as leader of the second revolt). If we know of this many messiahs and prophets, historians argue, there could very well have been many more. The historical evidence seems to weaken Christian claims about Jesus' uniqueness as messiah and his status as God incarnate.[6] History and theology do not seem to be compatible.[7]

Partly a result of these debates over the relationship between history and theology, partly a continuation of the privileging of science over religious traditions begun in the eighteenth century, some today—laity and theologians alike—claim that the idea of incarnation should be abandoned as antiquated nonsense. The classical language of the creeds formulated at Nicea and Chalcedon during the fourth and fifth centuries proclaims Jesus is "truly God and truly man" and "of one substance with the Father," "true God from true God," and "begotten not made." According to critics this is quaintly naïve at best, pure gibberish at worst. The early church appealed to the vocabulary and concepts of Greek metaphysics in speech about personhood and incarnation. As will be more fully explained in chapter 3, this appeal to philosophy led Christian theologians to develop what is called an ontological doctrine of incarnation.

Ontology is the branch of philosophy that asks about the reality status of things, and in existential psychology the word refers to study of the inevitable and formational features of life. The term is taken from the Greek words *eînai*, "be," and *logos*, "the study of." In Latin the word *ontologia* means something like the really existing things, or true reality. When applied to incarnation, it has been interpreted to mean that the reality of God is really present in a human being. In trying to explain how it could be that the creator of all reality has come to earth in the body of a human being, early Christian theologians found Greek philosophy helpful. They adopted concepts used to talk about the union of physical substances for their own talk about how the divine and human could be united in Jesus. This led to the "substance" language of the creeds (specifically that Jesus is *homoousios*—of the same "stuff" or substance as God) that has been subjected to centuries of critique. Meanings have shifted over the centuries, as have the dominant themes of discourse. Early Christian Greek metaphysical language about personhood has been replaced in today's post-Freudian world by the vocabulary and concepts of psychology. To find an idiom that communicates most effectively to today's believer, this experiment turns to recent research into human selfhood for its primary lexicon.

The doctrine of incarnation is central to Christianity. It is an extension of the Jewish belief that the creator of the universe is personally involved in human history: God is so deeply concerned about creation that God enters into space-time at a particular point in history so as to reveal the depths of divine love. To downplay this aspect of the tradition is to lose a foundational concept. If what Christianity tells us about God's concern for creation is valid, then there must be a better way to resolve the tension between theology and history.

JESUS AND INCARNATION

The goal of this work is to demonstrate that, contrary to much modern-day opinion, the concept of an incarnate divine being is quite intelligible for believers today. Given that all speech about christology and the incarnation aims to describe Jesus' identity in a

manner true to the tradition and credible to the times,[8] talk of
incarnation must begin with the humanity of Jesus and *a fortiori*
with the present state of knowledge about the human person.
Research into the historical Jesus can be understood to support claims
of incarnation and can do so most effectively with some revision of
the traditional language of incarnation.

Interpreted through the lens of faith, the flood of historical data
can be shown also to support Christian teachings. Yes, there were a
number of men who preached a messianic message around the
time of Jesus. The Romans executed some of these men, just as
Jesus was executed, for the threat they posed to the status quo. A
few were crucified, just as the Christian messiah was. Yet the life,
teachings, and death of only one of these men influenced his followers so profoundly that within a few hundred years of his death
the Western world believed him to be a true revelation of God.
There were other messiahs, other prophets, but only one whose life
and death demonstrated to the world that God so loved creation as
to make God's own self a part of it, through the incarnation.

I am attempting a revision that goes against the tide of recent
theological opinion. No one, except perhaps theologian Karl
Rahner (1904–1984), has even come close to a way of talking about
incarnation that preserves the ontological sense without the taint of
physical substance metaphysics. For this reason, I must clarify at the
outset the presuppositions upon which my argument is based. This
reframing of the doctrine of incarnation is an ontological one, but
not ontological in the sense imported from Greek substance metaphysics. Ontology is the study of being, existence, of true reality. I
claim that incarnation is somehow a part of what it means to be—
the incarnation of God in Christ can be understood as an ontological event, but not inevitably as an ontologically unique event. And
so this understanding of incarnation must necessarily allow for the
presence of some capacity for incarnating—making present—the
divine in all human beings. To make ontological claims about the
divine-human relation in Jesus, and at the same time to insist on
the absolute uniqueness of its occurrence in one man's life, is to
require that Jesus be understood as other than human. No matter

what language, no matter how elegant the philosophical arguments offered, if one says that Jesus was fully human and at the same time ontologically related to God in a way that substantially differs from you and me, it is impossible to avoid a docetic christology. That is, Jesus will merely *seem* human. We can speak ontologically of incarnation but only if all humanity is understood to possess the capacity for it, at least to some degree. Humanity as a whole—not just Jesus—is so constituted as to be capable of incarnating the divine. Correlatively, and in keeping with Eastern Orthodox Christian thought, we can say that as God continually incarnates the divine in and through humanity, human beings are enabled through the grace of God to become God.[9]

At first glance, to argue that each of us in some sense possesses the capacity to incarnate the divine might seem to obviate claims to uniqueness in the Christian understanding of Jesus as Son of God. But the uniqueness of Jesus' openness to God is not lost in this reimagining of the tradition. Something very like this understanding of the divine-human relationship, lost to the church in the West, remains central to the Eastern churches in their doctrine of salvation through deification, an idea to which I will return in the closing chapters. I agree with Marcus Borg's caveat on the human capacity to incarnate the divine: Any of us could be like Jesus, but in the same sense that any of us could be like Wolfgang Mozart or Albert Einstein or Mother Teresa.[10] Each of these individuals is every bit as human as you or I, and yet they differ in that each life expressed what is a normal human capacity—for music, for mathematics, for compassion—to an extraordinary degree. Jesus is fully human, and yet he is more than simply human. We can be *like* Jesus, but we cannot *be* Jesus.

Another presupposition has to do with the encounter with other religions. In the circumscribed world of previous centuries, it was possible to maintain exclusivist tendencies in Christian teachings on salvation. Jesus was seen as the only way to salvation. Christology faces a special challenge today in that credibility of absolutist claims for Jesus has disintegrated.[11] The more we learn of the history of world religions, and the more Christianity encounters other religious

traditions, the more difficult it becomes to claim exclusive ownership of salvation and even of divine incarnation. To claim that the
only true instance of incarnation happened in the life and death of
one man is not only naïve but also a gross limitation of the concept
and detrimental to the message of the faith. While it does remain
important to ground christology in the life and death of Jesus of
Nazareth, the Christian understanding of incarnation must be
revised to accommodate the fact that the idea of God's coming to
earth in human form predates the life of Jesus, and indeed appears
nearly universally in human religious history. This means that Jesus
is constitutive for the Christian faith and at the same time "normative but not constitutive" of Christian claims to truth. In other words,
Christianity exists by virtue of Jesus' life and death. His example and
teachings provide the focus for Christian faith and hopes for salvation. For Christians, Jesus is normative for our faith. He is also normative—provides the rules, so to speak—for Christian claims to
truth. But he does not *constitute* truth, meaning that he is not the
only possible truth of divine revelation.[12]

Corollary to this: as long as we limit the incarnate Logos to one
human life, our christologies will be (and have been) so thoroughly anthropocentric that we miss God's real presence, to the detriment of the rest of creation. This has led to an "objectification of
nature,"[13] the destructiveness of which we have only just begun to
comprehend. To correct the tendency toward indiscriminate use of
nature to the advantage of the human, we must speak of incarnation in broader terms than those of the human capacity for relation
with God. A broadened and deepened ontological understanding
of incarnation is needed to help correct Christianity's complicity in
the devastation of the environment. To say that God was, once and
for all, incarnate in a single human life requires a thoroughly
anthropocentric christology. It necessarily limits our ability, perhaps even our desire, to speak reverentially of all creation as manifestation of the divine. Given that the Christian tradition teaches
the divine origin and end of all things, one would expect that talk
of the incarnation would not, indeed could not, lead to a denigra-
tion of creation. That the doctrine has been interpreted so as to

support destructive anthropocentrism in relation to the nonhuman and material world points to problematic aspects of the traditional interpretation. Christian theologians have begun to attend to these issues, and a new specialization, ecological theology, has grown up.

Ecological theology necessarily begins with a doctrine of creation and God and offers a powerful corrective to the Christian tradition. But if it is to take its rightful place in Christianity, it needs to articulate an understanding of Christ, and its christology must be thoroughly and ontologically incarnational.[14] This is not intended as an ecotheological exercise, but it does have implications for such work. Material for a helpful christological perspective is already present in the tradition, and it will be brought together here in an understanding of the incarnation that opens our perceptions outward toward the entirety of creation.

THE CAPACITY FOR INCARNATION

One of the most enduring truths of the faith is Christianity's recognition that God is present to us in and through relationship: this, even more than the identity of Jesus with God, is the message of the Gospels. Jesus' words to his disciples in the Gospel of Matthew, "For where two or three are gathered in my name, I am there among them (18:20),"[15] have resonated through the centuries in theological formulations of God's revelation in and through personal encounter. Too often in Christian theology the doctrine of incarnation has been developed in isolation from theological understandings of personhood, not to mention theological doctrines of creation. Yet what context could be more crucial, when what is being posited is the ultimate form of human encounter with God? What is the encounter between humanity and the divine if not relationship? Incarnation is itself a relational concept. And so relationship becomes primary, and the humanity of Jesus crucial. We must ask how it is that we are able to enter into relationship with others. What is it about being human that makes relationship possible? In answering these questions we will find a path opening toward a coherent ontological theory of incarnation:

the living God is incarnate in the capacity for participating in the cognitive and affective lifeworlds of others.

The incarnation of God comes about in and through the experience of intersubjectivity, participation in the lifeworld of others. We now know, thanks to research in developmental psychology, that the human being is constituted by the capacity for relationship. Contrary to psychoanalytic theories that posit an originary state of fusion between infant and caregiver and development as a struggle for differentiation,[16] research shows that the infant is born with a rudimentary sense of itself as separate from others. This nascent sense of self matures through an elegant interplay of physiological and psychological processes that engage the infant in relationship with the caregiver. The sense of self matures in correlation with the capacity to enter into the experience of others. Early on, the infant relates to caregiver primarily through physiological entrainment (the process of synchronizing physical responses like heart rate and respiration to those of the caregiver) and affect attunement (a kind of mirroring of the emotional responses of the caregiver). In this early domain of existence, relation seems to occur primarily at the precognitive level—the other simply is, and the infant entrains and attunes accordingly.

As maturation progresses, interrelationality takes on more cognitive aspects. A firming-up of the sense of self coincides with the development of the ability to share in and respond to another's experience. The healthier the sense of self, the better one is able to enter into specifically empathic relation. In other words, the postmodern trend toward describing the self as fluid and without boundary is not entirely on the mark. Developmental research shows instead that we have something of a core self with flexible boundaries. If there were no core self, no deciding center that remained relatively constant over time, the self would be chameleonlike, becoming whoever the situation called for, without a place from which to make consistent moral decisions. The existence of this core self, understood as an ontological reality with fluid boundaries, but boundaries nonetheless, clearly has theological implications.

Participation will be explored as the larger process of which empathic and sympathetic relation, attunement, and entrainment are parts. Empathy is the higher-level cognitive aspect of participation, in which one enters into another's experience without confusion of selves. In truly empathic relation, individual autonomy is preserved. I comprehend your experience as your experience, without mistaking the experience as in any way my own. It will be explored as a multilevel process that incorporates sympathy, attunement, and entrainment. Sympathy is more aligned with feeling states than with cognition and brings with it a tendency toward fusion: in sympathy, one *feels* more than *comprehends* another's experience. In sympathy, the more primary responses of attunement and entrainment are at work. Something of a blurring of the line between self and other takes place in sympathy, and this is a double-edged sword. Because the lines between your experience and my own are blurred in sympathetic responding, I feel joy as if it were my own when you rejoice, and pain as if it were my own when you suffer.

This is not to say that emotional responding is less desirable than cognitive responding, but there is an important distinction. In sympathy, the other tends to be absorbed into the self, as the other's experience *becomes my own*. This means first, that sympathy is the domain of shared experience within which one is moved to act on behalf of another. Without this blurring of borders, impetus to find ways of relieving the suffering of another would be less insistent. Specifically, a sympathetic response to another's pain causes me pain, and so an immediate urge to relieve the pain. Because my response to another's experience is one of confusion, I do not cognitively identify the locus of pain as within the other. The motivation to relieve suffering is more a global reaction to pain perceived than an unselfish act aimed toward the other. In other words, because the experience is confused, it is not immediately possible to ascertain whether my being moved to relieve another's suffering is selfless or selfish in origin.

Shared experience within the domain of sympathy, and its concomitant impulse to relieve pain without differentiating whose pain it actually is, have led theorists and philosophers to argue that all helping behavior has a selfish origin. Thomas Hobbes (1588–1679), who insisted that the human being is a savage beast tamed only by social contracts, was able to explain away his own helping behavior facilely on the basis of this truth. When asked why, given his view of humanity as motivated by purely selfish urges, he gave money to a pauper, he replied," I was in pain to consider the miserable condition of the old man; and now my alms, giving some relief, doth also ease me."[17] But while it does seem true that helping behavior is tied at some level to a selfish urge to relieve one's own suffering, it does not necessarily lead to a pessimistic or godless interpretation of creation.[18] In a theological context, the theory of altruism's role in nature supports fourth-century theologian Basil of Caesarea's intuition that all of creation is united in cosmic sympathy: we are so created as to be moved to relieve the suffering of others.

As finite, embodied creatures, we are moved to act by the immediacy of personal suffering, and so we exist within a matrix of universal affinity, which is embedded in the genetic structure of creation.[19] The experience of participation is a movement, then, in which we unconsciously entrain physiologically, attune affectively, enter into the feeling state of another—literally experience the other's experience as our own—and then through cognitive processing come to know that the experience is another's, not ours, and to discern whether or not action on our part is appropriate.

A ROAD MAP

Because I want to show that this revision of the doctrine of incarnation is very much in line with the tradition, it will be necessary to lay foundations. Since it has been argued that the idea is itself obsolete, I begin in the second chapter with the argument that a strong (that is, ontological) interpretation of incarnation is possible today. The burden of the second chapter, "The Question of Incarnation," is that Christian theologians who insist that the doctrine of incarnation is obsolete fail to take into account the perduring importance of the idea of incarnation for many religions. I argue that the ubiquity of the symbol should suggest to us that speech about the divine as present to us in human form may well be vital to *homo religiosus*. In bringing together a brief overview of incarnational themes in other religious traditions, a summary of some ways Christian theologians have argued against the doctrine, and a look at the earliest Christian views on the subject, I argue that the idea of incarnation remains crucial to Christian thought. A symbol so central to the human religious experience should not be eliminated nor even watered down.

The third chapter traces the history of Christian thought about Jesus as God incarnate from its beginnings, through the gradual turning away from Greek metaphysical categories, to the Reformation's focus on Scripture and atonement, the nineteenth-century move to legitimize human experience as a source for theological reflection, and the twentieth century's existentialist and feminist turns. Although it is difficult, I try here—and throughout the work—to narrow the focus to incarnation, as much as possible. Doctrines of God, the atonement, resurrection, and ecclesiology are of course tightly interwoven with reflection on incarnation, but the purpose here is to speak of the event itself, insofar as it is possible to do so. My choice of representative theologians in this chapter was determined by the desire to show that although my use of contemporary psychological terminology and concepts will offer a seemingly new language for speech about incarnation, what I propose is not really new. The themes I am bringing together here have been a part of the Christian tradition from its inception.

The fourth chapter continues to place this work firmly within the tradition by way of historical overview of the roles that concepts of divine immutability have played in Christian thought. Ideas of God's relation to the world as empathy or sympathy have come to the fore in recent years, especially in process theology. The turn to human experience as a source for theology, begun in the nineteenth century, has been carried forward in existentialism, and has come to fruition theologically in renewed emphasis on God as absolutely relational. The theologies included in "The Empathic, Relational God" are a reflection of my attempt to reintroduce an understanding of the God-world relation as a dialectical one in which God manifests deep feeling for creation. The Jewish scholar

Abraham Heschel's work on the Hebrew prophets, and some process and process-based theologies, provide thematic material for my interpretation of God's relationship to the world. Heschel speaks of the prophets' relation to God as a sympathetic partnership, a union of feeling and will. For him, God is understood as radically immanent in transcendence. The immanence of God is revealed to us as God's own participation in our affective life: God fully rejoices, and suffers, with humanity. And yet God's transcendence is preserved, because affective participation, expressed most completely, always involves the elements of freedom and choice: God *chooses* to experience this world in all its beauty and its misery.

Chapter 5 involves a more comprehensive exploration of developmental and psychoanalytic psychologies' understandings of empathy and sympathy. In recent years, we have seen a gradual overturning of Freudian paradigms of human development. Developmental psychologist and psychoanalyst Daniel Stern advocates, on the basis of careful scientific observation of human infants and their caregivers, a revised understanding of how the infant develops and experiences his or her interpersonal world. His groundbreaking hypothesis serves as the starting point for the theological anthropology underpinning the theological proposition here.[20] Empathy is a central concept in Stern's hypothesis, as is the process of interrelatedness that he calls attunement, defined as the ability to mirror another by way of transient role identification. Using these themes, and expanding them to include the concepts of entrainment and sympathy, I will develop an "anatomy of empathy" as the capacity for relationship, the process referred to herein as participation.

I have chosen to refer to this process as participation because of the term's long history of use within theology and philosophy to describe the human relationship to God. Plato described the relation of individual objects to the forms as one of participation, *methexis*, "having in common" or "sharing." In Christian thought, we find the term first used in Scripture. In Hebrews 2:14; 3:14; 6:4, for example, *metochoi* and *metochous* refer to Christ's partaking in human nature and our partaking of Christ and the Holy Spirit. The Greek *koinonia*, or communion, is sometimes translated in Christian Scriptures as participation, as well.[21] The idea of participating in Christ is closely linked to the Eastern Christian theme of deification through assimilation to God, a point developed more fully in the text. As used in this work, an understanding of incarnation as participation means that Jesus, by entraining with, attuning to, feeling sympathy and empathy with humanity and God in such a way as to reveal the divine uniquely, makes possible our salvation by uniting us with God. The process of participation, intimately tied to the sense of self, is universally present in the human, and, it will be argued, is the means by which God can be understood as incarnate. To understand incarnation as occurring in and through our relations with others is to require right relation and action to ameliorate the suffering of others.

Further, I will show that participation is not limited to the divine-human relation. There exists in nature something very like the human capacity for entrainment—it is, in fact, called entrainment—and a tendency toward cooperation that seems to require some capacity for awareness of the plight of others. This biological reality, recently documented in scientific literature, is what Basil of Caesarea in the fourth century called cosmic *sympatheia*. The importance of extending divine incarnation to all of creation has been clearly demonstrated by recent ecological theologies. It is my hope that this revisioning of the doctrine of incarnation succeeds in showing how we can speak of God as incarnate in human form in such a way as to avoid the tendency to divorce the human from the rest of creation, a move that has historically allowed our desires to take precedence over the well-being of the planet.

In chapter 6, I bring together these themes into a theology of incarnation based on the belief that humanity reflects the reality of God in and through relationship: the capacity for affective and cognitive participation is truly the *imago dei*. Early Christians sought to express what Jesus was to them through various titles, one of the most important of which is "Son of God." This title, as will be more fully developed in the next chapter, is a relational metaphor—it expresses the reality that Jesus had a deep and intimate relationship with God. Originally a title referring to the nation of Israel, the king, or angels, it was sometimes applied to intensely spiritual people during Jesus' lifetime. Applied to Jesus, "Son of God" took on a biological sense in the Gospel narratives of the miraculous birth, and finally an ontological or metaphysical meaning in the credal formulations of later centuries. Through the symbolic language of incarnation, I seek to offer an interpretation that remains faithful to the intent of classical language of Jesus' two natures, while avoiding the materialist implications of substance language. Using the language of developmental psychology, I will show that the intuition of the creeds is correct: Jesus' relationship with God is and was ontological, embedded as it is in the capacity for intersubjective participation.

In the final chapter, I take up two important challenges that any theological proposal must meet: the question of practice, and the problem of evil. Good theology must be grounded in practice, and so I will show how this doctrine of incarnation as participation can be rendered practical. As for the second issue, theologies can no longer afford to gloss lightly over the gross injustices, depravity, and suffering that are so much a part of life. Speech about incarnation as constitutive of creation itself is confident but not facile. The very capacity that makes possible our sharing in the lifeworlds of others can be and often is perverted into a means for incarnating evil.

This is not intended to be a fully developed christology, my only intent being to explore the feasibility of ontologically incarnational language for today. Therefore some issues usually explored in christologies must remain undeveloped. The focus is on the idea that empathic relation, as developed herein, is a real possibility for humanity, although rarely achieved, and that in and through truly empathic relation to others, to self, to God, and to world we are brought into the salvific process of deification. Its fullest expression is found in the life, death, and resurrection of Jesus of Nazareth. Jesus as Christ manifests the epitome of relatedness: he entrains with, attunes to, feels sympathy and empathy with humanity and God in such a way as to be a singular revelation of the divine. Jesus as Christ is God's *pathos*, or empathetic participation in time and simultaneously our human sympathetic participation in the activity of God, whose self brackets time and extends beyond it.

INTEGRATING THEOLOGY AND CULTURE

I rely heavily on data from nontheological disciplines in developing this revision of our understanding of the doctrine of the incarnation. A brief note on method is, therefore, important. I attempt to adhere to what Ian Barbour calls the method of "integration," and more specifically his category "theology of nature."[22] Barbour's typology of options for the relation between religion and science suggests four alternatives: conflict, independence, dialogue, and integration. An integrative approach assumes the contents of theology and of science can be adjoined, at least to some degree. Integration can be done by way of natural theology, a theology of nature, or an attempt at systematic synthesis.

If this were a "natural theology," I might begin with data from developmental psychology and evolutionary biology, moving toward the doctrine of incarnation, deducing incarnation from psychology and biology. If I were attempting a synthesis, I would need to offer something of a metaphysics, as process theology has done. But my method here is a theology of nature, meaning that I undertake a more modest project, and begin with religious belief and experience, rather than with science. The incarnation of God in Jesus Christ is a truth for me, and so I begin there. Only after exploring the doctrine of incarnation as understood in the history of Christian thought do I undertake an examination of psychoanalytic and scientific research that might have a bearing on my theological convictions. I do not appeal to science in order to prove incarnation. I appeal to science in order to help articulate this theological reality.

I use this approach for a number of reasons, not the least of which is that I believe it to be the method employed generally by those believers who engage in critical thought about religious doctrine, and so it should be recognizable to a broader audience. One important underlying theme of the following chapters is that theological ideas necessarily undergo a process of inculturation, defined as "the incarnation of the Christian faith and life within the diversity of human experiences that are codified in the languages, ideas, values, and behavior patterns that make up a culture or subculture."[23] This means that we constantly seek to integrate inner with outer life, religion with cultural existence: for most of us that means not isolation of the secular from the theological but an attempt to bring the two together.

Because all knowledge is historically conditioned, it becomes necessary at times to go beyond a quest for more convergence and consonance between theology and science. At these points in history it is appropriate for us to revise theological doctrines in light of scientific data. But because the focus of this work is theological, these beliefs remain primary; if secular thought conflicts with theological insight so that no integration is possible, precedence will tend to be given to theology.

2

THE QUESTION OF INCARNATION

> And the Word became flesh and dwelt among us, full of
> grace and truth; we have beheld his glory, glory as of the
> only Son from the Father.
>
> JOHN 1:14

How can we understand the idea of incarnation today? Some theologians insist that christological doctrine and language have been
so contaminated by Greek philosophical concepts that any attempt
to speak of the nature of God's relation to Jesus as Christ is
doomed to failure. The philosophical theism of traditional theology has even been blamed for contemporary atheism.[1] Paul Tillich
believed the traditional theology of incarnation to be pagan, a
kind of polytheism. Other theologians, such as Gordon Kaufman
and John Hick, favor interpretation of Christ as symbol or metaphor.[2] Maurice Wiles has clearly expressed the problem facing theologians today:

> I am not claiming that one ought to be able perfectly to
> fathom the mystery of Christ's being. . . . We do not after
> all fully understand the mystery of our own or one anoth-
> er's beings. But when one is asked to believe something

which one cannot even spell out at all in intelligible terms, it is right to stop and push the questioning one stage further back. Are we sure that the concept of an incarnate being, one who is both fully God and fully human, is after all an intelligible concept?[3]

Wiles's important question cannot be properly addressed without attention to the thought world within which the idea of incarnation grew. The issues are complex, with at least two aspects of theology interwoven: speech about the nature of God and the issue of incarnation. Present-day criticism of the doctrine of incarnation tends to focus on the "substance" language of the creeds, but equally important is the ancient Christian emphasis on divine *apatheia*, God as impassible, immutable, utterly transcendent and unmoved by emotion.

But belief that the divine incarnates in human form is as old and diverse as religion itself: it is not unique to Christianity. In overlooking this truth, theology has failed to place the Christian incarnate God in a world-historical context. This failure contributes to (but cannot be held solely responsible for) the disillusionment of many believers. In this day and age, communication across the planet, indeed into outer space, can be accomplished nearly instantaneously. People no longer live in isolation, but many of our theological concepts do. The average person is today much more aware of other religious traditions than ever before. When incarnational themes present in other traditions come into contact with Christian claims to uniqueness regarding the incarnation of God in Jesus Christ, a crisis of faith can and does ensue.

In what follows, I hope to offer a way of speaking about incarnation that holds together the biblical picture of a God who is moved by and involved in creation and yet also transcendent, an important thrust of the Christian creeds. This speech about incarnation is first situated in the context of the world's religions. Before we can hope to express intelligibly how God was incarnate in Jesus, we first must acknowledge that divine incarnation has been expressed in other traditions.

The Many Incarnations of God

Incarnation of the divine is ubiquitous in the history of religions. Cave art from the Paleolithic Age depicts masked figures believed to be the divine animal spirit, and sacred visitors from the beyond are portrayed throughout the art and religion of premodern societies. Native American religions teach that souls of the dead return to earth in human or animal form and that the divine incarnates itself in this realm from time to time. Certain tribes in Australia teach that the human is made up of two souls, one mortal, the other immortal and believed to be a particle of the totemic ancestral beginnings.

The Gnosticism of the Hellenistic period taught that the human being is a duality of body and soul. Every person was a product of the immortal soul's fall from the divine realm, which resulted in its incarnation and imprisonment in the body. These ideas were combined in Greek thought with the mythologies of Olympus in which the gods were in constant commerce with humanity, very often in human or quasi-human form. Pythagoras, Empedocles, and Plato, for example, taught that the immortal soul fell from an original blissful state, due to sin, and suffered repeated incarnations until its final restoration to bliss. Pythagoras and Plato were themselves thought to have been gods incarnate.

Several centuries before the Common Era, the ancient Persians believed that Mithra, the God of light, would come in human form at the end of history. Mithra was to be a universal king and savior, God born from the womb of a woman. Human kings were believed to be divine in ancient Egypt, and in China it was taught that the emperor, as Son of Heaven, was the very representative of heaven on earth. Since the inception of Buddhism in China, emperors have from time to time been believed to be incarnations of the Buddha. For the ancient Japanese, the emperor was *akitsumi kami*, the god manifested in human form.[4]

Coexistence of divine and human in one person continues to be a prevalent theme in present-day religious traditions as well. The idea is so common that some type of objective relationship with the divine seems necessary for the religious life. This relationship takes the form of incarnation more frequently than not. In the *avatar* of

Hinduism we find what may well be the oldest clearly developed exposition of divine incarnation. In its earliest form, divine descent in Hindu thought was described as *pradurbhava*, manifestation. By the fourth century before the Common Era, the term *avatar*, from the words meaning "to cross over" and "down," had come into usage, primarily in relation to the earthly presence of the deity Vishnu. Although the term itself does not appear in the text, the *avatar* doctrine is most clearly expressed in the *Bhagavad Gita*, that popular epic tale of the god Krishna.[5] "To protect men of virtue," says Krishna, "and destroy men who do evil, to set the standard of sacred duty, I appear in age after age."[6]

In some forms of Buddhism, emphasis has shifted away from the life and example of the historical person Gautama Buddha to that of the Eternal Buddha, a transcendent being believed to embody universal truth. The Mahayana Buddhist doctrine of *Trikaya*, the "three bodies," teaches that the Buddha is known in these ways: as *dharmakaya*, True Body, the essential Buddha who *is* ultimate reality independent of all and yet the "thatness" of all; as *nirmanakaya*, Body of Transformation, that by which the earthly historical Buddha was enabled to work the good; and as *sambogakaya*, the Body of Bliss or celestial Buddhas and bodhisattvas, those who have attained enlightenment but choose to return to earth to help others reach *nirvana* as well.[7] In Japanese Buddhism, the doctrine is further developed into a cosmic theism in which all of creation is believed to be the embodiment of the Buddha Mahavairocana. This cosmic figure is both immanent, through embodiment of himself in the six constitutive elements of the universe—earth, water, fire, wind, space, and mind—and transcendent, absolute, eternal.[8]

Even in Islam, a faith based firmly in the *tawhid*, insistence on the absolute unity of God, there are sects that posit something very like incarnation. Although for the majority of Muslims the idea of incarnation is *shirk*—the compromise of God's unicity by association of other beings with him—the Shi'a speak of the Imam as both savior and human manifestation of the divine. Originally a ruler with the power to interpret the esoteric meaning of the Qu'ran, the Imam was believed to have inherited Muhammad's spiritual gifts. For many Shi'a this belief evolved into the idea that the Imam was the actual embodiment of the divine light. For some—the Druze of Lebanon, for example—the Imam came to be understood as the literal incarnation of God on earth.[9]

Finally we come to the question of Judaism. Because Judaism did not and does not accept the Christian belief that Jesus of Nazareth was God Incarnate, it is widely held that Judaism is adamantly non-incarnational. But Jewish scholar Jacob Neusner points out that Christians have found the Hebrew Scriptures to be a rich source of evidence supporting a God-concept amenable to incarnation, and they see the Christian Scriptures as a natural fulfillment of this. Yet, says Neusner, discovery that the texts of normative Judaism present God in terms of incarnation is "as jarring for Christian as for Judaic readers" of his work.[10] Indeed, incarnation as a concept is integral to Hebrew Scripture; therefore, any thought system that is an outgrowth of those writings must necessarily be shaped by this belief. Within formative Judaism the narrative itself operates as the medium of incarnation.[11] I do not presume to comment on Neusner's scholarship as regards the literature of the dual Torah, but I do find illuminating his examination of incarnational themes in these writings. In the Babylonian Talmud (*circa* 200 to 550 C.E.):

> In the Bavli in particular . . . God became man. . . . The incarnation, moreover, was not merely a matter of pointing to spiritual or other nonmaterial traits shared by God and humanity. God's physical traits and attributes are represented as identical to those of a human being. That is why the character of the divinity may accurately be represented as incarnational.[12]

I do not claim that all these religions "mean the same thing." But these examples underscore the significance of the idea that God, or gods, comes to earth in human form. The symbolic language of incarnation is the most powerful mode of expression available to humanity when faced with the need to express the experience of divine immanence.

Curiously, then, debate among Christian theologians in recent years has to some extent taken place within a vacuum of particularity. This is something of a paradox, given that those who advocate eliminating the doctrine from the faith often argue that to locate God so specifically in time and space entails exclusivist claims that are detrimental in Christianity's encounter with other religions. In arguing for radical revision or elimination of this central Christian concept, some have posited that the Christian doctrine of incarnation has been the cause of colonialism, sexism, or racism.[13] Some theologians have asserted the destructiveness of the idea of incarnation so adamantly as to leave us with the impression that they see this doctrine alone as the cause of wars and human suffering. These same scholars, who argue for the elimination of any doctrine that is implicitly particular, have so focused on Christianity that they fail to see that discourse about divine incarnation is not the exclusive property of Christianity.

This symbol should not be discarded simply because the language of its traditional Christian formulation no longer makes sense. Rather, we should delve more deeply into what incarnation really means and not abandon it because of perceived defects in the trajectory of Christian interpretation. Moreover, arguments pointing to the doctrine as the source of a host of destructive societal problems are far too reductionistic and, oddly enough, manifest a peculiar brand of imperialism. To imply that the Christian belief in Jesus of Nazareth as the very presence of God on earth is the primary source of conflict in the encounter of world religions assumes that incarnation can only be framed in its most exclusivist Christian form. This is to acquiesce in the privileging of one mode of discourse.

Insistence that the doctrine of incarnation is unnecessary to Christianity also misses the point of the symbol. Contemplation of the fact that it appears repeatedly in human history has led me to wonder why this theme is so insistent. At one level, it is an effort to understand the essence of God's relation to the human and to the world. At a deeper level, the symbol's currency supports my claim that the universe itself is hardwired for incarnation. The doctrine of the incarnation of God in Jesus matters greatly. To jettison the concept is to risk losing the very point at which Christianity potentially offers the world its most powerful expression of God's love.

Christian Exclusivity

The Christian use of the concept of incarnation emerged within a Greco-Roman cultural milieu and on Judaic soil. Frances Young points out how pervasive the idea of gods taking on human form was during this formative period, when even Roman emperors were deified. However, she goes on to say that "it is true that these examples [of deification of powerful people in the Greco-Roman world] should probably be treated as literary conceits with no very serious meaning" and that the idea of incarnation belongs "to a world in which supernatural ways of speaking seemed the highest and best expression."[14] Implied here is that (1) the idea of gods in human form for the most part is of minimal significance, and (2) to speak in terms of God's self-manifestation in humanity is meaningless outside the superstitious, antiquated worldview of the early centuries of the Common Era.

John Hick does point to the Mahayana Buddhist doctrine of the Cosmic Buddha to say "that there is nothing the least surprising in the deification of Jesus." He notes "a tendency of the religious mind" toward "exaltation of the founder" and offers an interpretation of incarnation as myth,[15] a move that leads him later to develop incarnation as a linguistic metaphor rather than an actual event.[16] Hick goes on to imply that it is the presence of these themes in Christianity alone that is the source of conflict in the encounter with other religions: "If Jesus was literally God incarnate, and if it is by his death alone that men can be saved, and by their response to him alone that they can appropriate that salvation, then the only doorway to eternal life is Christian faith." Theological attempts to circumvent the exclusivism implicit here are, says Hick, "anachronistic clinging[s] to the husk of the old doctrine [of incarnation] after its substance has crumbled."[17] He has recently argued that it is not possible to give the idea of incarnation any sort of "literal physical or psychological or metaphysical meaning" and so the concept must be completely discarded if not relegated to the status of metaphor.[18]

This is a frequently made but unfortunate and destructive move: Hick commingles the doctrine of incarnation and the teaching that salvation comes in and through Jesus Christ alone. It is certainly true that the concepts of incarnation and salvation go hand-in-hand: many, if not all, Christian doctrines are necessarily interdependent. It is also true that incarnation and soteriological exclusivity—salvation through Christ alone—have been uttered in one breath more often than not in Christian history. But to assume that belief in incarnation as an event (as opposed to a mythological or metaphorical expression) necessitates exclusivist claims is mistaken. By intermingling incarnation and soteriological exclusivity, revisionists sometimes create a situation in which it appears logically necessary that we abandon rather than reinterpret incarnational christology.

Those, on the other hand, who argue in favor of retaining the doctrine in its original ontological sense have, with perhaps the exception of Karl Rahner (for whom creation itself entails the incarnation) have thus far failed to come up with any meaningful alternative to the formulations of the early church. Texts that argue for preservation of the doctrine repeatedly claim that Christianity's interpretation is unique, and that is why it must be guarded. Michael Green's avowal of the Christian incarnation as one-of-a-kind exemplifies the kind of justification given by this camp. Green asserts no continuity with Judaism: "If you had looked the whole world over for more stony and improbable soil in which to plan [sic] the idea of an incarnation you could not have done better than light upon Israel!"[19] As we have already seen, recent Jewish scholarship takes specific exception to this claim of exclusivity. Jacob Neusner acknowledges that while the Christian interpolation of these themes cannot be equated to Judaic understandings of God as incarnate, it is a gross error to assume that Judaism is nonincarnational.[20]

Brian Hebblethwaite rejects any attempt to understand Jesus as one incarnation among many, claiming that to do so is failure to understand the classical doctrine. "If God himself [sic], in one of the modes of his being, has come into our world in person . . . we cannot suppose that he might have done so more than once. For only one man can actually *be* God to us, if God himself is one."[21] The Christian incarnation is unique, isolated in time from all other religious traditions and all other experiences in human history that have been understood to be encounters with God incarnate. In other words, the many ways in which humanity speaks of divine incarnation are not valid; only the Christian version is.

To Hebblethwaite's assertion that only one person can be God to us if God is one, the response must be, why? Why must we limit God in this way? Does this not imply that God is some sort of quantity or corporeal entity that can "be" at only one point within time and space?

Hebblethwaite insists it is nonsense to suppose that the God who incarnated in Jesus of Nazareth can have been incarnate in any other time or place and that it makes even less sense to posit that incarnation can be understood as somehow including all human- ity. "The main point of the incarnation is not a matter of relation at all. It is a matter of identity," says Hebblethwaite.[22] Yet in the chapters to follow I will show that the most powerful expression of Christian incarnation is to be found in a theological interpretation of relationship.

Christian incarnation is not about philosophical concepts of iden- tity. When placed in that framework, incarnation becomes an alien event. It becomes an insertion of God into human history that is without connection to past or future religious experiences of much of humanity. Emphasis on identity instead of relationship encour- ages a destructive supersessionist reading of the Hebrew Scriptures, implying that Christianity supersedes a no-longer valid Judaism. It leads to exclusivist claims in which what appears to matter most is adherence to right doctrine. The argument is less a defense of *Christ's* uniqueness than a defense of *Christians'* uniqueness.

Though at opposite poles, Hebblethwaite and Hick alike assume that we must retain the once-and-only-once character of classical interpretations or dispose of the concept entirely. As an alternative, some liberation and feminist thinkers endorse a shift in focus to only the acts and sayings of Jesus as recorded in biblical texts. These so-called functional christologies are reminiscent of Protestant reformer Philipp Melanchthon, who said, "To know Christ means to know his benefits, and not as *they* [i.e., the Scholastics] teach, to reflect upon his natures and the modes of his incarnation."[23] This makes for good preaching, but unfortunately leads to facile theology.

Melanchthon himself eventually had to return to scholastic thought in his attempts to explicate a coherent doctrine of incarnation.[24]

At this juncture, the problem of discourse about incarnation may seem insoluble. Given that the ancient ontological metaphysics of the Council of Chalcedon (addressed fully in chapter 3) has lost meaning or intelligibility for today's believer, and that traditional interpretations have tended toward exclusivist claims, some sort of revision is clearly necessary. I, for one, do not find it acceptable to jettison the concept altogether, nor do I find adequate interpretations that insist on understanding the incarnation as pure myth or merely metaphor. The basic truth of the incarnation is that the fully human Jesus somehow shared in God's own self so as to reveal the authentic character of the divine-human relationship.

INCARNATION IN A CHRISTIAN KEY

Incarnation, wherever it appears as a religious doctrine, is an attempt to express the nearly ubiquitous conviction that divinity embodied in human form is a reality in history. It is most certainly true that the intellectual universe of a present-day Christian is vastly different from that of a third- or fourth-century "father of the church," but that does not mean that all talk of Jesus as God incarnate is meaningless today. On the basis of the nearly universal appearance of incarnational themes in human history, it can be argued rather that to deny the importance of the symbol is to ignore an essential human insight or need, perhaps. Incarnational language expresses the immanence of God, the belief that God is accessible to humanity in and through the material universe. Do purely functional interpretations of Jesus' relationship to God and thoroughgoing emphasis on the metaphorical nature of language do justice to the message encapsulated in the event of Jesus' life, death, and exaltation? No. Do we lose touch with the original intent and message of Jesus Christ if we throw up our hands in frustration and refuse all attempts to express how God might really be incarnate in a human life? Yes.

For Christians the world over, belief in Jesus as the incarnate Son of God is professed in ancient creeds recited during worship. The

Nicene-Constantinopolitan Creed, formulated in 381 C.E., is the profession of faith used by the majority of Western Christians today. It was devised in an attempt to settle controversy over understandings of God as a Trinity of Father, Son, and Holy Spirit. The text as we now have it is the one creed for which universal authority and acceptance can be claimed, a status it has held in both the East and West since the council at Chalcedon, in 451 C.E.[25] It reads (in part):

> We believe in one God, the Father, almighty, maker of heaven and earth, of all things visible and invisible; And in one Lord Jesus Christ, the only begotten Son of God, begotten from the Father before all ages, light from light, true God from true God, begotten not made, of one substance with the Father, through whom all things came into existence, Who because of us men and because of our salvation came down from heaven, and was incarnate from the Virgin Mary and became man, and was crucified for us under Pontius Pilate, and suffered and was buried, and rose again on the third day according to the Scriptures and ascended to heaven and sits on the right hand of the Father, and will come again with glory to judge living and dead, of Whose kingdom there will be no end.[26]

But there is another creed more central to the debates about incarnation. The Chalcedonian Definition, written at the same council which ratified the above text in 451 C.E., was developed in response to the controversy over the relationship between Jesus' divinity and humanity that sprang up after the Nicene Council of 325. While it is this language that has been identified as problematic for "the average Christian," few outside academic theology have ever read the text or even know of its existence:[27]

> In agreement therefore, with the holy fathers, we all unanimously teach that we should confess that our Lord Jesus Christ is one and the same Son, the same perfect in Godhead and the same perfect in manhood, truly God and truly man, the same of a rational soul and body,

consubstantial with the Father in Godhead, and the same consubstantial with us in manhood, like us in all things except sin; begotten from the Father before the ages as regards His Godhead, and in the last days, the same, because of us and because of our salvation begotten from the Virgin Mary, the Theotokos ["God-Bearer"], as regards His manhood; one and the same Christ, Son, Lord, only-begotten, made known in two natures without confusion, without change, without division, without separation, the difference of the natures being by no means removed because of the union, but the property of each nature being preserved and coalescing in one *prosopon* [person] and one *hupostasis* [substance]—not parted or divided into two *prosopa*, but one and the same Son, only-begotten, divine Word, the Lord Jesus Christ, as the prophets of old and Jesus Christ Himself have taught is about Him and the creed of our fathers has handed down.[28]

The creeds are densely packed statements of faith, encompassing all of the major doctrines of Christianity but primarily intended to communicate in the idiom of the day how it could be said that Jesus was both man and God. We will explore the issues at stake for fourth- and fifth-century theologians in more detail presently, but for now the problem can be stated in capsule form: The major issue in these early christological controversies was the preservation of Jesus' divinity without compromise of his humanity.

The Chalcedonian Definition tells us that "Jesus Christ himself" taught the doctrine of two natures, that he knew himself to be concomitantly fully human and divine. But New Testament scholars tell us today that Jesus apparently did not in any sense believe himself to be God.[29] So before we can begin to understand the issues of Chalcedon we must attempt to discover the origin of this idea that Jesus was God incarnate. If he himself did not claim divinity, what were the leaders of the early church arguing about? In the face of what is now considered to be nearly incontrovertible New Testament scholarship, even so adamant a supporter of traditional incarnational language as Brian Hebblethwaite acknowledges "it is no longer possible to defend the divinity of Christ by reference to the claims of Jesus."[30] Neither can we find clear and indisputable evidence that the idea of Jesus of Nazareth as literally God incarnate was a part of the earliest teachings of the faith. The earliest believers did not question his humanity: they knew him as a man, albeit an extraordinary one. If neither Jesus nor those closest to him in time thought in terms of literal incarnation, how can it be that this idea has been so central and hotly debated in the history of Christianity?

Scriptural Origins
of the Doctrine of Christ as God Incarnate

From the standpoint of historical inquiry, little can be said about the life and death of Jesus. We can state with relative certainty today that the man Jesus was born about 4 B.C.E. and lived most of his life in the Galilean village of Nazareth. He was baptized by John the Baptist, gathered disciples, and taught in the villages and countryside near his home. His preaching centered on the coming of what he called the reign of God. Around 30 C.E. he went to Jerusalem for Passover, where he created some sort of disturbance in the Temple area. After a final meal with followers, he was arrested and questioned by Jewish authorities. He was executed on orders of Pontius Pilate, the Roman procurator. After his death, some of his followers had experiences that led them to proclaim that he had risen from death. They believed that he would return at some future time to institute fully the reign of God on earth, and they formed small communities to support one another as they spread the Good News and awaited his return.[31]

In addition to these few chronicled facts, scholars believe it possible to make a few statements about Jesus' own understanding of his mission and relation to God. For many centuries, it was believed that Jesus understood himself to be the incarnate Son of God, second person of the Trinity, right hand of the Father. The source for this is in John's Gospel. There, Jesus claims to be the messiah and implies that he has an awareness of his pre-existent unity with God.[32] The Fourth Gospel also served as the primary source for the

Chalcedonian writers' assertion that "Jesus Christ himself" taught that he was divine.[33]

Application of textual criticism to the New Testament has revealed that the Gospel of John was written well after most of the other New Testament texts and reflects beliefs held by a community separated from the historical events by at least a generation. Thus, heavy reliance on the Fourth Gospel for proofs of Jesus' self-understanding is no longer considered to be good scholarship. It is possible, however, to discern something of Jesus' own views by examining what James D. G. Dunn calls the "first century context of meaning," in combination with the Gospels themselves.

The New Testament record reveals a gradual enhancement of interpretations of the human Jesus. Earliest renderings speak of him as a human being who had a very special relationship with God. As time passed, readings of his life and work moved toward greater emphasis on the special character of this man's relationship to God, culminating at the end of the first century with the fully incarnational picture presented by John's Gospel. Actually, the Gospels present four different interpretations of the events, in a kind of progressive movement toward divinization. Mark, probably the earliest of the four texts, presents an overall portrait of Jesus as very much a human being. In Luke, Jesus is presented as a somewhat more than human figure, a development that progresses in Matthew to a man that makes claims to extraordinary powers. Finally in John, the latest of the Gospels, Jesus declares that he is the messiah and speaks of his relationship with God in terms of a kind of unity, presenting overall the impression of God incarnate.[34]

A theological tradition of long standing uses the titles given to Jesus by his followers as an entry into the question of Jesus' self-understanding. *Messiah, Son of God, Word, Logos, servant, prophet, savior, Son of Man, Kyrios or Lord, the Great High Priest*—these are the appellations found in Scripture. But few of these are used by Jesus in reference to himself. A brief look at the title *Son of God* is illuminating. Although we have no evidence that Jesus actually referred to himself as the Son of God, the phrase appears in the creeds and is central to Christian belief. In the first century, people were not infrequently referred to as sons of God in order to indicate their status as somehow specially pleasing to or favored by God. For example, mythological Greek heroes, like Hercules, were called sons of God. During Jesus' lifetime, Caesar Augustus was commonly referred to as such, as were the rulers of Egypt. Within traditional Judaism the title was used in various ways, as we see in the Hebrew Scriptures. Angels are sons of God, according to numerous texts—Gen. 6:2-4 or Deut. 32:8, for example. The king and other Israelites, even Israel itself, all received this title (2 Sam. 7:14; Exod. 4:22). Intertestamental Judaism developed the theme further, and it is found in the writings of the Dead Sea Scrolls as well.[35] Altogether then, it can be said that at the time of Jesus and during the early years of Christian formation, the term *Son of God* was widely known and used. To say that someone was the Son of God in antiquity seems to have meant something like "belonging to God."[36] Given its somewhat common usage, it is not surprising that the term came to be associated with Jesus. We have no evidence to support the claim that, when first used to speak of Jesus, *Son of God* meant anything other than its then-accepted meaning.

The title originally implied nothing like the Christian idea of Sonship as encompassing incarnational and trinitarian themes. It was a metaphor used to indicate the special character of Jesus' relationship to God. Although Jesus most likely did not consider himself to be the Son of God, it is feasible that he would have understood Israel and her people to be sons of God.[37] As conservative New Testament scholar N. T. Wright says, "I do not think Jesus [sat back and said] to himself, 'Well, I never! I'm the second person of the Trinity!'"[38]

Some have argued that Jesus did have a sense of distinctive relation to God, demonstrated by his reference to God as *Abba* or Father and his having taught the disciples that an appropriate form of prayer begins "Our Father . . . ." But this cannot be construed to mean that he thought of himself as the Son of God.[39] It was common during Jesus' lifetime for devout Jews to address God in prayer as *Abba*.[40] His use of *Abba* in reference to God is not evidence for a theory of Jesus' incarnational or pre-existent self-understanding.

Similar examination of the other titles used for Jesus can be and has been done,[41] but since the focus of this work is the concept of incarnation, and not the development of christological understandings per se, we cannot delve more deeply into this issue here. The evolution of incarnational themes in christology is a logical outgrowth of the endeavor to express the profoundly spiritual experience of those who encountered Jesus. John Knox sees a gradual unfolding of doctrine from (1) the early adoptionist view (belief that the human Jesus becomes Redeemer and Son of God after his death and resurrection, or perhaps at his baptism) to (2) *kenosis* (belief that Jesus was the pre-existent Son who voluntarily emptied himself of divinity for the period of his life on earth) to (3) the docetic Johannine Jesus who is more divine than human.[42]

The earliest christology of adoptionism obviously harmonizes with the experience of those who knew Jesus in his earthly life; for them there was no question as to his humanity. Peter's Pentecost sermon recorded in Acts 2:22-36 expresses the belief that Jesus was a man through whom God worked wonders, whom "God raised up" and who was "exalted at the right hand of God" (cf. Acts 3:12-26; 5:29-32; 9:22; 10:34-43; 13:28-41; 17:31; 18:28). There is in this understanding a very strong sense of God acting through the life and death of the man but no hint of the man Jesus actu-ally being God incarnate. As the early believers attempted to express the special impact Jesus' teachings and the event of the resurrection had on their lives, ideas of pre-existence came to be associated with Jesus. It would have made no sense to early believers to claim that God had serendipitously encountered a man with the qualifications to become the messiah. God would have known the identity of the messiah from before time, and so pre-existence would be implicit in the Gospel narrative.[43] But pre-existence was most certainly understood more in terms of God's knowledge than as some kind of ontological pre-existence.

There is no scholarly consensus about the apostle Paul's understanding of Jesus' relationship to God. Christological themes of adoption (Rom. 1:3; Phil. 2:9), pre-existence (Phil. 2:6-8), and recapitulation (Rom. 5:12-15—the "Adam christology" in which Jesus corrected the errors made by Adam) can all be found in the Pauline letters. John Knox argues that exegesis of Paul's writings suggests that he assumed the idea of pre-existence, so much so that he never makes a case for or against the idea.[44] Paula Fredriksen notes that Paul had very little interest in Jesus of Nazareth. He did not know the man and only came to belief in him as messiah sometime after the crucifixion through an experience of the Risen Lord.[45] It seems only natural, then, that Paul's focus is on the resurrection and on spiritual understandings of Christ—he was never a man to Paul. To claim Paul had a christology is anachronistic. He wrote to deal with problems encountered by groups of believers for whom he had pastoral responsibility, not to expound a systematic christology. We owe it to Paul and to ourselves to keep these issues in mind; we must allow "Paul to be a first-century Jew rather than a misplaced fifth-century Augustinian, sixteenth-century Lutheran, or twentieth-century existentialist theologian."[46]

Just when and how the idea of pre-existence came to be related to Jesus has been the subject of several books in recent decades. Larry Hurtado, A. P. Segal, Jarl Fossum, and others have examined the possibility that figures already accorded exalted status (angelic figures like Michael, patriarchs like Adam, Enoch, and Moses, and personified Wisdom, for example) within first-century Judaism may have provided the language and concepts for later christological developments.[47] However, it is important to remember that Judaism did not understand any of these figures to be "hypostases in any real sense rather than as simple literary personifications of God's own power and activity."[48]

For an embarrassingly long time, scholarship of Christianity was done in isolation from its roots in Judaism. That has changed in recent decades, and interesting discoveries are being made. It must be remembered that the Gospel record is a product of faith: the writers were first-century Jews who believed Jesus to be the long-awaited and resurrected messiah. They wrote to proclaim this belief, not to provide an impartial record of history. Further, compelling evidence now exists that during the doctrinal controversies of the second and third centuries, the very content of biblical texts was altered in transmission. Scribes apparently often took the liberty of deleting passages that conflicted with then-orthodox views and on occasion even rewrote some passages. The only method for textual reproduction during this period was copying by hand, and so it is perhaps not surprising that scribes not infrequently gave in to the temptation to change the texts "to make them 'say' what they were already known to 'mean.'"[49]

All of this is to say that we cannot uncritically and in isolation appeal to Scripture in developing a doctrine of the incarnation. Since what we have today are texts preserved by the winners of the christological controversies of the first three centuries of Christianity, we need to look at those disputes and the development of the creeds. As we do so, it behooves us to remember that "the winners not only write the history, they also reproduce the texts."[50]

In this brief survey of earliest Christian attempts to speak of Jesus' relationship to God, we have laid the groundwork for an exploration of the challenges that were to confront the church in its first few centuries of development. Questions soon arose about Jesus' relationship to God and the role of his humanity, as opposed to or in conjunction with the divinity incarnate in him. These issues took on more weight as theology struggled to place itself within the Greco-Roman world. In the first centuries battle lines were drawn and creeds formulated, all with the intent of explaining how it was that Christians saw the life and death of Jesus of Nazareth as especially revelatory of God's design for creation. In the next chapter, we will take an abbreviated look at the circumstances surrounding the formulation of the creeds and the development of christology, while we keep watch for themes that will prove useful in recovering some of the original power and meaning of a doctrine of incarnation.

3

A SHORT HISTORY OF CHRISTOLOGY

> The Father and I are one.
>
> JOHN 10:30

Controversy marked the development of Christianity, and one of the earliest points of conflict for believers was a direct result of the claim that Jesus was the incarnation of God. A major doctrinal challenge for the nascent church was how to reconcile belief in the resurrected Lord with the strict monotheism of Christianity's Jewish roots. From ancient times Judaism had struggled to eliminate polytheistic contamination and now, at the beginning of the Common Era, the tiny sect of believers proclaiming Jesus as Lord looked very much like a heresy of two gods.[1] To make matters worse, as theologies of the Holy Spirit developed within the context of third- and fourth-century trinitarian debates, the problems multiplied. In the eyes of many, talk of God as Father, Son, and Holy Spirit made Christianity look even less like monotheism than before.[2]

Along with these internal difficulties, Christian apologists faced the challenge of communicating their message to the non-Jewish world. The first century of the Common Era, a time of extraordinary cultural and political stability under Roman rule, provided a favorable climate for the dispersal of ideas, Christianity and Greek philosophy included. Although other profound traditions of thought flourished in Syria, Arabia, Egypt, and elsewhere, the dominant discourse of the world in which Christian orthodoxy grew was decidedly Greco-Roman. And so the emergent discourse of Christian orthodoxy was shaped by this thought world.

Assimilation of Greek philosophy into Christianity was at first a gradual, spontaneous process. A paradigmatic shift occurred by degrees in the first three centuries. This central shift involved movement away from the ethical reign-of-God focus in the religion of Jesus of Nazareth to a metaphysical, belief-focused religion by the time of Nicea. Emphasis on metaphysics was largely due to incorporation of Greek philosophical concepts, which had an especially powerfully impact on Christian doctrines of God and incarnation.[3]

This metaphysics remained primary for more than a millennium. The Reformation's return to Scripture, the Enlightenment's pursuit of reason and denial of the miraculous, and modernity's advance of historical-critical scholarship all converged in the nineteenth century in a turn away from Greek metaphysics and fomented a crisis for Christianity. Nineteenth-century theological attempts to renew religion and justify it to its "Cultured Despisers" re-emphasized the works of Jesus, the ethical implications of Christianity, and what those implications might mean about God. Twentieth-century thinkers would continue trends against metaphysical speculation but within the context of phenomenology, existentialism, and the growing skepticism of a post-Holocaust, postmodern world.

FROM NAZARETH TO CHALCEDON

> This is not a divine mystery but one that was created by a group of human beings meeting at Chalcedon in present-day Turkey in the mid-fifth century.
>
> JOHN HICK, *The Metaphor of God Incarnate*

In the first three centuries of Christianity, attempts to explain who Jesus was and how he was related to God took several different directions. The Gnostic challenge, with its vision of Jesus as a god clothed in the flesh of humanity, was condemned, along with the opposite view that Jesus was nothing more than a man adopted into special status as the Christ after his baptism. Numerous variations on these themes were condemned as well. Nascent orthodoxy contended that the full humanity of Jesus must be preserved and somehow held in tension with the full divinity of Christ. Interpretation of who Jesus was and how best to characterize his relationship to God took on new intensity as Christianity itself became a major force in the Roman world. When in the fourth century an Alexandrian presbyter named Arius (c.250–c.336) disagreed with his bishop over how best to interpret the divinity of Jesus, a controversy broke out that would culminate in the first ecumenical council of Christian bishops, the Nicene Creed and the development of trinitarian orthodoxy.

The Greek philosophical ideas that most heavily influenced the development of christology are the Platonic conception of God and the Stoic notion of *logos*. The Platonic God is a transcendent, impassible, absolutely simple and undifferentiated unity. The Stoic *logos* or reason is the active immanent principle that holds all things together and produces stability in all of being. In these concepts, Christian apologists found ideas that would translate the meaning of Jesus to the Greek mind. The Nicene and Chalcedonian creeds reflect centuries of effort aimed at harmonizing these concepts with the Christian belief that God's own self had become incarnate in the man Jesus.

New Testament texts referring to Jesus as the Son of God, the Logos, the Word of God who "was in the beginning with God," and "was God" (John 1:1-2) implied divine diversity. Christian theological ingenuity was required to reconcile these texts with the prevailing concept of God.[4] Arius, for example, was intent on preserving an absolute monotheism within the context of the widely accepted Greek metaphysics of God as an unchanging, impassive unity. In a creative but eventually condemned move, Arius insisted that Jesus could not be God. He said that logic requires four things of Christian monotheism: (1) The Word of God must be a creature—"made," not "begotten." (2) As a creature, the Word must have had a beginning: "There was when he was not." (3) The Son of God cannot have direct knowledge of God, since he is himself distinct from God. (4) The Son, unlike God, is capable of change and even possessed in his earthly life the potential for sin, although he never committed it. Arius and his followers believed that the titles attributed to Jesus were, therefore, titles of respect. Even though he is called God, said Arius, Jesus Christ is not really God but divine only by participation in grace. Jesus is God, and Son, in name only.[5]

For Arius, to say that the Father and the Son are "of the same substance," or *homoousios*, either obliterates any distinction between them or means that they are two gods. Needless to say, his ideas did not sit well with those who accepted the teaching that Jesus was in some sense God—"begotten, not made." Questions raised by Arius's teachings demanded answers framed in terms of the very being of God. Earlier, debates had centered on the relation of God to creation and the implications of Jesus Christ's life, death, and resurrection for the salvation of humankind. The Son, as second person of the Trinity, had been the focus of attention in terms of his role as mediator. In other words, the primary emphasis had been on God's relation to the world. Now, with Arius's insistence on the ontological question of substance, the issue came to be focused on the internal relations of the Trinity itself: Is Jesus, as the second person of the Trinity, of the same substance or being—*homoousios*—as the first person, God the Father? Is Christ the same as God, or only similar to God? Is Christ greater than or the same as humanity?[6]

Chief among Arius's opponents was Athanasius (c.296–c.373), who eventually became bishop of Alexandria and was frequently exiled for his efforts to defend the full divinity of Jesus. Athanasius took the argument into new territory by speaking of salvation instead monotheism per se. In *On the Incarnation of the Word*, Athanasius insisted that God became incarnate for soteriological reasons: the Logos became human in order that we might become God.[7] Unless Christ was "very God," salvation of humanity could not have been effected, for how could a mere man save humankind?[8]

The solution adopted by the council of bishops meeting in Nicea in 325 was influenced by this argument. It involved repudiation of Arius and his teachings, and the Son and the Father were declared to be *homoousios*, of the same substance. The term *homoousios* was questionable for many of the bishops since it is found nowhere in Christian Scripture. Furthermore, its having been suggested by and finally adopted at the insistence of the Emperor Constantine made many uneasy about opening the way to imperial influence on church doctrine. The resolution was expedient, then, but not comfortable for all.

Most of those in attendance at Nicea would have preferred to say that the Son and Father are *homoiousios*, "like in substance" (*homoi* means "similar"), not "of the same substance." Yet since Arius and his supporters argued that the Son was not divine, the core Christian claim of incarnation seemed to be at stake. This threat to the divinity of the Son and the oneness of the Trinity was too great, and so it was finally agreed that the ambiguous and confusing philosophical term *homoousios* was best: Jesus Christ was "very God of Very God, begotten not made."[9]

To say that the Son was of "like substance" would have allowed continuation of earlier heretical arguments that professed Jesus to have been merely human. It is perhaps unfortunate for the Christian tradition that the bishops at Nicea could not foresee the difficulties that their politically tactical solution to the question would bring. Rarely in the history of Christian thought has a single word generated as much controversy as *homoousios*.[10] In the end, the decisive issue was the need to refute those who said the second person of the Trinity was a creature. And so, in an ironic turn, the orthodox solution to a major doctrinal issue was found in an expression "coined by Gnostic heretics, dictated by an unbaptized emperor."[11]

Divine Substance and the Incarnate God

Affirmation of the divinity of Jesus, along with his humanity, created almost as many problems as it solved. The challenge of how to express the unity of person in Jesus, given that two distinct "natures" were united in one man, was met with appeal to the visible world. To the consternation of much modern theology, early reflection on the incarnation commonly used material analogies that carried connotations of tangibility. In the second-century Tertullian (c.160–c.225), for example, spoke of the incarnation as a deed in which the divine *logos* became incarnate by the "actual clothing of himself in flesh."[12] Another popular analogy was that of the relation of soul to body. This analogy was interpreted by theologians within an Aristotelian framework of form and matter—the soul is the body's form. Many early writers made use of this theme in discussing the incarnation. Augustine, for example, taught that "Just as man is soul and body so is Christ God and man."[13] Given that the early church existed in a Greek milieu, it was only natural that attempts to talk about Jesus' union with God would be shaped in that context.

The question of the union of physical things had been an important philosophical question for ancient Greek thinkers. It was said that material things could be joined in a number of ways. The differences depended upon whether the things joined retained their independent natures or not. For example, in a union of composition, the things united remain distinct, as when rice and corn are mixed. The resulting union is one in which the natures of the individual things united are unchanged. Some forms of union resulted in a *tertium quid*, or entirely different substance.[14]

This becomes very confusing for us because philosophers did not agree on meanings, and neither did theologians when they began to use this language to speak of the incarnation. For example, Aristotle said a mixture resulted in a *tertium quid*, but the Stoics thought a mixture was a juxtaposition of elements. If Aristotle placed a drop of water into a glass of wine, a new substance came into being that was neither wine nor water. If a Stoic philosopher did the same, the drop of wine remained wine, and the water was just water. Christian theologians wanted to avoid both of these outcomes—either a *tertium quid* or juxtaposition with no impact on the elements combined—in talking about the union of human and divine natures in

Jesus. So they used the terms of philosophy but meant by them something new. Tertullian, for example, used the term *mixture* but seems to have meant *composition*. Origen (c.185–c.254) used *mixture* and *composition* interchangeably but meant what is better termed *predominance*, a relationship of union between elements of unequal power in which the less powerful element is related to the greater as matter is to form (in an Aristotelian sense).[15] Applied to the incarnation, theologians often used the analogy of iron and fire. In Jesus the humanity is matter or potential—iron—and the divinity is form or realization of potential—fire. When iron and fire are joined, both elements remain. The fire makes the iron malleable, opening up the potential inherent in the iron. The iron is still iron, but it has been changed by the fire. The analogy is limited and imports terms that imply a physicality that confuses things further, but it did allow theologians to express the belief that God was in Jesus without destruction of his humanity and without loss of divinity.

Given that no single fully developed concept of personhood existed, and that understandings of the third person of the Trinity were elusive, this appeal to the concrete physical realm was unavoidable. Connotations of tangibility and materiality embedded in the philosophy of union of things combined with the unstable substance terminology adopted at Nicea. In the process, speech about the union of immutable divinity and changeable humanity in Christ became confusing, at best. Discomfort about terminology continued even after the Nicene settlement. The problem of substance language in reference to God and Jesus continued to arise, along with a new controversy about the role of the Holy Spirit.

A second ecumenical council was convened in 381 c.e., again at the insistence of an emperor, Theodosius I. The bishops, meeting this time at Constantinople, adopted an expansion of earlier statements regarding Christ's birth and death, along with a broader statement of the Holy Spirit's position as the third person of the Trinity. Arianism was firmly condemned and Nicea reaffirmed. Our present-day Nicene Creed was the product of this council. Sadly, the agreement reached here only served to clear the way for controversy over a different issue. The more the bishops tried to make sense of Christian ideas within the Greek metaphysical framework, the more questions arose.

To say that the Son was fully divine or *homoousios* with the Father meant that theology now had to deal with the fact of Jesus' humanity. If Jesus was fully God, how could it also be that he was a human being, a man who was born, grew to adulthood, ate and drank, wept, died? Did he have a normal human mind and will? How did the divine and human natures relate in the mind of Jesus? Did the two natures remain distinct, and if so, how did they interact? Did the two natures become one, and if so, how do we speak of this one nature? Did the union of divine and human make Jesus some new kind of creature, a *tertium quid*, neither human nor divine but something else entirely? Now that the issue of God as Trinity had reached some degree of resolution, the christological issue of Jesus Christ, the God-man, came to the fore.

Within a generation, controversy over the relationship between Jesus' human and divine natures threatened to rival the trinitarian debates of the previous century. The issues were incredibly complex, as the sample of questions above underscores. For the most part, theologians did not want to imply that Jesus was any sort of *tertium quid*: talk of the union of human and divine natures in him must not obliterate his humanity. Broadly speaking, theologians allied themselves with one of two interpretations: the so-called "Word-flesh" and "Word-man" christologies.[16] Terminology that had been used in the trinitarian debates was expanded and revised, which unfortunately made the situation all the more confusing.

The key terms were the same in trinitarian and christological language: *nature* or *ousia*, and *hypostasis* or *person*. Use of terms was messy, with *ousia* and *hypostasis* sometimes equated, sometimes not. The situation, then and now, is all the more confusing when we realize that in speaking of the Trinity, *nature* or *ousia* refers to that which is one, while *hypostasis* or *person* refers to that which is more than one: God is one nature, *ousia*, or substance in three hypostases or persons. In christology, the situation is reversed—nature or *ousia* refers to that which is more than one, while *hypostasis* or *person* refers to that which is only one: Jesus

Christ is two natures in one person.[17] To complicate matters further, *person* did not mean what it does today. For the apologists it could mean *persona*, the face one presents to the world or role one plays, or individual substance. These ideas are quite different from the current understanding of person as a psychological entity or self.

The churches of North Africa, particularly Alexandria, favored a Word-flesh christology in which the human and divine natures in Jesus formed an absolute unity. The union was considered by some Alexandrians to be so complete as to obviate discussion of the human nature or the need for a human mind or will. For this reason, it is sometimes called monophysite—one nature—christology. The relation between the divine and human natures was a *communicatio idiomatum* or exchange of properties. This means that, since Jesus had two natures, it was acceptable to attribute to either nature properties that are associated with the other. For example, to worship Jesus is appropriate (even though worship properly belongs to God) because the property of divinity has been "communicated" to the man Jesus. In its extreme formulation, Alexandrian thought proposed that the unity of the second person of the Trinity with human flesh precluded the need for a human soul in Jesus. Concerned to avoid any possibility that the incarnation might be interpreted as a special instance of saintliness or prophetic experience, the Alexandrians emphasized divinity to such an extent that it bordered on docetism, the notion that Jesus only *seemed* human.[18] Stress on the divinity of Jesus implied that he was not really human at all.

And so when an Alexandrian theologian like Apollinaris of Laodicea (died 390 C.E.) insisted that Jesus had no normal human psychology, his point was that salvation cannot be effected by a fallible human mind and will. The "Word was the sole life of the God-man, infusing vital energy and movement into him even at the purely physical and biological levels."[19] The death of a man on the Cross could not be efficacious. The death of Christ, understood as "one nature . . . a simple, undivided Person," was.[20]

The opposing Word-man proponents, motivated by a concern to preserve the real humanity of Jesus, said "that which he has not assumed he has not healed; but that which is united to his Godhead is also saved."[21] As Gregory of Nyssa put it, "By becoming exactly what we are, he united the human race through himself in God," and so, if he was not fully human, salvation has not been granted to us.[22] For the Antiochenes, so-called because their leadership resided predominantly in Antioch, the union of human and divine in Jesus was more a voluntary conjunction than a substantial union. Jesus Christ was clearly the God-man. Since he must have had fully functional human and divine natures, this was called dyophysite or two-natures christology. In its extreme forms, the dyophysite position was as problematic as the docetic tendencies inherent in monophysitism. Taken too far, dyophysite teachings could end up saying that the two natures in Christ were so distinct as to require something like a present-day diagnosis of multiple personality disorder.

Theodore of Mopsuestia (died 428 C.E.) taught that Christ "took not only a body [as the Alexandrian position implied] but a complete man, composed of a body and an immortal soul."[23] It was the created human soul in Jesus that formed the center of life and activity in him, including those actions that brought about our redemption. The Word of God and the man were united in Jesus by grace. This was not a moral union, like that of a prophet, with God; it was a permanent union in which the divine and human natures remained distinct and unconfused, and the person of Jesus one subject or unity.[24]

Although perhaps not immediately apparent, a major point at stake in these debates was God's impassibility, for the commonly accepted understanding of divinity was that God was changeless and without emotion. Within the philosophical framework of the early church, a divinity capable of emotion and change would be less than perfect. Only creatures could rightly be said to change, to be affected by time, to "become." Only God could be said to be unchanging, atemporal. God was all-powerful and perfect and so necessarily impassible. God was unchanging Being Itself. But to say, with Nicea, that Jesus was of the same substance with God logically required that "the Lord of glory" was crucified (1 Cor. 2:8), an impossible action for an impassible God. To say that Jesus and God were *homoousios* was to say that we might pray to be allowed to imitate the suffering of God (*pathos tou theou*).[25] Expressions like *God is born, the suffering*

God, or *the dead God* had become so commonplace in theological language that even the most ardent defenders of impassibility found it difficult to avoid using them.[26] The Alexandrian position that Jesus had one united nature and will logically implied that the divine Word was subject to change, suffering, even death. The christological controversy came to a head over just this problem, in the form of a debate over the veneration of Mary as the mother of the Son.

Given the doctrine of the interchange of properties between Jesus' human and divine natures it made sense to call Mary the mother of God, i.e., of Jesus who is divine. *Theotokos,* "God-bearing," was the title that was now widely affirmed in Alexandrian circles as an appropriate form of piety and theological doctrine. Nestorius, an Antiochene who became Bishop of Constantinople in 428 c.e., preached against this popular title. He rejected the exchange of properties concept and taught that Mary gave birth to a human being—to Jesus, not to God. The Antiochene position was that the human and divine natures in Christ must not be "con-fused," so Nestorius said that it would be appropriate to refer to Mary as "Christ-bearing," but never as "God-bearing" (unless one were to add "man-bearing" as well). His intent was to ensure that the Word, as second person of the Trinity, was not said to suffer or to change in any way. To his mind, the Alexandrian theory of hypostatic union—two natures joined in one person or *hypostasis*—advocated by Cyril of Alexandria unavoidably implied that the Word suffered all that the human Jesus endured.[27]

Since the philosophical ideal of divinity entailed *apatheia* (literally, "without *pathos*") such language could not be tolerated, and Nestorius' teaching was officially condemned in 431.[28] In an irony of history, the human defenders of the impassible God became so inflamed with emotion themselves that they sporadically engaged in physical violence with the supporters of Cyrilline monophysitism. Flavian, Patriarch of Constantinople, was apparently among those who died as a result of a particularly spirited enforcement of the monophysite position in 449.

As was so often the case in this period of church history, theological debates were deeply intertwined with imperial politics; and

soon the emperor, this time Marcian, intervened again. In 451, he
called another ecumenical council at which more than 500 bishops
were present. The emperor's intent in calling the council at
Chalcedon was to establish unity throughout the church, and so
compromise and diplomacy were again urged.

The precarious equilibrium achieved in the language of the
Chalcedonian Definition affirmed aspects of both the Alexandrian
and Antiochene positions. The union of human and divine natures
was defined by way of four negative qualifications— "without confusion, without change, without division, without separation"—in
apparent support of the Alexandrian stance. At the same time, the
phrasing made much of the distinction between the two natures,
which was so important to the Antiochene camp: "Christ, Son,
Lord, Only-begotten is made known in two natures. The distinction of the two natures is in no way taken away by their union, but
rather the distinct properties of each are preserved."

In the preceding century, Athanasius had characterized the
Nicene Creed as "a signpost against all heresies."[29] Some had hoped
it would end controversy, but as we have seen, it served then mainly to point the way toward the next doctrinal challenge, taken up at
Chalcedon. Although Chalcedon provided a boundary language
for christology, the settlement born of the council was no more a
permanent theological solution than had resulted from Nicea. In
a sense, its impermanence was inevitable. All Christian creeds
have two major purposes: rejection of error and an attempt to give
symbolic expression to the importance of Jesus for the Christian
faith. Since language is a fluid medium meanings constantly
change. Language "is always imperfect as a vehicle of meaning,
and thus a theological question is never put in a really perfect
form or in a form that will last forever . . . That is the perennial task of theology: to think out the meaning of the Christian
conviction that God was incarnate in Jesus, that Jesus is God
and Man."[30]

Theological reflection on christology in the West settled into a
kind of uneasy peace with the credal formulations of Nicea and
Chalcedon. It would be many centuries before real theological

innovation about the incarnation was to be seen again in Western Christianity. In the East, however, the struggle to verbalize the conviction that God was incarnate in Christ continued, and an exciting language of incarnation developed that was to remain virtually unknown to the West for centuries.

Eastern christological reflection remained grounded in the Chalcedonian definition of hypostatic union—two natures in one person—and at the same time evolved in genuinely creative directions. It had become *de rigueur* in the East to speak of the *communicatio idiomatum*, or the interchange of properties between Jesus' humanity and divinity. For Byzantine theologians, the true meaning of the incarnation was found in the doctrine of deification (*theosis* or *theopoiesis*), interpreted in light of the hypostatic union of divine and human natures. The idea of an interchange of properties naturally led to questions of volition: if the humanity and divinity in Jesus were joined, were Jesus' actions and decisions a product of the divine will, the human will, or some combination of the two? Scripture was not helpful here since in the Gospel narrative Jesus sometimes speaks as though he and God were one and sometimes as though he were fully and vulnerably human.[31]

Chalcedon had determined that in Jesus there are two natures. The logical corollary, christologically speaking, is that in him there are two wills and so the possibility of both divine and human actions. (If Jesus had only one will, it would belong to the *hypostasis,* or divine person.) Reversing the logic, we would be forced to accept that the Trinity, three hypostases or persons, has three wills. Clearly this conclusion is incompatible with monotheism. Obviously, for trinitarian monotheism, there must be a single divine will: Father, Son, and Holy Spirit are of one nature and so produce one action and have one will. To say otherwise would mean that the Trinity was composed of three gods.

Earlier, in the trinitarian debates, clear distinctions had been made between *theologia* and *economia*, speech about God's internal relations as a Trinity vis-à-vis speech about God's interaction with the world through the incarnation. The divine Logos referred to God's internal relations among the Father, Son, and Spirit, while

Christ referred to the economy of salvation, God's action in the world.[32] This trinitarian distinction was widely understood at the time, but in present-day thought the usefulness and intelligibility of talk of two trinities, immanent and economic, is debatable.[33] Then, however, it was an important distinction because it placed the controverted topic of christology into a trinitarian context. What matters for us here is an offshoot of the trinitarian distinction within the Godhead: if we say that God is a Trinity of persons, this implies a distinction of wills among Father, Son, and Spirit.

It is possible to resolve this tension, as the early church did, by saying that the will of each is actually one and the same with the will of God. The Trinity is, after all, the Christian way of speaking about how God manifests God's self in and to the world. But the situation is less easily resolved when we add the Christian contention that God's own self—as Son—is incarnate in the human Jesus. The will of the Logos incarnate must be the will of the Father in the Godhead: the economic actions of God in the world must undeniably affect the Trinity's internal relations.[34]

Deification, Incarnation, and the Energies of God

One of the most creative approaches to the problem of wills and incarnation—and a helpful resource for us—was offered by the Byzantine theologian, Maximus the Confessor (580–662). Taking as a starting point 2 Pet. 1:4, in which believers are said to "become partakers of the divine nature," Maximus taught that salvation means deification. All of creation participates in God through a dynamic process of *perichoresis* or mutual permeation that always begins in God, moves out to creation and back again to God. This is a reciprocal relationship between God and humanity within the process of deification. It is truly a "union without confusion" that is ours as a gift of the grace of God.[35] All humanity is capable of receiving this gift, but none has the ability to achieve deification independently of the grace of God. "All that God is, except for an identity in ousia, one becomes when one is deified by grace."[36]

"No creature is capable of deification by its own nature.... This can happen only by the grace of God."[37] We are wholly dependent upon grace for deification, but we do have an innate tendency toward this adoption into divinity. Deification is not antithetical to our natures and does not alter anything in human nature.[38]

For Maximus, the entire creation is engaged in a dynamic process of movement, with God as initiator and end of all *kinesis*. *Stasis* is an aspect of the divine but only in that as finite created beings return to God they experience the infinite (that which is beyond the finite) as static. God in God's self, however, transcends even infinitude. The movement of creation is not a gnostic cosmic fall into an evil material realm. Movement of finite creation is a movement upward to God.

The *logos* of God is the deifying presence of Christ in creation; it is expressed as *logoi*, the divine intentions or wills. The *logoi* are the pre-existent expression of God's plan for creation, summed up in the Logos. The world as we know it is brought into being in consonance with these *logoi*. The aim or goal or direction for each created thing is achieved to the degree that the creature is in conformity with its true being: "The definition of all nature is the *logos* of its essential activity."[39] Nature is in constant motion toward the goal but is always free in willing to move toward or away from God. We know God only through God's energies, *logoi*, wills, or intentions, not through contact with God's essence. Since we can never know God in God's essence, divine transcendence is preserved while the divine presence in creation is deeply affirmed. The created can never encounter the creator in essence but can know God immanently in creation through the divine energies.

Logoi are given for all things, and creation is brought into being in consonance with the divine purpose. This does not mean, however, that we exist in a predetermined universe. The human is completely free to conform to God's pre-existent *logoi* (intentions) or not. This is a necessary corollary to the teaching that we are made in the image of God: "if the divine nature is free, so is the image."[40] Therefore humanity has both a natural will, which is the freedom to respond to the divine *logoi*, and a deliberative—or free—will that became a reality for us as a result of sin. Before the fall of Adam and Eve, the human natural will functioned as a never-failing free movement toward conformity with God. After the fall, sin came to be intrinsically linked with humanity at the level of personal choice; it is here that the possibility for sinning resides within humanity.

Through the incarnation, God has restored the proper human mode of existence. The possibility for life in accordance with the natural will is ours as a result of the incarnation. Salvation is a double movement: of God toward humanity in the incarnation and of humanity toward God as a result of the incarnation. These two movements are united hypostatically—they become one existence, one reality—in the incarnation.[41]

As asserted in the Chalcedonian Definition, in Jesus are two natures. For Maximus this means that there are also two wills or energies, divine and human. The union does not come about as a result of the *hypostasis*. It is the union itself that *is* the *hypostasis*. In Jesus, the human "free" or "deliberative" will was in conformity with God's will, and so his humanity was in conformity with his divinity.

Maximus's christology is more helpful than the Chalcedonian Definition for understanding the parallel between Jesus' *hypostasis* and our own. Just as Jesus is a reality made up of two wills, divine and human, we likewise are two-willed in our one *hypostasis* of personhood. Our wills are, of course, both human. But the natural will, having been restored through Christ's incarnation, inclines us toward God in its responsiveness to the *logoi* (divine will or intention for us) that has existed in God from before all time. We move toward God in response to the kinetic character of the natural will. This movement is not a flight from the world but a return to God in completion of the perichoretic reality of our relation to the divine. By right use of the senses, right relation to this material existence, we achieve the *telos* of existence and discover God in the world. In this way individual salvation becomes a link in cosmic redemption.[42]

Maximus' interpretation of the incarnation in terms of will moves the discussion away from connotations of substance, of the juxtaposition or mixture of two things, as was implicit in Nicene and Chalcedonian theology, while remaining faithful to their intent. It is tragic that so creative a christology brought its author condemnation—a severed tongue and right hand, and exile.[43] Although still circumscribed by Chalcedonian metaphysics, his theology offers many possibilities for present-day speech about the incarnation. These possibilities will be explored in more detail as a part of my constructive proposal. But for now, we return to the West and its struggle to interpret the incarnation.

Western Revisions
of the Chalcedonian Paradigm

> Nicea and Chalcedon offer nothing for preaching, devotion, and catechism and so academic training in theology can place it in the background.
>
> Ernst Troeltsch

Many centuries would pass before true innovation in theology of the incarnation would be seen again. In the East, Maximus's innovations would form the basis for later theologies of deification and energies/wills. In the West, theology after Chalcedon generated only minor variations on the themes already presented and for the most part ignored or remained unaware of the East's innovations.

Theology of the incarnation during the Middle Ages was predominantly a repeat of the "one natures or two" debates that had led up to Chalcedon, now presented in the complex form of scholasticism. Scholastic interpretations of the union of human and divine natures in Christ tended to fall into three categories: the so-called *homo assumptus*, subsistence, and *habitus* theories. The *homo assumptus* christology insisted on a real distinction between the natures, to the extent that the humanity had its own existence as the man Jesus assumed into unity in the Word. The subsistence theory taught that body, soul, and divinity were all carried by the *hypostasis* of the Word of God. The *habitus* theory taught that Jesus' humanity was a mantle or covering in which the Word was clothed during the incarnation. The subsistence theory became predominant as theologians came to see that both the *habitus* and *assumptus* theories looked very much like kinds of thought condemned in earlier centuries.[44]

Theology of the Protestant Reformation tended to place emphasis on Scripture and in so doing could not avoid the fact that very little of Nicea's and Chalcedon's language of the incarnation was biblical. The two great thinkers of the time, Martin Luther and John Calvin, both found the Chalcedonian Creed and Medieval scholastic philosophical attempts to explain it especially problematic. Luther spoke for a deep concern in Reformation thought when, in reference to the two-natures doctrine, he declared: "What difference does that make to me? That he is man and God by nature . . . becoming my Savior and Redeemer—that happens for my consolation and benefit."[45] Foreshadowing twentieth-century functional christologies, the Reformers placed emphasis on Christ's saving work, relegating the incarnation to secondary status in favor of the atonement.

Nineteenth-Century Revisions

In the nineteenth century, the shift away from speculation toward more practical modes of reflection turned to human experience as a legitimate source for theology. The first truly new way of speaking about incarnation to appear in the West since Chalcedon came from the pen of Friedrich Schleiermacher (1768–1834). Concerned to translate Christian belief into an idiom acceptable to the time's "cultured despisers" of religion, he insisted that the incarnation was nonsense unless it was a natural occurrence, a possibility inherent in human nature. Echoing Eastern Orthodox writers of earlier times, he said:

> As certainly as Christ was a man, there must reside in human nature the possibility of taking up the divine into itself, just as did happen in Christ . . . even if only the possibility of this resides in human nature, so that the actual implanting therein of the divine element must be purely a divine and therefore eternal act, nevertheless the

temporal appearance of this act in one particular Person must at the same time be regarded as an action of human nature.[46]

Added to these deification themes is an evolutionary view of incarnation in which the human nature in Christ is interpreted as eternally "coming to be" within the process of the world.[47] The incarnation itself is a manifestation of "God-consciousness." This God-consciousness is present in all humanity, but it is only in Jesus that it is so strong and pure as to actually *be* the presence of God in him. In Jesus it is a "perfect indwelling." In us it takes the form of the "sense and taste for the infinite," or prereflective awareness of being "absolutely dependent" for our very being on God. This human awareness can evolve to greater and greater levels of knowing God. Christ differs from us in degree, not in kind; the difference in degree is located in "the constant potency of his God-consciousness, which was a veritable existence of God in Him."[48]

In the century after Immanuel Kant (1724–1804), theological responses took on the character of synthesis—attempts to unite theology and the sciences in ways that might support the contention that religion is integral to human experience. One of the greatest synthesizing minds of the century, Georg Wilhelm Friedrich Hegel (1770–1831), offered a philosophical system that would, for many, do just that. Hegel's emphasis on the virtual unity-in-difference of human and divine was a major stimulus to regenerating interest in the theology of incarnation. His work produced an immediate revival of talk about incarnation and made a major contribution to the development of evolutionary themes in theology.[49]

For Hegel, Christianity was the "absolute religion"—the final stage in the process of God's revelation, the most profound non-philosophical understanding of God yet achieved by humankind. The relationship of God to world is a panentheistic one in which the world process itself is the coming-to-be of God as Spirit. God "is a complex, dialectical, triadic process of self-actualization through time and history . . . the ultimate condition of possibility for the totality of experience."[50] The essential form of being is a dialectic of being and nonbeing; and so the distinction between God and humanity, infinite and finite, is a proviso of unity. Humanity, created in God's image, is spirit by nature, but finite and therefore alienated from God. And so "in order for it [this divine-human unity] to become a certainty for humanity, *God had to appear in the world in the flesh* . . . the substantial unity [of God and humanity] is what humanity implicitly is."[51] Intimating themes reminiscent of Eastern Orthodoxy's theological anthropology, Hegel says that:

> Human beings can know themselves to be taken up into God only when God is not something alien to them, only when they are not merely an extrinsic accident upon God's nature, but rather when they are taken up into God in accordance with their essence and freedom. The implicitly subsisting unity of divine and human nature must be revealed to humanity in an objective way; this is what happened through the incarnation of God.[52]

The incarnation is "a monstrous compound" that contradicts human knowing, an expression of the Spirit of God "without mediation . . . so that the divine presence is essentially identical with this human being."[53] "The divine in a particular shape [*Gestalt*] appears as a human being,"[54] becoming an immanent presence in the world. In the giving-up of transcendence, God reveals God's own self as love. Hegel's profound respect for the doctrine of incarnation would reverberate throughout the century in the thought of many others.

Isaak August Dorner (1809–1884) is credited with one of the more interesting interpretations of the incarnation to be offered after Hegel. Dorner's theology reflects the influence of both Schleiermacher and Hegel, particularly in his emphasis on human sensitivity to and receptivity of God's presence in the world. Human personality, for Dorner, is continually in the process of coming-to-be and is therefore historical, receptive to God, and aware of the need for God. This is so because God lives in us and we in God. Without this indwelling, God could only experience creation in all its possibilities, as potential but never as actual. And so the incarnation was a necessary event. The divine idea of humanity and world necessitates God-manhood.[55] The ground-work for the incarnation has been prepared by the presence of God's love from the beginning of creation.[56] Jesus, the God-man, is a new creation and the outworking of divine activity in the world. Incarnation is a developmental process, not a static insertion of divinity into space and time.

Incarnation is continual "since God as Logos constantly grasps and appropriates each of the new facets that are formed out of the true human unfolding, just as, conversely, the growing actual receptivity of the humanity joins consciously and willingly with ever new facets of the Logos."[57] Throughout all time, the Logos in Christ has been present, providing "ever more definite disclosures of his coming manifestation in the world." But this is not to say "that Christ was only the product of the generative forces of empirical humanity." Contrary to much of nineteenth-century Liberal Protestant thought, for Dorner the incarnation *is* miraculous, "an original and immediate act of God,"[58] not merely the manifestation of an exceptional morality on the part of Jesus.

Along with his idea of progressive incarnation, Dorner reinterpreted the classic doctrine of God's immutability. "God is not immutable in his relation to space and time, nor immutable in his knowing and willing of the world . . . there takes place also on [God's] side change, alteration, a permitting of himself to be determined." God is not, however, completely mutable. If that were so, God would be subsumed into the world process (a complaint often lodged against Hegel). In an intriguing move, Dorner insists that God is immutable in God's "ethical essence," rather than in terms of knowledge, power or presence. In fact, "true immutability and the livingness of God" are a unity,[59] just as in Christ the divinity and humanity are one. The highest possible God-concept is not one that speaks in terms of God's being. It is rather one that understands God as "absolute primal good." The ethical exists in God, not as an ideal but as a reality. It is the core of God's own self. It is in and through humanity that God forges a relationship of reciprocal ethical love.[60]

Throughout the nineteenth century christology was a major question for theology. The process, which began in the Enlightenment, of attempting to justify religious belief to the modern scientific mind expanded as questions of historical knowledge became more insistent. The turn away from the miraculous and supernatural to science and rationalism had culminated in Kant's eighteenth-century interpretation of Jesus as the ideal of moral perfection. Nineteenth-century Liberal Protestantism would follow Kant's lead in its tendency to relegate speech about Jesus as God incarnate to the past and to see him as the supreme moral exemplar. The language of Chalcedon was incompatible with the picture of the historical Jesus then emerging from critical biblical scholarship. Schleiermacher, Hegel, and those who followed sought to retain the sense of mystery and majesty communicated by the doctrine and at the same time speak credibly to an increasingly skeptical public. Their programs would bear unexpected fruits in twentieth-century thought.

Twentieth-Century Revisions

"To be a Christian is simply to be a human being."[61] "An expansive relational process constitutes the core of both the person and the divine."[62] These two sentences epitomize the ways in which twentieth-century theology extended the project begun in the previous century. The twentieth century brought much theological transformation, and any number of theologians could serve to illustrate the ways in which Christianity has continued the work of making sense of the incarnation. Yet, it is theologies that underscore the importance of human experience which offer genuine innovation for a doctrine of incarnation. I have chosen to focus on Karl Rahner because it is generally agreed that he came closer than any modern theologian to explaining the incarnation in terms that preserve the ontological sense of the classical doctrine while moving it away from the imbedded "substance" difficulties that are so problematic today. I have chosen to look at feminist christologies because they, more than any others, have revived speech about the importance of relationship as a theological category.

KARL RAHNER'S "CHRISTOLOGY OF QUEST." Operating within a framework that owes as much to philosophies of Hegel and

Heidegger as to medieval giant Thomas Aquinas, Karl Rahner (1904–1984) offered a theological scheme that led to rejuvenation of Roman Catholic theology very much like the nineteenth-century Protestant response to Schleiermacher. His existentialist approach, which he called the transcendental method, establishes the truth of Christianity by showing that the conditions for its possibility exist.

Since science has made God a question instead of an answer, and since biblical criticism has made Jesus a question, Rahner advocates an anthropological starting point, i.e., beginning by characterizing features of human experience.[63] He defines the human as "the being who, in history, listens to a possible revelation of God." We are ontologically constituted by the potential for hearing the word, when and if spoken by God.[64] Humanity lives in a state of reaching for but never grasping this horizon of consciousness: we are oriented toward the infinite horizon and in anticipation (*Vorgriff*) of it.[65]

In a reversal of most Western thought, Rahner sees true knowledge as surrender to holy mystery, rather than mastery over or understanding of objects. Being and knowing are a unity for him, but only pure being (God) is the absolute identity of being and knowing. Only absolute being is free from the questioning of existence. As finite being, human nature must probe the question of being and must have the potential to hear the answer, which is God: we are constituted by transcendence toward it and are, therefore, spirit:[66] Because of this openness, we must step out into the world in order to enter into ourselves and in so doing we encounter God.[67] It is only in knowing and loving others that we can possibly know and love God and ourselves.[68] The human spirit is ontologically engaged in a kinetic asymptotic longing for the divine; that is, the human spirit is forever in motion seeking that which remains just beyond its grasp in the finite realm—union with God.

Echoing Hegel's understanding of God as Absolute Being, which comes to be in the act of going out from itself in ecstatic love pouring forth, Rahner eschews the idea of created grace. God eternally offers grace. If the grace that comes to us is created, then change must occur in the human before the Spirit of God can be given. But for Rahner divine grace is the self-expression of God in which there is an ontological bestowal of God's own self in creation: Grace "is an interpersonal encounter. The giver is the gift."[69] Therefore, incarnation and grace are of a piece. This is Rahner's idea of the "supernatural existential"; neither grace itself nor God's own self but the offer of grace, which presupposes our natural receptivity to it. Although the supernatural existential is a constant structure of human being, it is freely offered by God and must be freely accepted as God's self-communication: this is no automatic justification due to divine indwelling. Besides, without revelation we cannot recognize the existential as supernatural.[70] We need the real symbol of Christ.

Through anticipation, *Vorgriff*, we transcend the finite in movement toward the infinite. Because the human is spirit—transcendence toward pure being—a revelation of "the depths of Divinity" and invitation "to share in the life of almighty God" is possible.[71] Revelation is not a divine interruption of human history. It is rather transformation of the human through the experience of God's presence. Revelation actually becomes a structural element of our experience—an existential—given to us ontologically as grace and experienced transcendentally in our affective and cognitive life.[72] The possibility for union of divine and human natures is "objectively identical with the essence of man [sic]" since the human already has at its core the condition for the possibility of this union.[73] Add to this Rahner's understanding of God as ecstatic, self-giving love, and the groundwork is laid for an ontological doctrine of the incarnation.

"Christology is the end and beginning of anthropology," says Rahner, and so "if God wills to become non-God, man comes to be."[74] The drive toward union with God is innate to humanity and the highest form of union—hypostatic union—is brought about in the incarnation. In Christ, God creates a "real symbol," a finite other through whom God comes to be. In this coming-to-be, God undergoes change in the other—Christ—yet remains immutable in Godself.[75] The incarnation underscores that human transcendence is transcendence into God.[76] The sacramental symbol of Christ is needed to reveal to us the possibility of fulfillment. A symbol, for Rahner, is "the highest and most primordial manner in which one reality can represent another . . . in which one reality renders another present." The true symbol is "an intrinsic moment of the thing itself . . . a mediation to immediacy."[77] Christologically speaking, the Logos is the absolute symbol of God: in Christ God is immediately, really present in the world. In Christ God becomes world and the world is divinized.

The traditional formula of nature and person is inadequate to explain the relation between human and divine in Jesus, since in him "*both* independence and radical proximity equally reach a unique and qualitatively incommensurable perfection," which is at the same time the perfection of relation between creator and creature. This must be the case if Christ is truly to function as mediator: in his life there must have been real freedom, not solely an instrumental function or passivity in the face of God's will.[78] In the incarnation we see complete divine self-bestowal and complete human acceptance. Now that the fullness of revelation and reception has occurred once in human history, it becomes a possibility for all humanity.

Within an interpretation of progress similar to Hegel's, Rahner understands the cosmos as attaining consciousness "in the individual totality and freedom which each individual" human realizes. This self-transcendence of the cosmos reaches final consummation when God creates something other than God's own self, and gives the divine self to this other. In this way, God becomes the "innermost life" of the world. The world exists for the purpose of God's self-communication, or becoming.[79] Creation and incarnation are two moments in the self-expression of God.[80] Through the supernatural existential, hypostatic union—the ontological assumption of human nature by the divine—is a real possibility for all humanity.

Hypostatic union is unique, the highest thinkable event, and at the same time a potentiality intrinsic to all of creation. Although the self-communication of God has been from before time, in the Savior we find "that subjectivity in whom this process . . . is *irrevocably* present as a whole" in acceptance as well as communication. Rahner insists that to speak of the incarnation of God is to say that God becomes "*material* . . . God takes hold of the world in the incarnation and in the fact of the Logos becoming part of the material world." In other words, the self-communication of God in Jesus becomes so decisive and irreversible that we cannot help but see it as given in this individual's history.[81]

As long as revelation occurs in finite form, through words, for example, it remains transitory. The finite always carries with it the possibility that it might be surpassed. Therefore, the true and absolute revelation must be unsurpassable. It must be the self-manifestation of God, must be God's own self—thus the hypostatic union of God in Christ. Although it is true that the hypostatic union is the greatest imaginable event, this is not to say that the union is a higher stage in an ever-evolving bestowal of grace—Teilhard de Chardin's "christification" of the universe, for example. The union of the Logos and human in Jesus is given (and only need be given) once in history, for Rahner. It is the "irrevocable reality in which God's self-communication proves itself not merely as a temporary offer" and through which it becomes "conscious of itself." Without it, we cannot conceive of the fullness of the possibility of divinization for humanity. Grace *is* the hypostatic union. What is signified here is God's free decision to establish the order of salvation.[82] The divine as supernatural existential remains always and only an offer and possibility of hypostatic union with God. The divine is actually present as offer: God is not always already in us. Rather, we are created with the *capacity* for union with God. The capacity is always already there: God is not.

RELATIONAL CHRISTOLOGIES IN FEMINIST THOUGHT. Feminist theologians have long argued against the classical language of Chalcedon, believing it to re-inscribe oppressive modes of thought that result in the marginalization of women and others. Contemporary feminist theologies have found a somewhat existentialist route to be fruitful in exploring the meaning of incarnation, and they combine this approach with categories of relationship to express the meaning of Christianity.

Elizabeth Johnson, for example, translates Rahner's thought into a feminist key through the ancient concept of Sophia, the Wisdom of God. God's power is relational, erotic, playful, empowering, persuasive, connected: "the liberating power of connectedness that is effective in compassionate love."[83] Sophia-God permeates the universe, encompassing all that is, and becomes incarnate in Jesus. Jesus-Sophia is constituted by relation to God and to humanity, whom the divine Wisdom makes into friends of God. The metaphors of sonship and the Word incarnate signify the relationship between Jesus and God in terms of solidarity, and reveal Sophia's suffering love for creation. Like Rahner, Johnson insists that God's power is that of love. Sophia-God experiences indignation, concern, sympathy, and compassion and enters into the world's sufferings so as to empower resistance, liberation, and healing. God, "She who is," is absolute relationality, "pure aliveness in relation."[84]

Rita Nakashima Brock interprets the relationality of God in terms of a christology of erotic power, or "heart." She picks up the age-old theological project of transforming Plato's idea of *eros* into Christian terms in her interpretation of the erotic power of interconnectedness.[85] "Brokenheartedness" is a central category, tied to her definition of erotic power as the "power of our primal interrelatedness."[86] Our society is damaged by patriarchy and power-as-dominance, she says. The result of this damage is that human infants in our society cannot develop healthy selves.

Psychological theory, specifically Alice Miller's work on dysfunctional families and Donald Winnicott's Object Relations Theory (ORT), provides the material out of which she constructs her understanding of Jesus. ORT posits that the human infant is psychically fused with the caregiver at birth and must develop through learning to differentiate "me" from "not-me." Brock sees parent-infant fusion as a product of the patriarchal family structure inherent in society and traditional Christian discourse, and she argues that our whole society is dysfunctional as a result.

Brock believes that christologies based in the man Jesus are not adequate for transformation of society, since they locate power in a single individual and reflect a male-centered fascination with hero-figures. Power as dominance leads us to search for a salvific lone hero figure that can absolve us of an original flaw—thus the traditional Christian understanding of salvation through the life and death of Jesus Christ.[87] Her remedy is the metaphor of "Christa/Community," which underscores that healing takes place in community and that through our collective memories we are sustained. Jesus the man participates in erotic power but does not himself reveal or embody it: "no one person or group exclusively reveals or incarnates it." That which is truly revelatory of incarnation and salvation resides in connectedness.[88]

Brock's christology offers themes that are helpful in developing the incarnation as participation. But it is also problematic at several points, to be taken up in greater detail in the constructive portion of this work. Most importantly here two points must be made. First, I find it problematic to displace Jesus so thoroughly from the center of christology. It is certainly true that at times the tradition has misused the maleness of Jesus in its attempts to re-inscribe oppressive social structures. Yet the core reality for Christian claims centers on this one man—God is believed to have been revealed in a radically new way through his life and death. Removing him from the center of christology begs the question. Regardless of the abuses tied to his gender, we cannot ignore the truth that Christianity is a historically mediated faith centered in Jesus. Second, there is convincing evidence that Winnicott's model of infant/caregiver fusion is not an accurate depiction of early human development. This is the subject of chapter 5.[89] For now, we turn to the broader question of the general efficacy of relational christologies.

Relational christologies have very nearly "become the 'canonical' position among feminist theologians."[90] Elisabeth Schüssler Fiorenza criticizes the existentialist approach employed by Brock and others for its failure to attend to the sociopolitical power structures embedded in religious concepts. The central metaphor of these relational christologies simply "dresses up" traditional feminine altruism in the garb of liberation, she claims, and thereby fails to challenge the oppressive sex/gender system. Although she concedes that the human is constituted by relationship, Schüssler Fiorenza insists that an existentialist approach is not compatible with a liberationist goal: relational christologies fail to recognize that relations are "power structures that not only situate the self but also shape and define it."[91]

Susan Brooks Thistlethwaite has also been critical of feminist theologies that speak of power-in-relation. Focusing on how white feminist thought has obliterated difference in its emphasis on connection, she insists that christology needs "clash" and "conflict." We must "confront the terror of difference" and to do so "makes a christology of relation impossible. Relationality without the shock of recognition of the uniqueness and difference" fails. Thistlethwaite criticizes Brock for finding "connectedness everywhere," while she finds "struggle and conflict." Instead of the ontic category of erotic power of connection, Thistlethwaite posits "an ontology of struggle" and a "method of difference." This gives primacy to separation, contest, and conflict, traditionally understood in Christian thought to be the products of sin. While Thistlethwaite is absolutely right in pointing out the ambiguity of creation and the presence of "connection and destruction, creativity and evil at the heart of the cosmos,"[92] christology is about the incarnation. This is not to say that christology has no bearing on a doctrine of creation or theodicy, but neither of these is the fundamental intent of a christology. Christology is an attempt to explain how God has acted in history to *heal* separation, to *overcome* sin and evil. Christology is about relation, not separation and difference. Christology is about how God is made known in a particular human life, in the relationships that one particular human being experienced with God and with other human beings. We know of Jesus because his way of relating to others was somehow revelatory of God.

While these critiques have uncovered important issues for relational christologies, they focus too intensely on particular aspects of these theologies and thereby overlook their strengths. To insist, as Schüssler Fiorenza does, that relationality is a feminine category and that christologies of relation threaten to maintain the status quo is to miss the truth that relationality is a human category and not the sole responsibility of women. It is true that feminist theologians have tended to assume relationality as feminine and to co-opt it as the preferred mode of speech for that very reason. However, as will be shown in chapter 5, relationality is constitutive of all of us. Each and every human self—male and female alike—is absolutely relational: human being cannot come to be outside of relation to others.

Men and women alike need to be liberated from power as domination. True freedom is never achieved unilaterally: oppressor and oppressed must be transformed. Typical theological arguments regarding power structures do little to show those who are on the top rung of the oppressive sex/gender ladder that they too are imprisoned within a destructive system. Feminist thinkers have often presented global critiques of sociopolitical ills. We would do well to heed Hannah Arendt's caution. There is a tendency toward paralysis that accompanies being socialized to awareness of guilt, she observes. "Where all are guilty, no one is; confessions of collective guilt are the best possible safeguard against the discovery of culprits, and the very magnitude of the crime the best excuse for doing nothing."[93] And so the way forward must provide a means for understanding that responsibility for transformation of sociopolitical ills lies at the level of the personal and particular. Only in this way can we empower individual enactment of healing.

Relation is not a purely feminine category, and if our goal is transformation of oppressive structures within society, we must not continue to allow it to be so interpreted. The essence of humanity and divinity is relation. The feminist turn to relationship and connectedness as the core human reality points the way forward for this revisioning of the theology of incarnation. An existentialist or experiential approach allows us to explore what it means to be human. The humanity of Jesus is one half of the incarnation equation, and the only side of the equation that either writer or reader can hope to grasp even partially. These themes offer powerful metaphors for understanding the intent of the original Christian doctrine of the incarnate God.

CONCLUSION

This chapter outlined an important trajectory in theological history. It began with the shift toward metaphysics in the first centuries of the Common Era, made necessary by the challenge of communicating Christian claims to the Greco-Roman world. It ends with the contemporary return to emphasis on the ethical religion of Jesus and on the intimacy of God's relation to creation, themes which were overshadowed for many centuries by philosophical debates over Jesus' consubstantiality with God. The return, marked by Dorner's insistence that incarnation is an ongoing manifestation of the divine within creation, continues to the present day. Rahner's insistence that human existence is imbued with the capacity for and longing after relation to God revived the deeply incarnational reality of Christian teachings. Feminist theologies, which refuse to accept that God's intent for creation could exclude portions of humanity on any basis, recover Jesus' own refusal to relegate the socially oppressed to lesser status in the reign of God. My own reconstruction of the doctrine of incarnation as participatory relation is part of this development. To take fullest advantage of the theological riches unearthed here, however, we need also to trace the radical shift in doctrines of God that accompanied these changing christologies. If my claims about incarnation are to stand up to scrutiny, it must be shown that there is a way of speaking about God that supports them.

4

THE EMPATHIC, RELATIONAL GOD

I am the LORD; I act with steadfast love, justice, and righteousness in the earth, for in these things I delight.

JER. 9:24

Some scholars have argued that the concept of God developed in the early centuries is alien to Christianity.[1] The early apologists, they argue, absorbed classical Greek notions of an atemporal, unchanging, absolute God, devoid of potentiality and unrelated to the world. The God of Judeo-Christian thought, in stark contrast, is deeply involved in and affected by all of creation. "The Greek deity is the final point of stability in a world of apparently senseless change. The Hebrew Lord is the initiator of significant change which transforms the character of historical experience."[2]

This demurral from the classic Christian synthesis of Greek and Hebrew ideas is relatively new. Until the end of the nineteenth century, theologians tended to accept traditional conceptions of divine immutability without complaint. Unchangeability was assumed to be an aspect of the eternal divine nature even for theologians who had challenged the classical doctrine of incarnation.[3] Yet the Jewish and Christian Scriptures are filled with imagery of divine mutability.

There we find portrayals of both utter divine transcendence and deep immanence. God is the "high and lofty One who inhabits eternity," who dwells "in the high and holy place" (Isa. 57:15-18) yet at the same time one who "changed his mind," for example, when the people of Nineveh turned from their sinful ways (Jon. 3:10). Yahweh's love, healing, and comfort for the suffering spirit are balanced with divine expression of anger, jealousy, and vengeful thoughts.

For theologians steeped in Greek philosophical concepts—Jewish and Christian alike—this latter tradition has been problematic. In Greek philosophy, divine immutability was the logical product of two basic ideas: the devaluation of emotions and the privileging of the ontological notion of *stasis*. Happiness, the goal of the Greek philosophical life, was usually interpreted to mean absence of concern or peace of mind. To be like God was the highest good and entailed being unaffected by emotion. *Apatheia* was the moral ideal since deity was "impassive and unalterable."[4] *Pathos* was a weakness that came upon the human from without. God, independent of all creation, could not be said to experience *pathos*. Contingency belonged solely to the human realm.

In Platonic and Aristotelian thought, the emotions were impediments to attaining true knowledge. Although Plato and Aristotle did not agree on the nature of the soul, they did agree that emotion was an aspect of unfulfilled existence and that rationality was antithetical to passion. For Plato, the human soul had three aspects: the rational, courageous, and appetitive parts. The rational component was immortal, located physically in the head. It was that which separates humanity from animals. The courageous aspect of the soul was located in the heart and lungs; although the natural ally of reason, it was a lesser part of the soul. The appetitive aspect was located below the diaphragm and associated with bodily desires or physical *eros*. Plato interpreted this tripartite schema dualistically, in that the rational aspect was thought to be closer to the divine. The other two aspects functioned to pull us away from God and toward the material realm of existence.[5] Aristotle differed from Plato in considering the soul and body to be a unity, with reason, the active intellect or *nous*, the impassible aspect.[6]

The Platonic conception of the soul would affect Christian theology powerfully in the fourth and fifth centuries through Augustine, while the Aristotelian notion of unity combined with impassible reason would reappear much later in Thomas Aquinas's scholasticism. The basic conceptual dissociation of reason from emotion, however, was influential even at the earliest stages of Christian theology, through absorption of the Stoic ideal of *apatheia*.[7]

For Zeno, the founder of Stoic thought, *pathos* was an irrational "violent fluttering" of the soul, literally disease, and so to be affected by *pathos* was to be mentally ill. Although later Stoic philosophers would disagree with his theory that the soul was made up of rational and irrational parts, the cornerstone of the system was equation of wisdom with freedom from emotion. The truly wise person was free from emotional influence: wisdom was *apathes*. Contrary to many modern interpretations, however, the true Stoic ideal was not total impassibility. Stoic wisdom required three stable emotional characteristics: joy, wishing or hopefulness, and a sense of caution. Stoic detachment focused on elimination of pity, pardon, or mercy. Since stability was of the highest importance, to pity or to have mercy on someone was unjust in that it could mean treating similar situations in disparate ways. Stoic justice was designed to improve the moral character of the one punished, and so to give in to mercy or to pardon an offense was itself an injustice.[8]

Platonic dualism of the soul and Stoic depreciation of emotion have profoundly influenced moral thought to this day. Despite the evident conflict between Stoic justice and the Christian concept of God, it is possibly true that no other system of thought has had as lasting an impact on Western ethics as Stoicism.[9] Dualism and divine *apatheia* appear in Christianity very early in spite of their conflict with the biblical vision of God. Already in Clement of Alexandria (d. 211 C.E.?), the ideal for Christian life was freedom from extremes in human passions. God, for Clement, was impassible and so human perfection consisted in being above courage, envy, fear, creaturely love, even cheerfulness. Since both divine and human perfection required *apatheia*, the incarnation had to be interpreted so as to divorce the divinity from the humanity in Jesus.

Clement's Jesus was docetic: "He ate, not for the sake of the body, which was kept together by a holy energy, but in order that it might not enter into the minds of those who were with Him to entertain a different opinion of Him. . . . He was entirely impassible, inaccessible to any movement of feeling—either pleasure or pain."[10] The Christian doctrine of incarnation combined with Greek impassible divinity necessarily transformed the man Jesus into an ethereal quasi-god.

We have seen that this issue of God's impassibility played a significant role in the fourth- and fifth-century controversies that led to the Nicene and Chalcedonian statements. And later influential philosophers continued to advocate Stoic-like anthropologies. In the seventeenth century, for example, René Descartes (1596–1650) described the emotions as disturbances of the mind. Baruch Spinoza's (1632–1677) opinion is clearly revealed in the title of the fourth book of his *Ethics*: "Of Human Bondage, or of the Strength of the Emotions." Immanuel Kant (1724–1804), in his eighteenth-century *Critique of Judgment*, insisted that "The principle of apathy, according to which the wise man must never succumb to emotion, not even to that of sympathy for the evils that befall his best friend, is a correct and sublime moral principle."[11]

Yet throughout the sacred writings of Judaism and Christianity—in the Psalms, in the writings of the prophets, in the Gospels—God is portrayed as emotionally involved in creation. The biblical vision does not teach that evil resides in the passions. If anything, evil is understood to originate in "hardness of heart." In the Hebrew Scriptures, an apathetic God would have been no God at all.[12] In the Christian Scriptures, God is love: "For God so loved the world that he gave his only Son" (John 3:16). The scriptural record directly contradicts the Greek ideal of *apatheia*.

The most distinctive term associated with Jesus in the Scriptures is *splanchnizesthai*, "to have compassion." Literally it means "to be moved from the viscera—or the heart—to have compassion."[13] Luke 1:78 refers to the "*heartfelt* mercy of our God." Jesus uses the word in telling the parables of the Good Samaritan in Luke 10:33, in Luke 15:20 of the father receiving his prodigal son, and in Matthew 18:27 regarding the king who forgives debts. Jesus was "moved by compassion" to heal in Mark 1:41, Luke 7:13, and Matt. 20:34. In Matthew and in Mark, the word appears as part of a formula related to Jesus' experience of the crowds of followers: "When he saw the crowds, he had compassion for them" (Matt. 9:36; 14:14; 15:32; Mark 6:34; 8:2). Karl Barth insisted that the intent of the Greek *splanchnizesthai* is much stronger than the meaning implied by our words compassion or sympathy or pity. Jesus was not simply moved by the sufferings of those around him, "but it went right into his heart, into himself, so that it was now his misery. It was more his than that of those who suffered it." It is in this visceral response to and participation in the sufferings of humanity that "[Jesus] was the kingdom of God come on earth."[14] This Jesus is a far cry from the Stoic sage unmoved by emotion.

Attempts to reconcile the biblical God of passionate involvement in creation with the unmoved God of the philosophers have required that theologians see the biblical record as anthropopathic. That is, they had to claim the textual references to God's anger, jealousy, and other feelings were erroneous attributions of human emotions to God. The Jewish philosopher Philo (died 50 C.E.) explained away the problem by way of his exegetical method. God's moods and feelings, he claimed, were pedagogical tools that should be interpreted allegorically rather than literally as references to God's nature. Moses, he said, spoke of God in human-like terms in order to teach. Christian writers would follow Philo's lead and so struggle along with philosophical Judaism "to find an apathetic God in the Bible."[15]

The problematic nature of Christianity's insistence on God as both loving and impassible found expression in Anselm of Canterbury's (1033–1109) writings during the eleventh century. Anselm knew that love necessarily includes sympathy—being moved by the experience of others—but found it difficult to reconcile the dichotomy between the philosophical vision of God's unchangeable nature and this necessary aspect of love. He sought a solution by proposing that although we experience God as compassionate toward us God is in reality unaffected by our sufferings and joys. How can it be, he asked, that God is:

> compassionate, and at the same time, passionless? For if
> thou art passionless, thou dost not feel sympathy; and if

thou dost not feel sympathy, thy heart is not wretched from sympathy for the wretched; but this it is to be compassionate. Thou art compassionate in terms of our experience and not compassionate in terms of thy being. . . . When thou beholdest us in our wretchedness, we experience the effect of compassion, but thou dost not experience the feeling.[16]

To the modern mind, removed as it is from the philosophical language of essence and attributes, this passage seems to mean that God is unmoved by our "wretchedness." This passage suggests that in the experience of our being forgiven, we mistake the effects of divine compassion—healing, peace—for signs that God is affected by our sufferings and joys. To maintain the philosophical concept of impassibility, Anselm offered a picture that contradicts what we know both of human love and of the God of the Scriptures.

A few centuries later, Thomas Aquinas succeeded better in reconciling the impassible God with love. In his *Summa Theologiae*, Aquinas posed the question of God's love in terms of passions. He first opined that "in God there are no passions. Now love is a passion. Therefore, love is not in God. . . . God loves without passion."[17] He then answered that love is the first act of the will, preceding all else. Obviously, we attribute will to God, and therefore we attribute love to God. Further, to love someone is to wish good for that person, to wish union with that good. Therefore we call love the unitive force, binding lover and beloved. God's love for us means that God wills relationship with us; and so God, whose essence is the good, wills for us the good. But God's love of all things is not the same as human love. Human love, said Aquinas, does not cause the good that we will for the person or thing that we love. Rather, our love is called forth by the good that is in that which we love. God's love is the cause of all goodness; human love is response to that goodness.[18]

Regarding God's mercy, Aquinas insisted that, although for humanity to be merciful entails a kind of sorrow, in God there is no sorrow. What we perceive as responsiveness on God's part to our sufferings is actually the replacement of defect with perfection.[19] And so the solution to the problem of maintaining God's absolute simplicity and unchanging essence is found in maintaining the gap between God and humanity. Although Aquinas offered a neat philosophical solution to the problem, theologically the issue was not changed. If we insist that human love is unlike divine love, where is our *entrée* into comprehension of what it means to have been created in the image of God? Where is the connection between our concept of God and the God of Abraham, Isaac, Jacob, and Jesus?

Philo and many others through the centuries have asserted the truth that biblical language is metaphorical, even allegorical at times. Since this is so, we must be cautious in appealing to Scripture when arguing for divine passibility. After all, in addition to description of God as capable of emotion, Scripture refers to God as an eagle (Deut. 32:11) and a rock (Ps. 31:2-3).[20] Surely no one would argue today that *these* passages are anything but metaphor. The question becomes one of criteria. Creative solutions that proclaim God's fully responsive relation to the world have been offered in recent decades, and they fall roughly into two broad categories: those grounded in the complex cosmology of process philosophy and those based in phenomenological or existentialist analysis of religious experience. Embedded in each of these approaches are key concepts supportive of my claim that incarnation is an ontological event tied to the capacity for intersubjective participation.

A MUTABLE GOD

Nineteenth- and twentieth-century theologies revived the concept of relationship as the primary category for speech about incarnation. Jesus' earliest followers spoke of him as a man who had been adopted into Sonship through the power of God, and theologians like Friedrich Schleiermacher, G. W. F. Hegel, and Isaac Dorner reminded Christianity that incarnation is about intimacy with God in relationship. They insisted that the capacity for incarnation is an aspect of creation itself and they thereby prepared the soil for revised speech about the divine nature. Relationship implies interaction, responsiveness, and changeability. Once the category of relation took hold in discussions of incarnation, it became well-nigh impossible to hold on to ideas of an unchanging, impassive, and immutable God.

Conflict between the concept of God's unmoved love and the biblical vision of God as intimately involved in and responsive to creation has become a point of intense theological reflection in recent decades. Since the focus here is on incarnation rather than the doctrine of God, I will not detail the many arguments about divine passibility and theopaschism.[21] But a genuinely believable theology requires that we speak of God as capable of sharing the sufferings of humanity. In the face of the actual and potential holocausts of our times, scholastic argument over whether God knows what a grapefruit tastes like or can ride a bicycle borders on the obscene. Love, as a mutual relation, implies vulnerability. If God is capable of love, God must be capable of suffering as well.[22]

Process Theology
and the God of Sympathetic Responsive Love

"God is the great companion—the fellow sufferer who understands," said Alfred North Whitehead.[23] Christian theologians following Whitehead and Charles Hartshorne argue that the classical theistic framework results in a kind of truncated divinity, in that nothing has an impact on God.[24] According to process thought, God is our companion in suffering who understands all of the agonies and ecstasies of existence. In process cosmology, all of creation is an everchanging series of events, the continuous transitional experience of "actual entities" or "occasions," one of which is God.

In *The Divine Relativity: A Social Conception of God*, Charles Hartshorne explored the implications of describing God's love as sympathetic dependence. Starting from the premise that perfection does not necessarily mean "that which cannot be greater" but rather "that which no other being could conceivably be greater than, but which could become greater itself," Hartshorne offered an idea of God as preeminently social, relational, and loving. He argued that to claim God is absolute in the classical sense means that God could ever only be a term and not a subject of relation.

If we are to make sense of the Christian claim that God loves absolutely, relativity must be an aspect of the divine. Human beings who remain unmoved by suffering are not admired by others—why then do we insist that this is a necessary aspect of God? To proclaim that God is absolutely independent and unmoved in every aspect is "metaphysical snobbery" and "spiritual blindness." Appropriately responsive dependence is true to human experience.[25]

Process theologians insist that to speak of God in this way, a panentheistic, dipolar conception of the divine is required. That is, God must be seen as having a fundamentally different kind of being and relation to creation than we usually conceive. In this cosmology, God is an "actual entity" or "occasion" in the world process, the entity that serves as an explanation for order and novelty in the world.[26] Everything that is exists within the boundaries, so to speak, of the two poles or natures of God: the divine primordial and consequent aspects. Everything in the universe is engaged in the process of becoming, from the most simple and immeasurable entity to the most complex, which is God. In God's dipolar nature, we find the organizational ground and teleological end of everything that is, ever has been, or will be. The primordial, or abstract, pole of God contains all possibilities for creation. It is the unchanging essence, the immutable aspect of the divine, from which the teleology of every entity comes. The goal of each and every entity in creation, referred to as the "initial aim" of God, constitutes the divine purpose uniquely intended for each "occasion" or individual "droplet" of experience. God's consequent or concrete pole is God-as-actual, God's action in the world. It denotes the mutable, responsive, changing aspect of God. In the consequent nature God experiences every event concretely, encompassing all experience. In this pole God is dependent upon the world. In the abstract pole, God is absolutely transcendent. David Ray Griffin understands the poles of God in trinitarian terms: the abstract pole contains the metaphysical traits traditionally attributed to God as Father, and the personal characteristics attributed to God as Son; the concrete pole, God as actually in the world, is equivalent to the Holy Spirit.[27]

Everything that is derives from God, in the sense that the divine primordial nature provides the initial aim or purpose for all aspects of creation. The initial aim works in consonance with the persuasive power of God, which "lures" each entity toward its fulfillment. God's "subjective aim" for all entities is that they experience greater value, which means increasing complexity and intensity of feeling. Each entity has absolutely free will to decide whether to align itself with God's aim for it. God does not, in fact cannot, interfere in the process except insofar as the initial aim has been provided.[28]

The question for us now is to consider how this understanding of God relates to a doctrine of incarnation. The christological problem in process theology is not how God and humanity can be combined in the life of a single human person, since God—as initial aim—is understood to be incarnate in every aspect of creation. Some process theologians adamantly defend the uniqueness of revelation in Jesus while trying to maintain Hartshorne's pantheistic cosmology. The question is how it might be possible to claim that there is anything unique in the incarnation as it occurred in Jesus.

Marjorie Suchocki believes that unique incarnation is consistent with process thought under these conditions: (1) the past has been a preparation for the event. In the case of Jesus, for example, his birth coincided with an intense restlessness among the Jewish people, a growing desire for release from Roman oppression, and expectation of messianic inbreaking. (2) The initial aim of God communicates the essence of God's character fully, and not in the "hidden" way God is present in general revelation. (3) God's initial aim must be adopted without remainder by the one in whom God is incarnate. (4) Since in process thought a person is a series of occasions and not a static entity, incarnation must be understood to be continuous: the one in whom God is incarnate would have to give assent to incarnation at every moment of existence.[29] David Ray Griffin believes that Jesus can be said to have been God's "supreme act" of revelation because (1) he presented a new message of love and forgiveness, (2) the content of God's aim was different for him, (3) he freely chose to conform to the divine initial aim.[30]

The process notion of God is not completely consistent with these interpretations of the incarnation.[31] Suchocki implies, and Griffin insists, that the divine initial aim for Jesus must be different in nature from the divine aim for all the rest of creation. If God cannot intervene particularly in creation, then how can there be intentional variation or degrees of God's presence? Griffin defines God's initial aim in Jesus as a "special act" which, he says, is a direct expression of divine selfhood.[32] Does this mean that the divine initial aims in every aspect of creation except Jesus are inferior expressions of God's own self? If the initial aim as perceived by the world is actually God's own subjective aim for eventual integration and harmony of all creation within the abstract pole of the divine, and if it is the case that God cannot act particularly in history, then does it make sense to claim that in Jesus God performed a "special act"? Griffin says that because God acts persuasively through evolution, divine intervention insofar as it could occur would necessarily be incredibly slow, in accordance with the timetable of evolution in nature. The God of process theology "cannot do much quickly to change things." God cannot intervene in disease processes, nor "directly get an aggregate to do anything." God can do no more than "present novel aims" to human beings.[33] In other words, Griffin's God is incapable of direct intervention in the world of time and space.

Process thinkers want to preserve the traditional Christian claim to uniqueness of revelation and insist that everything in creation has been given an initial aim that is consonant with the divine subjective aim. But since God is neither omnipotent nor omniscient, these themes are incompatible. If we accept that God has performed a special act in the incarnation, then either God intervened at that point in time to effect this unique event or God "decided" from all eternity to perform this act. But why would God have done so? Since God is not omniscient, God could not have foreseen the need for a special intervention. Does this mean the incarnation was God's way of hedging the divine bet, in the event that creation took a wrong turn in its evolution toward reunion in God?

Perhaps one reason that process theology is no more successful than the classical Christian doctrines is because it too adopts as its starting point a non-Christian philosophical system of metaphysics. More importantly for my thesis, however, is the truth that claims to ownership of a special event of incarnation disrupt the coherence of

Christian doctrine. Were these process theologians to acknowledge that incarnation appears again and again in religious history, and were they to explore the importance of this truth, exclusivity would be unnecessary. (I refer here to incarnational exclusivity, which usually, although not necessarily, entails exclusivity of salvation.) In attempting to preserve christological uniqueness, process theology ends up no more coherent than the classical "two natures" doctrine it purports to improve upon.

Under the restrictions offered by Suchocki and Griffin, the incarnation of God in Christ can only make sense if we say that Jesus is not so much a special act of God as he is a revelation of that which God intends for all humanity: perhaps a sort of evolutionary jump toward achievement of God's plan for us. This approach is not foreign to Christian history. The second-century bishop Irenaeus taught that God created humanity in an immature state, so that we can learn fully to appreciate good as opposed to evil. The incarnation recapitulated or summed up the history of the human race and made it possible for us to regain the image and likeness of God, which had been lost in Adam. It is interesting also to note that, for Irenaeus, God's power is persuasive not compelling.[34] Isaac Dorner's progressive incarnation (discussed in the previous chapter), Teilhard de Chardin's concept of Christogenesis (wherein the universe is moving toward "a hyper-milieu of Life produced by the coincidence of an emergent Christ and a convergent Universe"),[35] and Karl Rahner's attempt to place Christianity within evolutionary theory are other examples of this more inclusive approach to incarnation.

The main reason for giving attention here to process theology is not its problematic interpretation of divine power or of the incarnation per se. What matters most is the central role that sympathy and empathy play. In process thought God is sympathetic responsive love, humanity's companion in suffering. Whatever else might be said about the system, process thought has stimulated theology to reconsider its metaphors and return language of God's fellowship with us to its rightfully central place. In Suchocki's interpretation of the process God, empathy plays a vital role in the relationship between transcendence and the human self. This is an especially important insight made possible by Hartshorne's emphasis on sympathy, one which will be supportive of my own constructive argument. For now, the task is to explore other ideas of the divine that are amenable to an understanding of incarnation as the capacity for participation in the lifeworlds of others.

The Pathos of God

William M. Thompson has argued for recovery of a "Christic God-concept," one that encompasses the "essentially dialogic/relational dimension of the Divine" revealed in the Judaic and Christian traditions. To accomplish this, Thompson advocates that we start with a renewed valuation of the Jewish God-concept, particularly Abraham Heschel's understanding of divine *pathos*.[36] Says Heschel:

> The God of the philosophers is all indifference, too sublime to possess a heart or to cast a glance at our world. His wisdom consists in being conscious of Himself and oblivious to the world. In contrast the God of the prophets is all concern, too merciful to remain aloof to His creation. . . . These are the two poles of prophetic thinking: The idea that God is one, holy, different and apart from all that exists, and the idea of the inexhaustible concern of God for man. . . . He is both transcendent, beyond human understanding, and full of love, compassion, grief or anger. . . . God stands in a passionate relationship to man.[37]

Operating from the phenomenological premise that true insight comes from intimate engagement with the event in question, Heschel explores the prophetic consciousness as recorded in the Hebrew Bible. He distinguishes between what happened *in* the consciousness of the prophet and what happened *to* the prophet, explaining the structure of prophetic consciousness on two levels. At the transcendent level, content and form of the experience are *pathos* and event; on the personal level, they are sympathy and overpowerment.[38] The biblical record is the picture of God's "transitive concern" for creation. God's name, YHWH, is unpronounceable but it stands for "compassion."[39]

Revelation, says Heschel, is not a monologue.[40] The prophetic event reveals the *pathos* of God. Divine *pathos* expresses God's relation to humankind: it is not an attribute of God. For Heschel, *pathos* is God's involvement in human life: "Pathos, concern for the world, is the very ethos of God." The God of the prophets is revealed personally and intimately. This God experiences and expresses joy as well as sorrow, pleasure as well as pain: Pathos denotes "a living care."[41] In this relational understanding of revelation and prophecy, human agency is as important as divine action. If we speak of the *pathos* of God, we speak of the human as able to evoke a divine response. This is a dialectical relationship of "God's participation in the predicament of [humanity]. . . . [The human] is not only an image of God; [he or she] is a perpetual concern of God." The gulf that separates us from God is transcended by God's own *pathos*. It is God's response to us that bridges the abyss between human and divine. The divine *pathos* is the "focal point for eternity and history, the epitome of all relationships between God and [humanity]."[42]

The prophets possessed an intuitive grasp of the unspoken message of God's concern. For them, meditation on the meaning of divine expression resulted not so much in knowledge as in increased sensitivity to the presence of God. To know God was, for the Hebrew prophet, to be in fellowship with God and in sympathy with the divine aims for creation. The prophetic experience of sympathy with God's *pathos* was an opening "to the presence and emotion of the transcendent Subject."[43] In this notion of the human experience of God, we find hints pointing us toward a way to understand something of the experience of Jesus.

Divine *pathos* is a dynamic way of relation, involvement, participation. As a functional reality, God's *pathos* is "the unity of the eternal and the temporal, of meaning and mystery, of the metaphysical and the historical." The anthropological significance of this understanding is profound: we are relevant to God, God participates in history. The human has an ultimate dignity and intensely humbling responsibility to God and to all creation. The divine *pathos* demands a human response. Heschel tells us that this

response is sympathy. The prophet serves God by harmonizing his
or her being with God's call. This is an *unio sympathetica,* an "accord
of human privacy and divine concern," an experience of God's
pathos as a part of one's own soul. In sympathy is found "fulfillment
of transcendence."[44]

A religion of sympathy is appropriate, says Heschel, for a faith in
which the human is called to love God with all one's heart, soul, and
might. Religious sympathy is a self-dedication, redirection, and
active cooperation, a "harmony of the soul with the concern of
God"—not self-conquest, suppression, subordination, or aspiring
to the being of God. It is openness to divine presence and not an end
in itself. To be in sympathy is to live with another. Sympathy is a
challenge, a commitment, a call to action. It is tension and trepida-
tion, requiring courage, faith, and love. Divine *pathos* and human
sympathetic response are demands.[45] Jürgen Moltmann describes
Heschel's theology as a "bipolar theology of the covenant," a sort of
dialectic between God's *pathos* and the sympathy of the Spirit in
humanity. God is in essence free, but at the same time intricately
covenanted with creation.[46] The divine *pathos* is not identified with
God's being. The *pathos* of God is the form of the relationship of
divinity to humanity.[47]

Thompson suggests that Christian theology reappropriate this
God-concept in christology. In this context, when we proclaim that
the life of Jesus reveals the divine, we mean that Jesus' life in sympathy with God was encountered by those who knew him as divine
pathos. The Jewish cognizance of God's *pathos* was mediated
through the covenant; the Christian, through Jesus of Nazareth.
Jesus is in line with the prophetic-divine *pathos.* Thompson argues
that at the time of Jesus, "the implications flowing from the Jewish
consciousness of God were still ambiguous, mainly because
Judaism linked access to God to the covenant. In the case of Jesus,
however, the note of universal access to God comes through clearly." It is this aspect of Jesus' teaching, perhaps, that brought him
into opposition with the Judaism of his day.[48] This means that Jesus
does not represent a divinely intended supersession of Judaism.
Given that present-day Jewish philosophy struggles, just as

Christianity does, to reconcile the impassible God of Greek philosophy with the God of the Hebrew Scriptures,[49] we cannot say how history might have been different had the implications of divine *pathos* been fully realized by Jews and the earliest followers of Jesus. The point cannot be made strongly enough that this is not a supersessionary interpretation of Jesus' life and work in relation to his Jewish faith. We cannot, however, hope to understand anything about Jesus as historical figure or as mediator of the Christian faith unless we declare firmly his Jewishness.

Jesus was a Jew who believed himself to have a new understanding of the Jewish God. As far as we can tell, he had no intention of creating a new religion. He understood himself to offer a new interpretation of the tradition, not a new tradition.[50] The earliest Christians also understood themselves to be in continuity with Judaism, not founders of a new religion. They did unfortunately come in time to preach a supersessionary message. As a result, the history of Jewish-Christian relations is a sad story of prejudice, distrust, and violence. Very early, Christians developed the tendency to divorce themselves from their Jewish roots. Failure to assess honestly the nature of Christian continuity with Judaism has played a significant role in encouraging and perpetuating anti-Judaic and anti-Semitic tendencies in our history. With centuries of deliberate distancing from its formative roots, Christianity has led itself astray doctrinally. Twentieth-century recognition of anti-Semitism within Christian thought has led scholars to exercise extreme caution when attempting to recover meanings embedded in Christianity's continuity (and discontinuity) with Judaism.

Sadly, even today the statement, "Jesus was a Jew" produces intense reaction—often shock—among some Christians. It is theologically embarrassing that we have only just begun to recognize how thoroughly Jewish Jesus was and what that means for Christian doctrine (a point clearly illustrated in the previous discussion of Jesus' referring to God as *Abba*). Appeal to a Jewish theology of God in revisioning a doctrine of the incarnation is risky business. But it is a necessary risk, one that must be taken in order to recover the essence of Jesus' relationship to God.

Besides, Jesus was crucified not by the Jews who opposed him (who had no such power under Roman rule) but by the Romans, and in the manner preferred by the Empire for executing political criminals. His was a politically motivated execution.[51] Jesus' teachings were threatening to the chief priests and considered seditious by the Romans. His message was not well-received by those in authority, and this implies that Jesus was seen to represent an overturning of the power structures of his day more than the replacement of one way of worship with another. This is the great insight of Latin American liberation theology, that in Jesus we see not an omnipotent God unmoved by the plight of creation but an unequivocally and wholly relational God who has experienced the evils of humanity's will-to-power firsthand.

Thompson calls the particular kind of panentheistic interpretation implied here "theopathy." The divine immutable essence (which he interprets as "fidelity," but I, following Dorner and Heschel, interpret as ethical unchangeableness) and human mutability are reciprocal, a sort of Hegelian universal correlation in which we understand everything as defined by virtue of relation to something else. In this way we can say that it is through relation to others that we know ourselves as unique. God's transcendence as Immutable Other is preserved while at the same time allowing for a supremely immanent understanding of the divine.[52] Jesus reveals the divine as Pathos and Sovereignty, as a permanent dialectic of immanence and transcendence. What this means is that God's transcendence is relational: "Without *pathos*, sovereignty becomes mere power; without sovereignty, Pathos becomes tragedy."[53]

Farley's Jesus:
The "Through-Which" of Redemption

The most theologically rigorous treatment of empathy as the divine-human relation to date is Edward Farley's *Divine Empathy: A Theology of God.*[54] His thesis is that God reveals God's self in and to the world through the "facticity of redemption." Redemption, transformation in the direction of the good, is "a founding that imparts courage to anxious and idolatrous agents, a reconciling love imparted to human relations, and an emancipating norm of justice for oppressed groups. . . . a kind of compassion."[55] And so the metaphor of empathy is valid. Empathy implies "the understanding of God's activity in the world as an 'efficacious suffering'" or "concerned suffering participation in the life of a genuine other," which is manifested through the incarnation as "empathic union . . . that arises with a human sensibility to the divine empathetic suffering."[56]

Although Farley's project is a doctrine of God, he does offer an analysis of Jesus as the empathetic "through-which" of God's redemptive activity in the world. The task of christology is to discover *how* the event of Jesus functions as the through-which of redemption. His ground rules for interpretation are two: first, Jesus is fully and unqualifiedly human; second, the way in which God is in Jesus is not unique—there is no difference between the way God indwells Jesus and the way God can be present in and to others. In this way, Farley seeks to avoid ontological versions of Jesus' uniqueness. The uniqueness and finality of Jesus come about with the new universal community of believers, which is an outgrowth of the life and death of this man. But "the trace or tone or piety in Jesus' life is a being-founded in God that releases him toward various human freedoms . . . that . . . carries him into public life on behalf of the marginalized of his day." This "being-founded means a sensibility to the divine empathy that opens him empathetically to those around him. . . . Jesus thus appears to be one with the divine empathy." The divine empathy is infinite and therefore without restriction: "its *as such* character" is unqualified and "coincides with creativity itself."[57]

Farley compares his view of the incarnation to the formulas of the early church period. Just as in the Nicene and Chalcedonian definitions the divine dwells within Christ, here the divine empathy, God, dwells in him. What has been classically understood as *logos* becomes empathy. The "immanent, world-moving aspect of God, God in relation" is empathy. Jesus' death and exaltation are the through-which, the precipitating factors leading to the universalization of the Hebrew faith in the new community. The new community is the "resolution of the event of Jesus as Christ" and at the same time is "the faith of Israel in universal, that is, nonethnic form."[58]

In a footnote, Farley indicates that the *as such* character of Jesus' relationship to God is like the prophetic response to God described by Abraham Heschel. However, he sees the *as such* relationship of Jesus to God as "a union that arises with a human sensibility to the divine empathetic suffering."[59] Farley's interpretation here is somewhat narrow and to some extent misleading: he has equated sympathy, love, compassion, empathy, and *pathos* with suffering. This is a move that, as we shall see, it behooves us to avoid.

Farley believes his reduction of *pathos*, sympathy, compassion, and love to empathy is appropriate for a doctrine of God.[60] Abraham Heschel took pains to avoid this reduction in his talk of divine *pathos*, but Farley says that since we can never know the exact mechanism of God's activity in the world it is meaningless to make these distinctions concerning God. Yet I find Farley's reduction problematic for a number of reasons. First, when attempting to speak of the incarnation, we are concerned with the human as well as with God. In what follows I will show that the very distinctions Farley avoids open up possibilities for understanding how it is that the life of a single human, who died nearly two thousand years ago, continues to have meaning for us today.

Equating empathy to suffering is problematic from another standpoint. Through empathy, God functions in Farley's system as "the ground of the cooperative, directional aspect of world processes," influencing and drawing the human out of an innate tendency toward solipsism and into cooperation with others by means of a process we can never explain.[61] Farley's contention that we are innately solipsistic is not supported by recent developmental psychology. The discussion in the next chapter demonstrates that even in infancy, the human is innately other-oriented, radically *non*solipsistic.

Further, in this move to speak of God as the support and ground of human inter-relationality, Farley adopts process theology's view of suffering, which leads him to understand God as drawing us into ever more intense realms of suffering: "God Godself is implicated in the tragic character of world process [which is] enormously intensified" as God allows and even encourages suffering in the same way parents do as they "will and guide their children toward maturity." While one may agree with Farley that "few parents would wish their children to die in childhood or be lobotomized in order to avoid the suffering that comes with the increased sensitivity of maturity,"[62] his equation of empathy with suffering eviscerates the categories of joy and hope that are so central to Christian eschatology.

Farley's account of divine empathic involvement tells us much about the nature of God and contains the germ of a fruitful christological interpretation. But it fails to take fullest advantage of the possibilities it opens up. He tells us that the way in which God was in Jesus is no different from the way in which you and I experience God, but in collapsing several important categories, he reduces empathy to suffering or cosuffering. This leaves us without a means of transcending the tragic. And it is not suffering and death but the power over it that is central to the Christian message. Jesus' suffering and death on the cross are important to Christians, but the potency of the Christian message is found in the message of hope that is the resurrection. The way forward lies in recasting empathy in contrast to sympathy, and in configuring more precisely the categories of interaffectivity, the task of the next chapter.

God's Fellowship with Humanity

The doctrines of God reviewed in this chapter support the claim that God is an intensely relational personal being who fully engages creation in all its passion and glory. The Pathos and Sovereignty of God are revealed time and again in history by an experience of the divine that is mediated through a human life. God—ethically steadfast, constitutively related to and affected by creation— eternally calls us out of ourselves and into relation with one another, with the world, with God. The human being, drawn outward asymptotically toward the divine, comes to be fully human in response to the divine *pathos*.

Divine ecstatic love pouring forth into creation is a coming-to-be of consciousness in which God is truly united to the world as offer and possibility. "The universe, both matter and spirit, is encompassed by the matrix of the living God in an encircling which generates uniqueness, futurity, and self-transcendence in the context of the interconnected whole," says Elizabeth Johnson.[63] In the Byzantine theology of Maximus the Confessor the *logoi* for all of creation exist in God and are poured out as possibility. Creatures have the freedom to choose how closely to align with the divine intention. Everything originates in God and mutually interpenetrates with God. Through alignment with the divine *logoi* the creature attains deification and union with God.

We do not need the complex process language of divine dipolarity in order to say without contradiction that God in God's essence is ultimately unknowable. The divine essence appears to the creature to be a static reality but is in truth always in motion. All of creation is in a constant state of perichoretic movement initiated by God and aimed toward union with God. Through God's energies, the divine is and always has been intimately involved at every level of creation.

With Isaak August Dorner and Abraham Heschel, I say that God is morally and ethically changeless, impassible in sovereignty. With process and process-based theologies, I say that God is deeply moved by the exigencies of existence, that God is revealed to us as "living care." I suggest that we can understand all of these attempts at speech about communion between creation and God—the divine aims of process thought, the energies, wills, or *logoi* of Maximus, Rahner's supernatural existential—in terms of the capacity for participatory relation. This is the mechanism of incarnation, known to us as empathy.

In these first chapters I argue for revision of traditional Christian understandings of the divine-human relation. Even so, the argument remains rhetorical and so runs the risk of failing to connect with the experience of today's believers. The theologians selected in this chapter express God's fellowship with humanity through relational terms like *pathos*, empathy, sympathy. But unless we clearly define terms and differentiate between the feeling states of sympathy and empathy, speech about God may remain as remote for today's believer as the language of Chalcedon.

We have seen how theologians speak of God's capacity for involvement in creation. My thesis that God is made incarnate through participatory relation assumes that both humanity and

God are capable of such experience. If this is so, then the capacity
for participation in the lifeworlds of others must be inherent to
humanity. To make the strongest possible case for an ontological
understanding of incarnation as participation, we need now to turn
to the human. Our next task is to develop an understanding of the
human that incorporates the relational character of human beings.
In service of this, we will need to distinguish between states or
phases of shared affectivity. We will also need an "anatomy of
empathy." Once these tasks are accomplished, I will extend the discussion to evolutionary biology's interpretation of altruism in
nature, which will allow us to speak more broadly of incarnation as
an ongoing ontological event in creation itself.

5

THE EMPATHIC, RELATIONAL HUMAN

> Theologians should listen to what scientists are telling us about
> reality, and use it in reformulating doctrines.
>
> SALLIE MCFAGUE

Our understanding of the mental world of infants has been hampered by the fact that historically developmental discoveries have been constructed in isolation from psychoanalytic theory. The developmental psychologist studies the human infant and for the most part refrains from generalizing about later stages of life on the basis of those observations. The implications of observed behaviors in infancy have been left there, with little effort toward correlative theories of adult life.

Yet psychoanalysts, for their part, have not hesitated to theorize about infancy on the basis of adult psychology. Psychoanalysis, as the treatment of dysfunctional ways of being in the world, obviously can only be done with someone who has well-developed verbal and communication skills. It is most often undertaken with adults whose lives are in some sense troubled. Psychoanalytic theorists have displayed no hesitation in speculating about the infant's experience of selfhood on the basis of research done with adult clients in therapy. Most psychological theories of infancy are based therefore not on observation of infants but on the experiences of adults suffering from psychological problems significant enough to have brought them into therapy. We now know that this approach has led theorists to formulate inaccurate theories that completely miss the true nature of infancy.

For many decades theorists believed the sense of a self as separate from others was not present at birth. They believed the self as a discrete "core entity" develops only gradually with the unfolding of psychic separation that comes about through breaking the bonds that tie infant to mother. It was assumed that the infant had no real sense of self, in other words, until many months of life had passed. As a result of reading back into infancy from work done with adults in therapy, events that require symbolic capacities—abilities we now know are not possible before the acquisition of language—have been attributed to the preverbal lifeworld. For example, the very mother-infant fusion so important to psychoanalytic theory and the psychic defense of "splitting" another into "good" and "bad" other are capacities now believed impossible before language acquisition.[1]

Today, by contrast, the self is understood to be "a dynamic relational system" that is present from the outset of life.[2] There is a rudimentary human self that is not so much a thing or entity as it is an organizing awareness, a non–self-reflective experience of agency, physical cohesion, temporal continuity, and intention.[3] The self is, in a sense, a process rather than a thing.[4] The "sense of self exists long before infants recognize their own image in a mirror, before the acquisition of language or symbolic abilities. The prelinguistic self is believed to be based on the direct perception of the self as a part of a relationship with the physical and social environment."[5] The infant is prewired, in other words, with a sense of self.

Corollary to erroneous ideas about development of selfhood are mistaken ideas about the capacity for interpersonal relatedness and intersubjectivity—the mental ability to symbolize or represent another's state of mind. Influenced by Sigmund Freud's theory of id, ego, and superego development, which posited that there is no capacity for prosocial behavior until around four to six years of age, and Jean Piaget's thesis that the child is incapable of understanding the needs of others until six or seven years, psychologists have until recently believed that sympathy was a very late achievement. In truth, the human infant is quite capable of responding to the distress of others: babies even in the first two years of life actively attempt to comfort others in distress.[6] Other-oriented behavior develops gradually over time: a fully developed capacity for sympathizing in the abstract comes about by the time children reach the teen years. Once measured in terms of separation and individuation, maturity is now gauged in terms of "the capacity to enact altruistic behaviors based on internalized moral principles and [the child's] understanding of the perspectives of people who are unknown" to them.[7]

In this chapter we will examine this new way of understanding the development of a healthy self and its relationship to the capacity for empathy. We will take a look at psychological theory and confusion over meanings of words for sharing in the experience of other living beings in order to develop an "anatomy of empathy." This anatomy will uncover a connection between empathy, the human being, and creation itself.

DEVELOPMENTAL PSYCHOLOGY AND SELVES IN INFANCY

Although much debate continues within psychology over the nature of the self, clearly understandings of it have changed dramatically during the past two decades. This shift is due in part to the groundbreaking research into human development reported in Daniel Stern's book *The Interpersonal World of the Infant: A View from Psychoanalysis and Developmental Psychology*. Stern presents an enlightening survey of the inner life of infancy and early childhood. He offers a vision of the infant as an individual from birth, possessing some sense of self and an innate drive toward wholeness, which is realized within the matrix of interpersonal relation. In the developing self we find progressive *domains of interpersonal relatedness* that remain operative throughout life.

THE EMERGENT SELF. From birth until about two months of age, the infant exists in the realm of the emergent self. Psychoanalytic theory focuses on physiology at this stage of life—the regulation of feeding, bowels, and so on—and so has historically missed the point that whatever regulation does come about during these early months of life happens through social interaction with caregivers. Freud, for example, decided that the self is shaped primarily by physiological tensions. It is true that the infant's body is the first reference point for development of the sense of self (46). But it functions as a reference point in the encounter with others, not as an island of self-referential experience.

The emergence of a self is a learning process for which the infant human is predesigned. This development is not, however, a cognitive process in the way that we usually tend to characterize learning: thoughts, perceptions, and actions as particular events do not yet exist for the infant. At this age, these experiences are encountered directly as patterns or shapes or intensities rather than discrete happenings (67). It is not possible for infants to know *what* they do not know or *that* they do not know; and so we cannot claim that infants exist in an undifferentiated fusion with the caregiver, as had previously been thought.

Infants exist in a state of perceptual unity in which they are able to take information received in one sensory mode and translate it into a different one. We do not yet understand just how this "amodal perception" operates, but research shows that the ability is present in the first weeks of life (47–48). For example, infants can translate tactile information into visual understandings. In one study, blindfolded three-week-olds were given two different pacifiers. One pacifier had a spherically shaped nipple, the other a nipple with nubs on it. After allowing the infants to touch one of the pacifiers only with the mouth, the researchers removed it and placed it alongside the other. When not blindfolded, the infants looked quickly from one pacifier to the other and then gazed longer at the pacifier they had been allowed to touch.

Infants at this age seem to experience the world globally and directly. Qualities like shape, motion, rhythm, and intensity, and emotions like anger, sadness, and happiness are all experienced as global amodal perceptions (51–55). What this means is that the infant can make abstract representations of qualities that he or she perceives. The two-month-old is already integrating information received and organizing experience into patterns of "me"—"not me."

This comprehensive internal world of emerging organization is the most basic domain of human subjectivity. It operates unconsciously as the experiential matrix from which thoughts, forms, acts, and verbalized feelings will come later in life. It is also the origin of ongoing emotional assessment of events. It is the vessel for creative experience, and it remains active during the formation of each of the succeeding aspects of self development (67–68). This stage is not purely passive receptivity: infants do also engage in a kind of constructive activity. The infant apparently senses that other humans are somehow different from the rest of the world, but it is not until that experience is ordered into "constellations" of relation that maturity develops.

THE CORE SELF. At about two months of age, the infant becomes a noticeably more social being. From two to six months, the infant is experiencing the evolution of a sense of self-versus-other and self-with-other. Classical psychoanalysis claims that the infant at this stage lives in symbiotic psychic fusion with the caregiver and does not develop a sense of self until the end of the first year of life. We now can say, however, that through a process of identifying unchanging elements within experience, the infant comes to reside in a more ordered mental universe. The basic experiences crucial to development of a core self are "invariants," things that remain constant across experiences and time: agency, self-coherence, self-affectivity, and self-history or memory (69–76). At this stage the sense of self is not a cognitive construct or a kind of knowledge. It is, rather, experiential integration that takes place at the unconscious level.

Agency is the most fundamental of invariants. It is a deeply unconscious experience in which three things converge: a sense of will or volition that comes before motor activity, proprioceptive (sensory) feedback, and predictability of consequences following the action. Through the elegant and repetitive coming together of will-to-move, sensation of movement, and consequences of movement, the infant develops a sense of being the author of actions.

Self-coherence is the experience of self as a separate physical entity. It comes about through the experience of recognizing that the sound of a voice originates from the same visual location as the face, for example. It comes to be through coherence of motion, of intensity, of form, and of temporal structure. Accurate sensing of temporality is closely related to maintaining a core self in social encounters. Infants are incredibly adept at timing. Research shows that they can detect departure from simultaneity to the microsecond. For example, three-month-old babies were shown video tapes of their mothers. If the mother's voice was out of synchrony with facial movement, delayed by only several hundred milliseconds, the babies became distressed (107). The baby's ability to track temporally is a major factor in differentiation of self from other.

Self-affectivity is made up of sensory feedback from muscle action, internal patterns of arousal, and feeling qualities related to the various emotions an infant experiences. In other words, for each emotion, like fear or anger or joy, the infant comes to expect certain things to happen. Different sensations accompany the intensity associated with joy as opposed to fear, for example.

Finally, self-history or memory provides the means by which self-continuity is achieved and maintained. The human infant is equipped with memory systems that are not dependent upon language: motor memory, perceptual memory (especially for voice and smell), and affect memory are a few examples (76–94).

Through encounter with variety, an infant begins to "triangulate" invariants: that is to say, he or she begins to differentiate unchanging aspects of self from invariants belonging to others. The caregiver operates as a "self-regulating other" to some extent, providing mutual experiences that allow the infant to develop feelings like attachment and security (104–5). Through integration the infant develops generalized representations of interactions. Whenever these representations of being with another person are activated or remembered the infant has an experience of being-with another. Stern calls these experiential memories "evoked companions," since the memory is very like actually being with the other. The evoked companion is not an imaginary friend but a way of making the other present "in the form of an active memory . . . they are a record of the past informing the present," and are "permanent, healthy parts of the mental landscape that undergo continual growth and elaboration" (116–19). Anyone who has ever experienced the loss of or prolonged separation from a loved one has encountered just what Stern means here—we can call up memories so strong that the other is a real presence in our lives, even though the person is not physically present. This capacity to be with another in the abstract is already a part of lived experience in the human infant between two and six months of age.

Core relatedness, then, establishes that the infant's physical and sensory experiences are distinct from yet shareable with others. This capacity is the necessary prerequisite for more sophisticated ways of being-with others, and remains operative throughout life. "It is the existential bedrock of interpersonal relations" (125). Once this core self has taken shape the foundation has been laid for a quantum leap in development.

THE SUBJECTIVE SELF. Around seven to nine months of age, the infant begins to experience a sense of subjective self, constituted by the growing awareness that her thoughts are shareable with others. With emergence of this awareness that mental contents can potentially be shared with others, the infant is capable of true intersubjectivity, which is the deliberate seeking of shared experience about events and things (128). Since language skills are not yet developed, what is shareable are experiences that do not need to be translated into words. Intentions ("I want that toy"), attention ("Look at the dog"), and feeling states ("This peek-a-boo game is exciting") are the kinds of mental contents that can now be shared.

We cannot explain this amazing leap forward in development. In fact, intersubjectivity seems to be an emergent property that is a byproduct of maturation. An emergent capacity is a unique way of functioning that is possible only in the presence of and interaction between certain lower-level abilities but cannot be explained on the basis of these lower abilities.[8] In other words, intersubjectivity cannot exist without the capacities for amodal perception, ordering of experience in terms of invariants, calling up evoked companions, temporal tracking, and so on; yet it cannot be explained simply through examination of these capacities. These nascent capacities come together in the human infant at this time to give rise to something more than strictly explicable on the basis of prior capacities.

Until now the infant has existed in a world in which only empathic *responses* were noted; now, the infant becomes aware of the *process* itself that bridges her mind to that of others (124–37). The first and most important aspect of this process is the ability to share emotional states. Stern calls this affect attunement (125–41).[9] Attunement is a sort of translation of subjective states into behaviors, or creation of an analogue for feeling in behavioral form (161). Although imitation does play a role in infant development, affect attunement is clearly a higher-order activity. The distinction between imitation and affect attunement is important: in imitation, there is no referent to internal feeling state, while in affect attunement there clearly is (124–42). Affect attunement, then, is an unconscious process whereby some kind of cross-modal matching of behaviors related to another's feeling state is performed. It is a vital aspect of communication among human beings of all ages.

Stern makes an interesting observation here, although it is relegated to a footnote: pure imitative behaviors, like mimicking and "shadow-talking," are intuitively recognized by children to be irritating behaviors. They produce a "negative intimacy" that tends to "infuriate peers or adults. . . . There is something intolerably invasive" about them (107 n.3). Few adults have never had a young child deliberately mime actions or mimic behaviors. This nearly always ends in intensely negative responses on the part of the one imi-tated. The activity, seemingly only an irritating game designed to annoy adults, is in truth an important experiment in developing separateness. In exaggerating the normally unconscious attunements that are part of human relation, the child is underscoring her self as separate from the other. For the recipient of imitation, however, making attunement a deliberate and conscious process seems to violate the intimacy of true relatedness.

There is no fusion of selves here, but there *is* fusion of affect. This fusion of affect—affect attunement—is possible very early in life, as Stern's research has shown. Children are capable of displaying sympathetic responses at a very early age: offering of one's own "blankie" or comfort item to soothe another or bringing one's own mother to comfort an injured friend even though the injured child's caregiver is present, are examples of early sympathetic responding. Nancy Eisenberg's research into prosocial behavior shows that by the age of ten to fourteen months infants clearly respond to the distress of others, but the responding usually takes the form of seeking comfort for themselves. Infants only gradually come to differentiate between their own and another's distress. By eighteen to twenty-four months, comforting behaviors directed toward the distressed other begin to appear, with children becoming "more overtly and self-consciously other-oriented and less self-oriented with age."[10]

It should be clear at this point that the ability to share one's inner thought world with others is integral to the development of a healthy sense of self. The self is formed in and through relationship to other human beings. Without the capacity for intersubjectivity, the self cannot mature. Since our goal here is to lay the foundations for a theological anthropology that allows for an ontological doctrine of incarnation, I want now to build on Stern's theoretical insights into the interconnectedness of self-development and the capacity to share in the lifeworlds of others. This will require some theorizing of my own about the mechanism through which we are able to participate in the lifeworlds of others.

Entrainment or Interpersonal Synchrony

When we say one thing entrains another, we mean in simplest terms that one pulls the other along in tandem. In the human, synchrony of physical responses occurs between fetus and mother, infant and caregiver, and even among conversation partners (e.g., heart rate and respiration shift into similar rhythms and rates). Social psychology has generated a substantial body of research documenting the phenomenon of entrainment at the microcultural, macrocultural, and biological levels. There is much documentation in support of the theory that people living and working together enter into forms of temporal synchrony.[11]

William Condon is one of the foremost researchers into the relationship between human communication and entrainment. He has found that each of us exists in an elegant realm of self-synchrony, wherein the body moves in synch with one's own speech.[12] Interactional entrainment is a recent discovery of science, made possible by the advent of the film industry. In the early days of filmmaking, it was necessary to record sound separately from the visual portion of the movie and later synchronize voices with actions. Observation of body language and group interaction in frame-by-frame sequence revealed the astonishingly complex nature of human interaction. Stern acknowledges the importance of self-synchrony in temporal coherence but discounts the possibility of interactional synchrony. Since each individual lives within his or her own temporal structure (self-synchrony), Stern believes it to be impossible that timing of behavior can be influenced by another (83–84). Yet he notes the reality of "self/other similarity," which occurs between lovers, mothers and infants, even groups of people (107 n.3). He does not explain how these behaviors contradict the concept of interactional synchrony. Stern claims that Condon's research on interactional synchrony has not been replicated and that the phenomenon "has not stood the test of time" (84). A survey of the literature, however, indicates otherwise.[13]

Conversation partners have an incredibly intricate and complex mode of interaction. The listener in conversation "moves with the speaker's speech almost as well as the speaker's body itself." Infants apparently entrain to the voice almost as well as do adults. This elegant interactional display occurs outside of awareness, and with amazing precision.[14] The more in synchrony that listener and speaker are in terms of posture and body movement, the greater the degree of rapport experienced.[15] Something very like this conversational linking is present in the human infant almost from the moment of birth, and may well exist *in utero*. It has been experimentally demonstrated to exist within an hour of birth. The human infant is so adept at entraining to speech that should a different language be spoken, the rhythm of the baby's movements will change to match the new language.[16] There is a "precisely shared communicational dance" between infant and mother, says Condon. "This early entrainment may be an aspect of the development of empathy."[17]

The Anatomy of Empathy

> The self is not an unchanging entity with fixed borders but a fluc-
> tuating confluence of relationships. It is a dynamic integration
> that emerges in and through love.
>
> LINELL E. CADY

Empathy has become something of a buzzword in psychology. It is a relatively new word for English speakers, coined in German as *Einfühlung* (*ein* = one; *fühlung* = feeling) in the late nineteenth century.[18] It was first used in aesthetics to describe how we respond to art but was quickly taken up into the vocabulary of psychology as a descriptive term for "feeling oneself into" a situation.[19]

Until this new word appeared, the English-speaking world used sympathy to refer to any sort of shared emotional state. According to the Oxford English Dictionary, sympathy comes from the Greek, *sympatheia*, meaning "having fellow feeling." It is "the quality or state of being affected by the condition of another with similar feeling . . . entering into or sharing the feelings of another; conformity of feelings . . . community of feelings; harmony of disposition." Empathy is "the power of projecting one's personality into (and so fully comprehending) the object of contemplation."

Sympathy has been an object of philosophical inquiry for several centuries. David Hume and Adam Smith explored its role in moral development. Charles Darwin, influenced by Adam Smith's work, considered it to be an emotion that was vital to survival. Partly as a result of Darwin's attraction to the concept, late nineteenth- and early twentieth-century social psychologists integrated it into theories of instinctual behavior, as a product of operant conditioning rather than inheritance. Developmental psychologists in the late nineteenth century noted a correlation between sympathy and parental affection, and between sympathy and altruism. But again, sympathy was nothing more than a learned response. With the advent of empathy as a new concept, interest in sympathy waned.[20]

Empathy eclipsed sympathy in theoretical exploration. Interest in the concept was directly proportional to development of psychoanalysis. Soon after empathy entered the vocabularies of psychology and philosophy, confusion erupted. Meanings varied so widely that they were at times contradictory. Empathy has been called a form of knowing, of communicating, of perceiving, of understanding. It has been said to be role-taking, mimicry, a process, a learned ability, an expression of ego, a form of emotion, a cognitive act, a classically conditioned response, or a genetically transmitted innate response.[21]

Psychology is indebted to two theorists for the current emphasis on empathy in therapy and in human development. Carl Rogers's technique of unconditional positive regard and Heinz Kohut's insistence that empathy is "the essence of the psychoanalytic cure" and "the major constituent of the sense of security in adult life" fixed empathy at the apex of psychoanalytic theory.[22]

Today, theorists who distinguish between sympathy and empathy generally define sympathy as a somewhat inferior reflex-like response or a quasi-manipulative emotional event in which the sympathizer lacks control. Empathy is usually interpreted to be a superior mode of relating in which the empathizer maintains separation from the object of one's empathy. One theorist calls sympathy a kind of "immature, imperfect empathy."[23] Another begins his essay delineating the differences between sympathy and empathy and ends by conflating the terms so that empathy becomes "attenuated sympathy."[24]

Given these widely variant and even contradictory understandings of a concept that is generally believed to be the defining aspect of psychotherapy, one wonders how conversation among theorists occurs at all. Developmental and social psychologists see empathy as constitutive of the healthy human[25] and have struggled unsuccessfully to develop accurate tools for its measurement in adults. This inability objectively to measure the individual capacity for empathy is due in part to lack of agreement on just what empathy is and in part to the fact that empathy as an event is itself unstable. Studies show that situational factors like mood, sex, length of interaction time, and setting have a definite impact on empathic responses. Nonverbal cues have also been shown to influence empathy. Empathic abilities emerge developmentally, can be learned, vary considerably between people and also from situation to situation in the same person, are present in inverse relation to personality disturbances, and are important to the therapeutic milieu.[26]

Steven Levy says that empathy has become a "superordinate" term that should be employed to describe the different ways an analyst interacts with the analysand. Present-day confusion is the result of theorists having taken "a part for the whole."[27] Theorists have confused a way of being-in-relation with the entire process of psychoanalysis. Although the usefulness of these terms in describing a particular technique of psychoanalysis may be debatable at this juncture, our concern here is with the role of empathy and sympathy in interpersonal relation and not the therapeutic milieu per se.

Empathy has been linked to entrainment in an essay by Richard Restak, in which he describes possible neurobiological associations for the empathic process. There *is* an innate human tendency toward some sort of shared rhythm of life, which reveals itself at the biological as well as communicational levels. Although he stops short of postulating the eventual discovery of actual neurological explanations for empathy, Restak does believe that the empathic process is intimately connected to those processes that drive the human tendency to entrain, or live in synchrony.[28] Other theorists argue that empathy entails a communication process that is based in biology and fundamental to all living things—in simple organisms it is rooted in preattunements and innate displays, while higher social beings must learn how to use these innate capacities.[29]

I suggest that, for humans, the process whereby one is able to feel what has been perceived in the other operates in and among four interrelated domains: entrainment, affect attunement, sympathy, and empathy. These four domains are best understood as aspects of a more global process, which I call the capacity for *participation*. It may be helpful at this point to review the definitions outlined in chapter 1. *Entrainment* is the earliest and more biological means of entering into the lifeworld of others. It is found throughout nature, in the most elementary and the most complex forms of life. I will say more about this astonishing capacity in the next section of this chapter, but for now we can define it as an innate biological response in which an organism brings itself into harmony with its environment. In the human infant, entrainment with caregivers involves physiological synchronizing of biological responses like heart rate and breathing. It is the first and most basic step toward participatory relation. Entrainment is an unconscious event involving biological responses.

Attunement involves the matching of one's emotional state to that of others, and as such assumes a more highly developed sense of self as different from others. It tends to begin cross-modally: I may first match your excited tone of voice with rapid body movement, for example. In infants, it sometimes looks like mimicry, as the child matches his or her facial expressions, tone of voice, level of excitability and so forth to others. Attunement can be done deliberately to enhance communication. But mothers and infants, lovers, and close friends engage in unconscious attunement that is part of the elegant rhythm of deep communication.

Entrainment and attunement pull us physically into the mental experience of shared emotion, or *sympathy*. The conformity of one's feelings with those of another is a type of fusion. In sympathy, we experience the emotions of another person as though those emotions were our own. Sympathy is "an immediate flow of experiences *undifferentiated as between mine and thine*, which actually contains both our and others' experiences intermingled and without distinction from one another."[30]

Empathy is a somewhat removed way of responding to others. It seems to be an innate capacity for some and more a learned skill for others. Empathy is the more conscious and linguistic aspect of sharing in the lifeworld of another. When it occurs as a natural response, entrainment, attunement, and sympathy all come into play in a kind of sequential flow of unconscious physical and psychological events that culminate in felt comprehension of the other's experience. But because it is a cognitive event, it is possible to generate empathy by choice. In this case, the sequence is to some extent reversed. The decision to relate empathically can be made fully consciously, as when a therapist enters into counseling with a client, or quasi-consciously, as when a parent "steps back" from the urge to solve her children's problems for them. When the decision for empathic relating is conscious, the first step in the process becomes imaginative projection. Through the imagination, the emotional responses of sympathy and psycho-physiological responses of attunement and entrainment are stimulated.

Sympathy does not require imaginative projection. In sympathetic responding, one is with the object of sympathy. Sympathy is an innate and somewhat automatic response, and as such can result in confusing one's own needs with those of the other. In fact this blurring is an important aspect of motivation to alleviate the suffering of others. As Thomas Hobbes said, "My alms, giving some relief, doth also ease me."[31] Experience is organized into patterns of thought prior to linguisticality. Language is, in a sense, an outgrowth of rather than the basis for thought.[32] Sympathy, as a quasi-linguistic emotional response to the experience of another, is best characterized as more basic than empathy, which requires some degree of linguistic ability and higher-level cognition. Empathy and sympathy are not identical, nor are they antithetical.

To speak of empathy and sympathy as aspects of the larger process of being-in-relation-with others (more specifically in the sense of being able to share the intrapsychic lifeworld of fellow human beings) allows us to talk of these processes without the confusion that has ensued from the last century's engagement with the psychoanalytic process. Locating the processes of entrainment, attunement, sympathy, and empathy under the umbrella of *participation* allows us to speak now of the whole, rather than just the parts. Each of these is one aspect of the elegant and finally incomprehensible way in which the human person is able to be a self while knowing the experience of another. The broader framework offered here allows attention to be shifted away from semantic issues toward the more powerful questions of human relationality that form the core of the theological project for which this exploration provides foundation.

Entrainment and affect attunement are the primordial domains of participation. They occur at the earliest stages of human life and continue throughout. They are preverbal processes that form the ground out of which intersubjectivity grows. Without entrainment and attunement, social interaction would not be possible. With them, the human is able to enter into a region of deep relationality long before the advent of linguistic abilities. It is only by virtue of the processes whereby we are able to synchronize and attune physiologically and affectively to another that we are able to *feel* the emotion of sympathy or *think* the cognition of empathy. So it is through an elegant interplay of sensuality (entrainment and attunement) and intellect (sympathy and, more so, empathy) that we are able to share another's lifeworld.

Cosmic Sympathy: Entrainment and Altruism in Nature

> [God] joined the whole cosmos . . . by an unbroken law of love into one communion and concord, so that things . . . appear to be united through a universal affinity, that is sympatheia.
>
> Basil of Caesarea

A further, deeper dimension of participation is cosmic. The human being comes to knowledge of self in and through relation to other human beings. Participation, the capacity for experiencing and responding to another's intrapsychic lifeworld, links us to one another and to existence itself. Through entrainment we "are organizationally linked with and part of the universe in which we evolved." From birth we are "naturally receptive to the structure of the universe."[33] There seems to be an underlying rhythm of creation, into synch with which all of life moves. There are "populations of nested rhythms which select and entrain [us] in the form of different species and their individual members, ranging from

Mozart to his mitochondria." This rhythm is available to us through entrainment, which some have proposed as the meta-model for all knowledge.[34]

Evolutionary Biology and the Ecological Self

Entrainment as a biological concept is not new. It has long been recognized that many creatures physiologically entrain to their environments and to other members of their species. The underlying rhythm of life reveals itself in, for example, the universal human tendency to dance: one researcher explains that music is actually an extension of the rhythms that already exist within the individual, and not the source of the rhythms to which we respond.[35] The chameleon's ability to camouflage itself through changing coloration and the seasonal migration patterns of birds are two widely known examples of entrainment in nature. The so-called "biological clock," co-regulation of menstrual cycles among women living in close quarters, courting dances of some species of bird, responsiveness of human and animal fetuses to light, sound, and maternal circadian rhythms are only a few examples of the ways in which higher forms of life are known to entrain with environment.[36]

Entrainment plays a role in time perception, as well. Biological time, or the temporal integration of physical bodies, is the means by which living beings stay in step with their worlds. The biological clock, or circadian rhythm, determines sleep patterns, mating behavior, hunting, and accounts for phenomena like jet lag. Studies of fetal circadian rhythms reveal a neurological connection that involves the hypothalamus of mother and fetus. The maternal biological clock plays an important role in regulation of the fetus's physiological rhythms.[37] The phenomenon of entrainment, so important to the human capacity for sharing the lifeworld of others and development of the self, is integral to nature itself.

Entrainment is vital to survival. From the primitive response of a plant that turns to maximize exposure to sunlight, to the elegant interactional synchrony among humans in conversation, all of life displays the aptitude for entraining with environment and with other living beings. Even sensory perception is an elegant participatory experience in which a kind of entrainment between knower and known occurs. The other, be it human or another form of life, confirms my own reality in and through the activity of perception. The human self is "ecological" in this sense, that perception is by its very nature participation in creation.[38]

Reciprocal altruism, another fascinating and important natural phenomenon that has theological implications, is tied to this capacity for interrelation. Creatures traditionally believed to operate out of a selfish drive for individual survival exhibit collaborative behaviors that bear striking resemblance to altruism among humans. Biologists have documented cooperation in which animals even risk injury and death in order to ensure the survival of other members of the same species. Even more surprising are documented cases of nonhuman creatures risking their own lives to save the lives of members of other species, one of which is discussed below.

Altruism in humans is linked to the capacity for empathy.[39] Although empathic ability in and of itself does not account for truly altruistic action on the part of human beings, it is influential in the process of risking one's own well-being for the sake of another. Since we know that entrainment in human behavior is foundational for the experience of empathy, it is likely that entrainment in nature is linked to the drive toward altruism among nonhuman species. Although there are to my knowledge no studies linking entrainment with the capacity for altruism in nature, I want to explore the possibility that a connection does exist, one that mirrors the connection drawn in our analysis of the human capacity for sharing the lifeworld of others.

Operating within a Darwinian model of evolution as "survival of the fittest," biologists have found the presence of altruism in nature quite puzzling. Like *empathy*, the word *altruism* has different meanings in the literature. Sometimes it is used as a synonym for cooperative or prosocial behaviors like giving and sharing. It differs, however, from these behaviors. True altruism means that an individual sacrifices fitness in order to maintain or increase the fitness of another.[40] Altruism as sacrificial behavior aimed at supporting the survivability of another has been found throughout nature, and in the most surprising places.

In 1984, biologist Gerald Wilkinson published a study that documents reciprocal altruism among Costa Rican vampire bats.[41] The vampire bat survives by drinking the blood of larger animals: given that this is accomplished by making small cuts in the skin of creatures many times larger than the bats, a night's foray can often end unsuccessfully. On average, young bats fail in the search for blood one out of every three nights, while older bats fail about once every ten nights. Since starvation sets in for the bats after going without blood for sixty hours, young bats are in real danger of death should they fail to obtain food two nights in a row. (Since the mammals are nocturnal, to fail two consecutive nights would mean going at least sixty hours between meals.) However, a form of reciprocal altruism has evolved that reduces the chances of death from starvation.

When a bat is successful in feeding, he drinks more blood than is needed at the time; upon return to the roost, he regurgitates some of the excess blood to feed those who have failed in their nocturnal hunt. Since it is possible for them to starve quickly, their sharing excess blood is antithetical to the bats' natures within a Darwinian survival of the fittest model. Individual bat survival would be enhanced by building up nutritional reserves to tide them over the nights of no success. But the bats engage in a more exquisite and less selfish form of survival insurance.

The bats apparently engage in a kind of score keeping—"You give to me and I'll give to you. You cheat me, and I'll cheat you."[42] Since the bats live in close proximity for many years, they develop individual relationships in which bats that have shared blood in the past receive blood when needed from the recipient of past generosity. Even the grooming behavior of the bats seems to have developed to support sharing. When grooming one another, the bats spend an especially large amount of time with the area around the stomach, which means that cheating is easily detected—an abdomen distended by a large meal cannot be hidden in this situation![43] And so nature has evolved a complex system of helping behaviors that supports both individual and group survival. This striking example of

reciprocal altruism helps us to see that the tendency toward cooperation is inherent in nature—survival is dependent upon it.

Selfish Genes and Killer Whales

Evolutionary biologists have found that the only way to make sense of
altruism within a Darwinian paradigm is to insist that the "selfish
gene," in fact, drives even the most self-sacrificing behaviors. Oxford
biologist Richard Dawkins popularized this concept in the 1960s: individuals act not for the good of the group, or even for the self, but for
the good of their genes.[44] In this paradigm, altruism is nothing more
than genetic selfishness, explained in terms of reciprocity, kinship, or
group selection.

For these theorists reciprocity or reciprocal altruism is a form of
barter in which the implicit assumption is that if I do a good deed
for you, someday when I am in need you will return the goodness.
Here altruism is actually a short-term strategy aimed at long-term
gain, as we saw in the example of food sharing among vampire bats.

In a group selection framework, altruism happens because it is
beneficial to the group's survival. The sacrificial act of one member
of the group ensures continuation of the group as a whole. Groups
that have some members who act altruistically have survival advantage over groups without at least some altruists. Within the group,
selfish behavior is most successful, but a few altruistic members will
be encouraged so that their giving can be exploited for the overall
advantage of the group. In order to encourage altruism within
groups, sanctions are levied against members who take advantage
of altruists for personal gain, and incentives are given to members
that behave altruistically. In this model, having too many altruists
would be as dangerous to group survival as having none, and so the
incentive and sanction process is a sophisticated evolutionary
mechanism.

The kinship selection model sees genetic material as the driving
force behind altruism. Self-sacrificial acts ensure the survival of
genes. In this mode, I would be prone to take care of myself and
members of my immediate family first, since this is where my

purest genetic material resides. Once my own survival and that of close relations is assured, only then might I consider providing assistance to others in need.

But what about cross-species altruism? Biologist Lyall Watson reports an amazing incident, which simply cannot be explained by means of traditional reciprocity, group, or kinship models. In 1976 twenty-nine false killer whales beached themselves on an island off the Florida Keys. Watson participated in a rescue effort along with private citizens and other scientists. A large male whale was obviously ill, bleeding from one ear, and unable to remain upright in the shallow water. The other whales were trying to prevent his drowning by supporting him to keep his blowhole above water. The altruistic whales were in danger of death themselves, as the water was very shallow. Try as they might, the human rescuers could not find a way to force the healthy whales back into deeper water. In the end, the human helpers gave up trying to get the whales to swim away and resorted to trying to keep the whales wet and sheltered so they would not sunburn. On the third night, the ailing male died, and by dawn the group of whales had begun to disband. The whales knew that their companion could no longer benefit from their help, and so they quietly swam away. Watson believes these whales displayed true concern for another. Although this anecdotal evidence is not as highly valued as controlled studies in the realm of science, he insists that the word *concern* is appropriate, for not only did the whales risk death for the sake of their ailing group member: during the three days of attempting to help the whales, the humans were themselves "rescued" a number of times by the sixteen-foot long whales.

> Each time one of us swam anywhere near the group wearing a snorkel—through which we make noises that do sometimes resemble those of a whale with a waterlogged blowhole—we would promptly be "rescued." One of the whales would detach itself from the group, slide underneath the human swimmer, rise so slowly that he was lifted almost clear of the water, and carry him further into the shallows. It was a humbling experience to be so propelled, able to do little to interfere with the effort

until one could stand and take out the mouthpiece and stop making such distressed and distressing sounds.[45]

How do we explain this cross-species altruism? "Helping across the species lines argues very strongly against a simple genetic explanation for altruism," says Watson. In this environmentally conscious age, we have made some advances in understanding ourselves as dependent upon the ecosystem for survival, and so the human actions make sense. But what about the whales? How can we explain their actions toward the humans? Watson answers in terms of reciprocity: when one encounters altruism it is very difficult not to reciprocate, and so the whales would somehow have known that they "owed" the humans like action. But it truly is not this simple.

Even though he appeals to reciprocity to explain the whales' willingness to save the divers, Watson notes, "There is a ratchet in the works, a mechanism which allows something more generous to grow out of indifference, something 'good.'"[46] Even Richard Dawkins, promoter of the selfish-gene theory, has noticed this tendency in nature. "As Darwinians we start pessimistically by assuming deep selfishness, pitiless indifference to suffering, ruthless heed to individual success. And yet, from such warped beginnings, something . . . close to amicable brotherhood and sisterhood can come."[47]

DRAWING NEAR
TO A THEOLOGICAL ANTHROPOLOGY

God created humankind in his image, in the image of God he created them.

GEN. 1:27

Empathy is crucial to the human capacity for self-transcendence and therefore to the human experience of spirituality. Self-transcendence is the capacity to reflect on the totality of life and to transform one's natural self by virtue of spiritual freedom.[48] Transcendence is both a natural (or "horizontal") and a spiritual (or "vertical") reality.

In nature it is relative and relational, in that each entity transcends all others by virtue of difference, and at the same time transcends itself in and through empathy. "Empathy is the de-absolutization of the self and therefore the transcendence of the self by knowing the self as one center among many centers, participating in a universe of centerless centering. Empathy requires a 'feeling-with' that mediates the sense of interconnectedness" and makes possible the willing of well-being of others.[49]

Vertical, or spiritual, transcendence involves a knowing of the self in its openness to God: in other words, an entraining, attuning encounter of sympathetic awareness that human actions truly matter to God. Simply put, it is participation in the divine. Horizontal transcendence within the realm of the finite is grounded in difference. It is the act of participation with other finite beings. In self-transcendence, participation in the lifeworld of another, we can be moved to act for the well being of others by virtue of our encounter with their experience. "Transcendence through empathy draws on infinity within relation."[50] Or in the words of Karl Rahner, "In knowledge and freedom, which are the concrete realization of life, the I is always related to a Thou, is primordially as much with the Thou as with the I, always only experiences itself as differentiated from, and identified with, the other in the encounter with the other person."[51] The human being has a dual capacity for self-transcendence: the vertical, cognitive openness to the horizon of being (God), and the horizontal, moral openness to the being of others. We are created with the capacity to know God and as such have the moral capacity, indeed obligation, to know the finite other.

Human beings are the world's first potentially truly ethical creatures. We are certainly to some extent at the mercy of our genes but apparently much less so than any other species presently alive on this planet. In our decisions, in the choices we make and the institutions we create, we can and sometimes do transcend biology. Motivated by participatory relation we can choose to engage one another in compassionate action.

Biblical scholarship has shown that the Hebrew word for compassion originates from the same root as that for the womb, *rhm*.

As a singular noun, *rehem* means uterus or womb. In the plural, *rahamîm*, it can mean compassion, love, and mercy.[52] When we speak of God as capable of compassionate care, or empathy, "the semantic tenor of the word indicates that the womb is trembling, yearning" and that God loves the world with the costly love of a mother for the fetus within. The prophet Isaiah portrays God's suffering due to human evils in the graphic language of child-birth: "For a long time I have held my peace, I have kept still and restrained myself; now I will cry out like a woman in labor, I will gasp and pant" (42:14). And so God's love for the world is perhaps best characterized as "womb-love."[53] Just as the human mother and fetus entrain with one another physiologically, God entrains with the world through womb-love.

Perhaps science will always find it difficult to explain the altruistic tendency in nature. But for theology, this is not so problematic. Just as the human being entrains with others, thereby engaging in the process of developing the absolutely relational self, nature entrains and engages in processes not unlike the human capacity for participation. The ratchet in the works that drives nature on toward generosity, toward brotherhood and sisterhood has its source in the divine. The cosmos is a boundless system of discrete but interrelated parts that are harmonized through a universal affinity that has its origin in God. The unity of the cosmos in divine love, says Basil of Caesarea, is *sympatheia*, the kinship or harmony of all creation.[54] God is most deeply connected to the world process. To describe God's presence in the world as participation allows us to consider God's impact at all levels of creation, from the most basic rhythms of life to the most sophisticated of cognitive acts. The universe is united through divine participation, a truth most clearly revealed through the incarnation of God, to the discussion of which we now return.

6

The Incarnation as Participation

> Always and in all his Word God wills to effect the mystery of
> his embodiment.
>
> Maximus the Confessor

It is time now to fulfill the intent of this work. I want to offer a new
symbolic language of incarnation that captures the intent of
ancient creeds and at the same time preserves the ontological sense
of the Christian doctrine. The christological, theological, and
anthropological insights we have explored will now be interlaced to
show how we can say that God is made incarnate through participatory relation.

This will involve several steps, the first of which is to construct a
word-picture of the human Jesus. To do this, I will place what the
tradition tells us about Jesus into the context of chapters 4 and 5:
the discussion of ideas of God as deeply involved in and moved by
creation and of the human capacity for participation in the lifeworlds of others. If the Christian conviction that Jesus' human
nature was not different from yours or mine, theories of selfhood
and altruistic behavior in human beings should illuminate our
understanding of his relationship to the world. If I am on the right
track with this revision, theological insights into divine *pathos*

should be harmonious with the picture of Jesus that begins to emerge. Then I must assemble a bridge to span the gap that remains between psychological theory and the theology of incarnation. The materials out of which I build the bridge include what we know of the symbolic nature of language and Karl Rahner's splendid (but up to now little-known) theology of the symbol. Rahner's concepts of the plurality of being and the Logos as symbol of God provide the ground out of which a fully developed theology of incarnation as participation will grow.

Jesus the Man: Fully Human

> He took with him Peter and James and John, and began to be distressed and agitated. And he said to them, "I am deeply grieved, even to death; remain here, and keep awake." And going a little farther, he threw himself on the ground and prayed. . . . He said, "Abba, Father, for you all things are possible; remove this cup from me, yet not what I want, but what you want."
>
> Mark 14:33-36

We have no direct information about the formative influences in Jesus' life. But if we believe, as Christian doctrine insists and Scripture demonstrates, that Jesus was fully human, we must assume that throughout life Jesus was subject to and shaped by the same kinds of developmental influences that affect all human beings. Although those who quest for the historical man lament the paucity of historical facts, in the context of this work, absence of information underscores the power of the narratives that we do have: Jesus simply appears to us, having been shaped by his human experience, ready to offer a new revelation of the divine. Beyond what can be inferred—his Jewishness, for example—there is nothing specific we can say about how Jesus' human nature came to be uniquely open to the divine. We are shown in the Gospels that this was so, but we cannot on the basis of specific historical evidence say much about how Jesus came to be the man he was. In terms of proof, "Absence of evidence is not evidence of absence."[1]

Douglas Ottati says that Jesus the man must be seen as constituted by his genetic makeup and environmental influences.[2] Jesus is the clearest expression of God's grace and incarnates not the divine nature, as in the sense of *ousia* or being, but incarnates God in his "radical devotion to God." In and through the presence of grace in Jesus, God is constitutive of who Jesus is. Jesus' life corresponds to the divine; it participates in and gives expression to the reality of God. Although he argues against substance language, Ottati's exploration of the formative influences on Jesus' humanity is useful here.

Operating under the assumption that human subjectivity is to a great extent expressed in behavioral patterns, Ottati argues that we must assume at least some degree of congruity between an individual's actions, speech, and inner commitments. In order to understand one another, we correlate behaviors with affections and commitments. When another's speech does not correlate with his or her actions, we find it difficult to understand who that person is. Each of us has an emotional constitution (what Ottati calls "heart": patterns of feeling or affections) that is a result of one's genetic makeup, social influences, and one's organizing or integrative center of reason. Our understandings of one another are largely based on actions: we infer another's heart, affections, priorities, and commitments, from her or his actions. So although we have no direct information in the Gospels about the early influences on Jesus' development, we can say that the narratives reveal Jesus' character and something of his subjectivity by way of the behaviors and words recorded.[3] The Gospels give us "sharp access to Jesus' affections" as perceived by those who knew him.[4] That said, what does this perception mean for a doctrine of incarnation?

As noted earlier, the most distinctive term used in the Scriptures to describe Jesus' involvement with others is *splanchnizesthai*, to be viscerally moved, to be affected in the gut, to have compassion. His extraordinary openness to the lifeworld of others is symbolized, for example, in the report of his sensing the touch of the woman who bled for twelve years before being healed in her encounter with Jesus (Mark 5:29; Luke 8:44). On the basis of our exploration of human development, we can say that the human Jesus was so shaped by his own early life experience as to be able to enter into deeply empathic relation. That this is so is recorded in the Scriptures: Jesus was perceived by those who knew him to act out of a viscerally felt "feeling with" those to whom he reached out. Since reference to his capacity to enter into the experience of others is mentioned frequently in the Gospels, we can assume that this ability must have been quite striking, even unique among his peers.[5] On the basis of what is now known about the development of human selfhood, we can say that Jesus had what we today would call a healthy sense of self and a highly developed capacity for empathy. This capacity led him to a self-giving career of teaching and preaching for the liberation of the soul and the relief of suffering.

We explored in chapter 5 how it is that one enters into the life-world of another. The impetus to relieve another's suffering is an outgrowth of the process by which the sense of self develops and by which we are able to comprehend the experience of others. Helping behaviors, then, are grounded in the capacity to share in the life-world of others. But as noted in the previous chapter, there is a kind of helping behavior that appears to go beyond the bounds of this paradigm—altruism. An uncompromised willingness to risk personal well-being for the sake of others is an important aspect of who Jesus is. The radical character of his self-giving and its relationship to the "ratchet in the works" of creation are material to this ontological interpretation of incarnation.

Altruism, Empathy, and Jesus

Altruism is of special interest to a variety of theorists today. We saw in the previous chapter how important it is to psychology and biology. Political theorists concerned with ethical behavior have begun to explore it as well. Like genetic theories, most political and social theories explain helping behavior in terms of self-interest. Our lives are assumed to be directed by selfish motives, and yet selflessness endures. Kristan Renwick Monroe, a political theorist at the University of California, insists that although self-interest provides a starting point for understanding humans, it fails to explain many behaviors. She studied people who offered assistance to others, ranging from generosity based in self-interest (like giving money to charity) to true selflessness. She concluded that "ethical political action emanates primarily from one's sense of self in relation to others."[6] The motivating force behind ethical behavior appears to be primarily a product of intuitions related to the sense of self: "identity is more basic than conscious adherence to moral values" (219). This means that if an act is in tune with our sense of self, it is not so much a choice as a recognition of the act as a reflection of who we already are (214–20).

Monroe came to these captivating conclusions through empirical study. She conceptualized behavior along a continuum, with pure altruism at one pole and pure self-interest at the other. She then identified subjects and divided them into groups descriptive of their performance of helping acts. Criteria for classification included degree of risk to self and family as well as expectation or likelihood of reward: the greater the real risk to personal and family well-being and the more likely the act would go unrewarded, the more altruistic the behavior. In the study itself, Monroe placed entrepreneurs at one end of her spectrum because they are "paradigmatic self-interested actors." Generosity of entrepreneurs is based on a kind of calculus in which benefits, like tax deductions, potential praise or publicity, or future likelihood of payback (reciprocity) are evaluated. Their giving is therefore clearly linked to self-interest. Philanthropists are next along the continuum, defined as those who engage in significant acts of giving—usually financial—that reduce but do not obliterate well-being. Heroes and heroines are next, distinguished by their status as ordinary citizens who risk their lives in a single act to save another. Finally, true altruists are those who place themselves at risk over a period of time to perform helping acts that offer little or no possibility of praise or reward, and that entail risk to significant others.

Monroe interviewed people who had rescued Jews in Europe from Nazi persecution and found that they most closely fit the classification for true altruism. Many rescuers housed Jews for months or years at a time. Obviously recognition for these acts was out of the question since when discovered by the Nazis these actions were often punished by imprisonment and execution. The consequences more often than not extended to include the rescuers' families and neighbors (15–18).

Important to an understanding of altruism is the fact that these people often lacked the things that traditional theories based in self-interest say are prerequisite for selflessness: safety, emotional support, even food and fuel (155). The act of helping was the end itself. No other motive could be identified: in-group or kinship concerns were not operative since Monroe studied only non-Jewish rescuers. The desire to help was so strong that many of the rescuers gave food to Jewish refugees even when it meant their own families had to go without (166). Because the danger of imprisonment, torture, and execution extended to their families, many altruists isolated themselves from loved ones and friends (176). The altruists often found it necessary to violate learned ethical standards in performing acts of self-giving—lying in order to protect the refugees, for example (194). Bluntly put, there was absolutely no incentive to assist the Jews, and tremendous incentive not to. Why, then, did these people act as they did?

Monroe looked for developmental factors in the histories of her sample group that might reveal similar circumstances of life and upbringing that play a part in psychological shaping, such as economic status, race, education, or religious affiliation. She found none. There was no consistency in parental relationship. There was a tendency among altruists to have identified with a role model in development of ethical values, but overall the altruists' experiences of parental and societal influences mirrored that of the general population. Just like the rest of us, altruists' relationships with parents ranged from abusive to supportive (179–84).

The perspective of the altruist diverged from all others in one respect: "Altruists see the world as one in which connections exist and extend through nature, beyond the death of any one particular individual" (123). Because of this, altruists acted without regard for consequences, and perceived themselves as having no choice in the situation. They *had* to act as they did. The core of altruistic identity is a perceived link to humankind as a whole: "All life concerns them. All death diminishes them. Because they are part of mankind" (216). This is not a singular empathic response to the needs of one individual, although the capacity for empathy is an integral part of it. Altruism seems to arise from a global participatory relation to humankind as a whole.

The altruist somehow entrains and attunes with humanity at large so as to respond immediately, reflexively even, to the need of another. The altruist seems to pass through the affect-laden sympathetic domain instantaneously, taking hold of the stimulus to action while automatically engaging the other empathetically. The capacity for empathy is so complete in the altruist that it is possible for him or her to stand outside of the most basic human categories of in-grouping, like family, in responding to another's need. The altruist transcends not only self but also the human propensity for narrowing helping behavior to those most "like me." The altruist is able to transcend difference in order to preserve the unique, the singular person.

The Gospel record of Jesus' behavior portrays him as very like Monroe's true altruist. He, like those who provided sanctuary for Jews during the Nazi regime, forsook the emotional ties of family in the interests of what he perceived to be a greater human need. Like Monroe's altruists, Jesus found it necessary to violate learned standards of behavior and to disobey the authority of the rabbis. Out of a sense of loyalty to a greater and more universal ethical standard he broke the basic teachings of his faith regarding work on the Sabbath (cf. Mark 3:-6; Matt. 12:1-14). Jesus also seems usually to have wanted no praise for the good that he did. He often directed those he healed "to tell no one" (Luke 5:12-16). Just as the altruist acts without regard for consequences to family and self, Jesus went so far as to respond, when told his mother and brothers were waiting, "Who are my mother and brothers? . . . Whoever does the will of God is my brother and sister and mother" (Mark 3:31-35). Knowing full well the dangers, Jesus continued to preach and to teach publicly, even to the end. He prayed, as death approached, that if it be God's will, he be relieved of the burden (Luke 22:39-42). For him, the choice was God's, not his own.

Jesus clearly fits the identified pattern of altruistic behavior. He was inordinately capable of self-transcendence on the horizontal plane. But the Christian interpretation of Jesus' life insists that he was much more than an altruist, that his life and death were somehow revelatory of God in a new way. The Christian tradition teaches that his ability to transcend self went beyond the horizontal, so much so that we speak of him as having vertical transcendence into God.

Asymptotic Longing for God

To understand the human capacity for vertical transcendence into God, or deification, we begin with the theological insight that creation generally and humanity particularly are kinetic, not static, entities. Everything is in motion toward God in a perichoretic, mutually penetrating, relationship that has as its end the salvation of all creation, understood as union with the divine. Deification is a real possibility for all but is accomplished only through the gift of grace. As Friedrich Schleiermacher insisted, there dwells within creation the "possibility of taking up the divine," the implanting of which is "purely a divine and therefore eternal act." This possibility can be understood in terms of Maximus the Confessor's concept of *logoi*, seeds of God's plan for each created entity, or what Karl Rahner called the supernatural existential. This means that all of creation is imbued with the grace of God, that grace is "loose in the world."[7] The giver is the gift: the divine is really present as possibility and as end.

There is within each of us the potential to stand outside ourselves to share in the joys and sufferings of others. Not only can we, but apparently we must, having been so constituted that even our health is improved physically and psychologically when we actively and intimately share in the lifeworld of others.[8] The nascent human self, present at birth, reaches full maturity only in and through relation to others; and in this process, the possibility of divine encounter resides. Rahner posited that human knowing is receptive, and that to know is not first to grasp an object distinct from the self, but to be self-reflective. "The nature of being is to know and to be known in an original unity, in other words, self-presence."[9] The very fact that we ask what it means to be shows that we already have a provisional knowledge: it is impossible to ask about something that is entirely unknown to us. The nascent sense of self identified by developmental research—self-presence or subjectivity—forms the ground for the going-out-from-self that makes possible the encounter with God. We first know others only in and through the dialectical process of self-presence and going out from self to other: and so, too, by extension to God. "We go out toward God only by entering into the world . . . only by stepping out into the world can we so enter into ourselves that we encounter being and God."[10] The means by which we go out into the world to encounter the divine and nondivine other is participation. At the most basic level we entrain and attune with nature, with other forms of life, and with one another. The core self moves outward in a triangulation of sorts, through which the two known points, "self" and "other," are used to orient our asymptotic longing in the direction of God. As the self triangulates, participation takes on the shape of emotionally sympathetic and cognitively empathetic interaction, with other and with God, who is encountered as grace.

Self-other triangulation is kinetically oriented toward the infinite. Each truly participatory encounter with an other provides a glimpse of the asymptotic horizon of all transcendence. Each glimpse of this horizon serves to fuel our anticipation of the *telos* of creation, union with God. And so we live with hearts restless until they rest in the final salvific union. The offer and possibility of union with God, what Rahner called the supernatural existential, is constitutive of all creation. Revelation itself becomes a structural element of our experience. God in God's self is not always already within, but the potential always already exists for the absolute revelation.

Human Transcendence into God

Within Judaism, there has always been awareness of the possibility of a special kind of participatory relationship with God: that of the prophet. The Hebrew prophet is unique among humanity for his or her ability to become so entrained with and attuned to the divine will as to feel intensely—be in sympathy with—God's pain in the face of human disobedience. The *pathos* of God is revealed in the words and actions of the prophets. The prophet, so open to the divine, so capable of vertical self-transcendence, reveals God to us as Pathos and Sovereign, morally and ethically changeless, intensely moved by human experience.

The Hebrew prophet, in speaking as the mouthpiece of God, uses the first person pronoun because he feels God's *pathos*.[11] He is so in sympathy with God's desire that Israel obey the covenant, and God's distress at the Israelites' transgression, that he can legitimately speak as God. One of the most intriguing and conspicuous themes of prophetic speech is the threat of punishment.[12] Perhaps the words of the prophets are so often focused on chastisement because these men, as human beings in sympathy with the divine, were overwhelmed when faced with the gap between what God intended for the Jewish people and the reality of life.

Abraham Heschel says that Jeremiah, for example, occasionally suffered from "hypertrophy of sympathy for God" or "sympathy gone absolute."[13] At times, Jeremiah became so angry at the intransigence of his people that his own emotion conflicted with God's intention. In over-identifying with God, Jeremiah took on God's anger as his own. This is an error of sympathy that can only be corrected by the distancing that comes about through empathy. Jeremiah was overwhelmed by his sympathy for God and came into conflict with God's *pathos*. At these times he did not reflect the *pathos* of God; rather, his anger exceeded God's own response. Divine mercy and human rage conflicted, and so God rebuked Jeremiah, reminding him that the goal was discipline, not destruction, of his people.[14]

In Jesus, as in the Hebrew prophets, we see a human being capable of radical sympathy with God. The tenor of his teachings, however, differs from that of the prophets. For the most part Jesus conveys divine punishment less intensely than divine love and forgiveness.[15] The prophet's "words are designed to shock rather than to edify," says Heschel, and were aimed at "the life of a whole people."[16] Jesus taught a message intended for a people—the Jewish people—but that empowered the individual to transformation. When we speak of Jesus' ability to participate in the divine, we find that the difference between his relationship to God and that of the prophets implies that he was less prone to becoming overwhelmed by God's *pathos* than the prophets tended to be. With the exception of the cleansing of the Temple, Jesus is not reported to have displayed the kind of anger that plagued Jeremiah, for instance. It may be that the cleansing of the Temple was an instance for him of "hypertrophy of sympathy" with God in which he lost sight of God's mercy and became overwhelmed with the anger that more properly belonged to God. The cleansing of the Temple and surrounding narrative in Matthew's Gospel underscore the intensity of the man's relationship with God. Jesus' entry into Jerusalem appears deliberate and carefully planned. Matthew's Jesus throws down the gauntlet upon entry into Jerusalem in an apparent direct challenge to Jewish authorities that they deal with him and his message. This story is not the tale of a reluctant messiah. This Jesus is a man who knows what he is about and who surely knows what the likely consequences of his actions will be.

Both the intensity of his relationship with God and his complete humanity are clearly communicated here. Jesus' humanity erupts forth, overwhelmed at times with the difficult task of living in sympathy to God's plan. In the cleansing of the Temple, and then again the next morning, we see him struggling with the demands of an intense relationship with the divine. On his way back into Jerusalem on the day after causing the disturbance in the Temple, hungry, probably afraid of what awaits him in the city, Jesus looks for a fig, but the tree is barren. In what might be interpreted symbolically as a second instance of hypertrophy of sympathy, or overidentification with the divine will, he curses the tree; it dies. The tree, like the Jewish authorities, refuses to bear fruit in the face of God's plan, and so Jesus takes on himself that which properly belongs to God, the role of judge and the pronouncement of punishment. The disciples' amazement at what he has done serves to call Jesus back to his proper role as revealer of God's plan for creation.

These instances are examples of times when Jesus, like the Hebrew prophets before him, became overwhelmed by the experience of God's *pathos*. But Jesus differed from the prophets in that he was somehow better able to maintain a sense of who he was in relation to God and so able to withstand, to a greater degree, the intensity of emotion that came from being so in sympathy with God. "God is raging in the prophet's words."[17] And also, occasionally, in Jesus' words. But more often, God is forgiving in Jesus' words. The picture we have of Jesus in the Gospels leaves us with the distinct conviction that his relationship with God had a different character than that of the prophets'. We can understand this difference in terms of our taxonomy of participation: Jesus was the embodiment of cosmic participation. His relationship to God and to humankind went beyond sympathy, the ability to experience the other's feeling-states or emotions. Self-transcendence for him was well established horizontally, with fellow human beings, as well as vertically, with God. Precisely because of his humanity, Jesus' ability to transcend vertically into God was not always free of contamination. However, it remains that in him we see the manifestation of the highest form of human sympathy for God's desires, combined with an ability to comprehend cognitively God's *logoi* or will.

Ordinarily we correctly hesitate to ascribe to a human being the ability to empathize with God. This is so because in full empathic encounter one moves from sympathetic emotional flooding and projective identification[18] into a more cognitively distant and deliberate state of awareness. This implies a cognitive separating of oneself from the other. To empathize with God, it would be necessary to *think* the divine experience, something that is not possible short of deification. Empathy requires that one maintain the sense of self-as-distinct-from-other at the same time that one is moved by the other's experience. It is here that the distinctions between entrainment, attunement, sympathy, and empathy take on theological significance.

Jesus entrained, attuned to, and lived in sympathy with fellow humans, the divine cosmic *sympatheia*, and with God. He saw himself as distinct from yet intensely in relation with God, and he lived a nearly empathic relation with God, a deeply empathic relation to others. In other words, Jesus' relationship with God and humanity was one of full participation. Jesus was the Logos of compassion, the Logos of participation, in that his life was a fulfillment of God's plan, sowed in him at birth. Jesus, as Logos and revealer, was able to mediate between humanity and God such that he, in time, was rightfully and authentically understood to be the presence of God on earth. Because we are finite, it is necessarily true that the experience of the infinite God is always mediated. Jesus was the symbolic means through which God has been revealed as the matrix of relationality.

JESUS AS SYMBOL: FULLY DIVINE

> I am the resurrection and the life. Those who believe in me, even though they die, will live, and everyone who lives and believes in me will never die.
>
> JOHN 11:25-26

In the first two chapters of this work, we saw how the idea that Jesus was God incarnate gradually developed out of the faith responses of the earliest Christians. As these first believers struggled to express the impact that the life and death of this one man had on their own lives and understandings of God, the underlying conviction grew that in Jesus, God was somehow more fully present and revealed than in any other human life. And so, as happens in human history when the divine is revealed through a human life in a startlingly new way, thoughts turned to the symbol of incarnation.

That all human language is symbolic has been well established within the Christian tradition. Second-century philosopher and theologian Justin Martyr, for example, wrote in his *Second Apology*, "these words, Father, and God, and Creator, and Lord, and Master, are not names, but appellations derived from his good deeds and functions . . . . 'God' is not a name, but an opinion implanted in the nature of men of a thing that can hardly be explained."[19] From Origen to Aquinas to postmodern thought, the metaphorical and symbolic character of speech about God has been acknowledged.[20] Even the framers of the Chalcedonian Definition did not intend that the substantialist language of Jesus as *homoousios* with God be understood completely literally. They struggled within the confines of the language of the day to express as distinctly as possible that which can only be approximated in linguistic terms.

Even so, until recently there has been a tendency in theology to avoid speaking of Jesus as symbol. Paul Tillich is perhaps the theologian to whom we owe the deepest debt for reviving speech about the symbolic nature of religious language for the present age. He believed the teachings of Christianity could be most meaningful with a clear understanding of the nature and interpretation of symbols.[21] Words can ever only symbolize or represent: just as the word *table* brings to mind or represents the object so called, the phrase *God incarnate* symbolizes the experience of God-made-manifest in a human life. Human language can never fully reveal the divine. The infinite can never be fully comprehended by the finite. The biblical record tells us that God remains forever hidden from the finite world, even when manifesting the divine presence: "You cannot see my face; for no one shall see my face and live . . . I will cover you with my hand until I have passed by; then I will take away my hand, and you shall see my back" (Exod. 33:20-23).

Since all language is symbolic, and religious language especially so, we have recourse only to symbol in speaking of the divine. Therefore the most coherent way of speaking about the full divinity of Christ within a nonsubstantialist ontological framework is to be found through an exploration of the theology of symbol, the fullest exposition of which is found in Karl Rahner's writings. Because this project relies heavily on nontheological disciplines and insists on an approach that approximates negative theology with regard to God's self, it is important to highlight points at which this thesis is tied to the Christian theological tradition. The symbol as a theological concept helps to integrate the insights gleaned from psychology and biology into a theological construct for speech about incarnation.

Rahner's Theology of the Symbol and Incarnation

Christology is self-transcending anthropology and anthropology is deficient christology.

KARL RAHNER

Karl Rahner's theology of the symbol is the most thoroughly developed attempt to explore the ways in which symbols can be said to function ontologically within christology.[22] In Joseph Wong's characterization of Rahner as a mystic "seeking conceptual clarity in a philosophical system in order to convey his religious experience," we have a concise and accurate statement of Rahner's method.[23]

Rahner begins with the premise that all beings are multiple and therefore symbolic in nature. The nature of human knowing is receptive and self-reflective, rooted in an original unity that is known in the making-present of self through entry into the world. Since Rahner's is an existentialist theology, the notion of symbol arises naturally in his reflections on the phenomenology of presence.

A symbol, says Rahner, is "the highest and most primordial manner in which one reality can represent another." A true symbol "renders another present . . . allows the other 'to be there.'"[24] This interpretation goes far beyond more familiar definitions of symbol. To help uncover the depths of meaning here it will be useful to briefly recall Paul Tillich's use of the term, since his is probably the most widely used definition. Symbols, says Tillich, are more than mere representations of things. A symbol—as object or idea—is also a sign, signifying what it concretely is, and at the same time is "transparent." A symbol can be seen through, so to speak, so that whatever it symbolizes becomes visible. Since symbols bring us into contact with the symbolized, Tillich says they participate in that to which they point.

The American flag is a good example: the flag is in reality nothing more than pieces of cloth stitched together. Yet emotionally charged, even violent confrontations have happened between people over how this fabric is treated. Intense reaction to "desecration" of the flag by burning it or using the pattern for clothing comes about because of the flag's status as a symbol. The cloth takes on something of the reality it represents (in this case the American way of life), and so desecration of the flag is in some sense an attack on democracy. In religion, symbols mediate the divine to us.[25]

At first glance Rahner's and Tillich's definitions of symbol appear similar. But Rahner goes beyond Tillich to claim that a "real symbol" makes that which it symbolizes really present. A real symbol does not just mediate the divine—it makes the infinite really present within the finite realm. The true symbol is "an intrinsic moment of the thing itself." It "is a mediation to immediacy." It is, in other words, the self-expression of the divine. Rather than pointing toward God, moving from the finite toward the infinite, as in Tillich's theology, for Rahner the true symbol is a movement from God toward creation, an expression of God's self-giving love.[26]

Some have claimed that Rahner's interpretation of the symbolic nature of being is inadequately substantiated in his writings, but the difficulty in understanding this is perhaps due more to the inadequacy of existentialist philosophical language than to deficiencies in the concept.[27] What Rahner was trying to express is more adequately established by Stern's developmental research than by phenomenology or existentialism. Rahner intuited what Stern and others have demonstrated empirically. Rahner begins with the premise that all beings are multiple, made up of diverse elements. Since all of creation comes from God, there is an original unity from which the multiplicity of being flows. Even the simplest of beings is multiple since everything that is has at least an essence (or core nature) and its existence. When placed in conversation with the understanding of human development offered in the previous chapter, Rahner's interpretation of being as symbolic and plural opens up new possibilities for an ontological doctrine of the incarnation. The limitations of language are once again problematic, since Rahner is speaking of being in a way intended to disallow substantialist interpretation while insisting on ontological implications—precisely my goal in this book.

With the Christian trinitarian understanding of God as a basic assumption, Rahner can say that ultimate being is itself a plurality in unity: God is one, revealed in three modes of expression. The multiplicity of God is revealed to us in divine self-communication as Holy Mystery and Source, as Act within history, and as Gift.[28] Since absolute being itself is plural, each individual being can also be said to be constituted by a plurality that is more than the distinction between essential human nature and finite existence. Finite multiplicity is a consequence of the divine plurality in unity, not due to fragmentation that originates in the fallen nature of finite existence, as Paul Tillich thought.

Understood as "an intrinsic moment of the thing itself," a symbol is much more than simply representation or making-present. When he says that the symbol "is the self-realization of a being in the other, which is constitutive of its essence," Rahner is saying, first of all, that being—finite and infinite—must venture out from its original unity, interact with and encounter another, in order to execute or accomplish or put into effect its own reality or identity. Rahner uses the terms "self-realization" and "self-expression" frequently. He insists that the plural moments of a being are its "self-expression" (*Selbstausdruck*), necessary for its "self-realization" (*Selbstvollzug),* and that "being present to itself" (*Beisichselbersein*) is the mediating point between self-expression and self-realization. For the present-day reader, these terms can be somewhat misleading and have, I think, contributed to misunderstanding Rahner's point here. "Self-realization" has come to be associated with popular psychology's notions of self-fulfillment through focus on one's own needs, fears, and desires. "Self-actualization" has likewise tended to be interpreted at the popular level in terms of "finding oneself," an accomplishment achieved through focus on one's own needs to the exclusion of others. Implicit here is a selfishness and passivity that are not consonant with Rahner's intent.

The English translation of these terms has erroneously implied an individualist sense not present in Rahner's thought. The German *Selbstvollzug*, translated as "self-realization," can also be translated in a more active sense, as "self-execution" or "self-carrying out," and these alternate translations give clues as to what Rahner was attempting to express. To speak of "self-execution" rather than "self-realization" is to underscore the active nature of existence. To execute means to "put into effect; to perform; to create in agreement with a prescribed design; to make valid; to carry out what is required."²⁹ But since "execution" is commonly used in English as a synonym for "putting to death," perhaps "self-fruition" is a more faithful rendering of Rahner's meaning than self-realization or self-fulfillment. Being is oriented, then, toward self-fruition—bringing the self into accord with the divine intent.

Humans truly are relational beings. The healthy self comes to fruition only in and through the give-and-take of participatory encounter with other beings. That said, we stand in a better position to uncover the power in Rahner's words. The core unity of being is a plurality that arises from within the unity, just as the human person only comes to know itself in and through others. The plurality ("plural moments" of a being)³⁰ is so constituted that, as it is in agreement with the original unity, it is an expression of that origin—a symbol of it, in other words. In going out from oneself into full encounter with the other, the other reflects back to us who we are. In the encounter with another, in the going-out-from the enclosed unity of self into the open plurality of self and other, we see the self for what it truly is, in all its selfishness and in all its glory. Here is the being-present-to-itself to which the self responds.

Response ideally involves adaptation to that which has been made present and, in this way, the self becomes composed of ever more plural moments of being as these plural moments return to and are processed by the original core unity of self. Rahner is describing the dialectical character of the human self as constituted by the drive toward self-transcendence. The self is an ever-changing process of becoming. Self-fruition is a dynamic, perichoretic process of movement, a spiraling asymptotically toward God.

Otherness is constitutive of human being. As we come to realize ourselves in this otherness, the intrinsic plurality is understood to be expressive of who we are: we are constituted by all others with whom we have entered into relationship. The expression of this self, this plural unity, is the symbol of the original unity. "The symbol is the reality in which *another* attains knowledge of a being."³¹ The symbol "is the self-realization of a being in the other, which is constitutive of its essence."[32] Psychologists have described the inter-subjective and projective nature of empathy in strikingly similar terms: "in searching for the other in an active fashion, we come to our own reflection, the fundamental projective nature of empathy, and the dialectical quality of finding and creating meaning."[33]

Participation, as the highest form of encounter with the other, is an expression of the symbolic nature of being, in that being "gives itself away from itself into the 'other,' and there finds itself in knowledge and love, because it is by constituting the inward 'other' that [the self] comes to (or: from) its self-fulfillment, which is the presupposition or the act of being present to itself in knowledge and love."[34] Participation, as the mode by which we transcend self into other and self into God, becomes the means by which the symbolic nature of being comes both to reveal and to know the presence of God. Participation is the mechanism of transcendence, and the goal of human transcendence is God. The dynamism of self-transcendence at the heart of creation's becoming is the first step toward the incarnation.[35]

In trinitarian terms, the Logos as symbol of the Father becomes the means by which God effects the divine self within time and space. The Logos is God's own ability to express the divine in history.[36] It is not a "thing" but the symbolic representation of divine self-communication and the blueprint for the unfolding of divine creative activity. Were we to say that the Logos assumed a human nature, in the sense of putting on something ontic or static, the Logos could not be a true symbol of God: "The assumed humanity would be an organ of speech substantially united to him who is to be made audible: but it would not be this speech itself."[37] Jesus' actions would, in this case, be revelatory of God, but Jesus himself would not be. But Jesus as Christ is the self-utterance of God. In the going out from the divine self, God becomes human.[38] The Logos is the relationship. The symbol, as the going-out-from-unity, becomes in this divine context the medium of expression of the selfhood of God. The essential nature of God can never be known except to God's own self, and so it is made present to creation in and through the symbolic expression of participatory encounter with that-which-is-other-than-oneself.

THE INCARNATE GOD

> This world is so filled with God that it gives God to us.
>
> KARL RAHNER

Just as Maximus the Confessor understood God's will to be really present in the world as pre-existent seeds, *logoi,* or divine intentions, God is understood here to be constitutively present in the world as possibility. God's offer of self in the supernatural existential, cosmic *sympatheia,* was fully accepted by the man Jesus, and in this event, God came to be fully present within time and space. Rahner says that "[t]he humanity is the self-disclosure of the Logos—the relationship—itself, so that when God, expressing himself, exteriorizes himself, that very thing appears which we call the humanity of the Logos."[39] This is as close as we can come to describing the full divinity of Christ. The finite is a moment within the infinite: short of deification, the human mind can never comprehend the divine. When we say as Christians that God's own self is made incarnate in Jesus of Nazareth, we mean that Jesus as an ontological reality functions symbolically to make present giver and gift. Jesus embodies the relationship between humanity and God.

It has been argued that to understand incarnation in these terms fails to preserve Jesus as "consubstantial" with other human beings, that God's presence to Jesus is qualitatively different than God's presence to the rest of humanity. If this were so, metaphysically we would be required to say that Jesus is ontologically different from us, relative to God's presence.[40] But we are saying here that God is present as an offer that can be accepted or denied. What is offered is participation in the divine, the means by which we find union with God. In Jesus, we find the offer fully accepted.

Having said that what was offered and accepted was God's own self, it is logical to assume that this event, in which a finite being implemented full acceptance of infinite reality, must have effected a change in the ontological reality. It is therefore not so much a question of Jesus' being ontologically unique prior to the full acceptance of the reality of God, as it is that to become fully united with the divine intent is to become related to the divine presence in a new way. In fully accepting the divine gift, Jesus' humanity was ratified in the fullest expression of freedom and thereby became a true symbol of God. In him God is made actually present in and to the world, to the fullest extent that it is possible for the infinite to be contained within the finite. This symbolic expression of God—the making present of God's own self—was only possible because of the full acceptance of the gift. The full freedom of God, to offer or not, and the full freedom of humanity, to accept or refuse, are preserved.

Because incarnation, for the Christian, is understood to mean that the reality of God is revealed in a man's life, and this particular interpretation of the notion incorporates salvation through deification, we must return to what we know of the human again and again to flesh this meaning out. The human has, from the very beginning of life, something of a sense of self. We, at a deep physiological and psychological level, join with others through entrainment and attunement. In sympathy we first know ourselves as a plurality in unity: in our own experience we enter into the experience of another, encountering it as if it were our own. The self is constituted by the capacity for participation in the reality of other human beings and is only known to itself in the encounter with others. Participation is the process by which we know ourselves, through transcendence of the boundaries of self/other distinction in communication. The plurality of I and thou thus becomes the means by which I know myself. True empathy is experienced when, once we are able to know ourselves as a plural unity, we transcend the boundaries of the distinction between self and other without obliterating them. Self-knowledge is an outcome of the relationship between knower and known.

So, on this account, we see that being realizes itself through plurality in unity. Although there is a basic unity of self, a knowing of self that seems to be always already a reality for the human infant, this is a kind of precognition rather than anything like full self-knowledge. We have seen how it happens in human development that this self is always and only known in and through relationship with others. So we can say that we actually know ourselves only in terms of a plurality that symbolizes or makes present the original unity. Only in this way, then, does the human know itself in anything like its pure original unity—through the symbolic making-present of the unity within the multiplicity of relation. It is in the going-out-from-self into participation with others and coming to know that experience as our own and yet not our own that the self is known.

God, on the other hand, knows God's own self—the fullest expression of participatory relation, what we call love—from eternity, as a unity gone out to fullest self-presence in the plurality of being. Thus self-fruition is not self-knowledge as such but participation in the reality of otherness. God is, at one and the same time, that toward which human love is pulled, and love itself. God is fully and completely other-oriented, as we are created to be.[41] God is ecstatic being: the divine self, as love itself, overflows and pours divine love out into all of creation. This divine love or self-communication is the grace of God, the capacity for participatory encounter with others. The divine self-communication is an ontological event in which God gives God's own self as participatory encounter: the giver is the gift, grace is God's own self.[42]

What, then, does this tell us of God? We have said that the most coherent interpretation of divine immutability is in terms of ethical steadfastness. God is Pathos and Sovereign, morally and ethically unchanging yet at the same time intensely involved in and moved by the exigencies of created existence. Attempts to speak of God in metaphysical terms have tended to devolve into abstract philosophical speculation or into incoherence at the level of the everyday. Presently theological consensus is that the most adequate God-talk centers on the nature of God's relationship to the world. "God is" can be rightly interpreted to mean "God is known to us as." God's own self cannot be fully comprehended within the created order. Traditionally this truth has been expressed in terms of divine transcendence. In this understanding of God as Pathos and Sovereign, *pathos* refers to divine immanence and sovereignty is representative of the transcendent God. To say that God is Sovereign expresses the truth of divine supremacy and ultimate incomprehensibility. To speak of the *pathos* of God is to recognize that the divine-human relationship is a passionate one in which God reveals an inexhaustible concern for creation through participation.

We know the immanence of God in creation as divine participation. Just as the finite is a moment within the infinite, so participation—divine immanence—is our means of encounter with the transcendent God. Participation is the inbreaking of infinity into the spatiotemporal realm. God is present to the world in participatory encounter, or perhaps it is more accurate to say that God is hidden in creation as cosmic *sympatheia* and the possibility of participation. This is what it means to say that God is ecstatic being, love overflowing into all of creation. Rather than saying that God is empathy itself,[43] we say that participation is the mechanism of transcendence for the created order, the means through which we are able to understand anything about God at all. Grace, the offer of God's own self, is teleological empathy, drawing us asymptotically toward deification. We do not possess God in the acceptance of the offer, but we do possess the possibility of union with the divine.

Participation involves two kinds of openness: receptivity and revelation.[44] This serves as shorthand for the complex multiphasic process developed in chapter 5. In receptivity, we suspend our perspective so as to filter the other's experience through our own "grid" as little as possible. The healthy self is able to suspend itself as definitive or, better, is able to allow the experience of the other to enter into its own reality rather than be filtered out. Participation is a perichoretic process of reciprocity, of receiving and revealing, in which union but not fusion with God is offered. Truly participatory relation requires also a revelatory openness, the response of self-disclosure as well as opening of oneself to the other. At the level of the divine, we can speak of a mutuality and openness in God. "This *receptive* openness in God is complemented by the *revelatory* self-disclosure that Christians know as the incarnation."[45] Through participation, the divine permeates all of creation, offering through grace the possibility of deification for all.

This is not to say that, as potential recipients of the gift of God's self, we are therefore able to comprehend God. God's divine self-communication is always mysterious precisely because God is encountered as immanent yet remains ultimately unknowable. The human, although sensing its origin in unity, is always known to itself only in a plurality. God, as the original unity, is revealed in plurality. In the encounter with God through divine *ekstasis*, the prereflective awareness of that primordial unity (the supernatural existential) reveals to us both the reality and the incomprehensibility of God—thus the asymptotic character of our finite longing. This is so because the rudimentary human self is not an entity, but more an organizing reference point or state of perceptual unity in which there is an experience of agency, intention, temporal constancy, and physical cohesion. The self is a dynamic relational system, an experiential matrix within which resides the longing for self-transcendence into God. Grace, offered eternally, is intrinsic to creation.

The language of gift and offer is vital to this ontological understanding of the divine-human relation. The gift of God's own self is always already presented, the offer is made eternally. Embedded in the rhythms of the universe is the evocative call of the divine. The human is, however, completely free to turn away the gift, to refuse the offer. We are called to collaborate with God, to seek synergy between the divine will and our own. This collaboration is always a gift of grace, never ours to possess nor ever merited.[46]

For Rahner, in the incarnation the "humanity is the self-disclosure of the Logos itself, so that when God, expressing himself [*sic*], exteriorizes himself, that very thing appears which we call the humanity of the Logos."[47] If we understand the humanity as the capacity for participatory relation, we can say that Jesus is the absolute symbol in that in the going out from self he found full receptivity to the divine exteriorization and thereby transcended into God. We are so constituted as to be able to transcend ourselves into the sufferings and joys of others. In Jesus, self-fruition was so complete as to have been in harmony with the divine *logoi*. He, more fully than any other human being, accomplished transcendence into God as well as humankind and so achieved deification.

In other words, the very humanity of Jesus is revelatory of God. Obviously, then, any attempt to speak about the divinity of Christ as separate from the humanity of Jesus is artificial at best, though of course they are distinct. In the end there is still mystery: even to say that in Jesus the divine self-offer was wholly taken up and that in that taking up of the divine *ekstasis* the reality of God has been revealed fails to do justice to the gift of incarnation.

JESUS AS CHRIST: FULLY HUMAN AND FULLY DIVINE

> In him, all the fullness of God was pleased to dwell, and through him God was pleased to reconcile to himself all things.
>
> COL. 1:19-20

Jesus the human being is "the medium of God's actual self-gift."[48] In transcending himself vertically through full participation in the life of God, and horizontally through full participation in the life-world of humanity, Jesus came to be the means through which gift and giver are made present for the Christian believer. The divine *pathos* is God's concerned and loving involvement in the life of humankind. Moved by a sympathetic sharing in the plight of humanity, God makes God's *pathos* manifest by an empathetic projection of God's own self into time and space.

The lives of the Hebrew prophets show how it is possible for a human being to live in sympathy with God, to share in the divine feeling state and at times become so overwhelmed as to take it on as one's own. Jesus as Christ is God's *pathos* or empathetic participation in time. He becomes our human sympathetic participation in the activity of God, whose self brackets time and extends beyond it. As the "God-receiving man,"[49] Jesus is the symbolic reality, the focal point for eternity and history, the exemplary embodiment of all relationships between God and humanity. Like the Hebrew prophets before him, part of Jesus' uniqueness lies in the fact that he possessed a great capacity for entry into the divine *pathos*. But Jesus' uniqueness extends beyond the ability to hear and express God's Word. In him we find more than the prophetic ability to harmonize his soul with the divine concerns. In Jesus as Christ we find harmony of soul with God extended to harmony of soul with his fellow humans. In Jesus full collaboration with the divine aims is achieved. His life and teachings, his lasting influence on the world are the products of the synergy between his inner world and God's. Jesus was somehow so open to the entraining rhythms of the divine that, more so than any other human, his inner world was attuned to the grace that is loose in the world.

The Fullness of God Revealed

Now that the bridge between psychological theories of human development and theological interpretations of the symbolic nature of being has been crossed, we can see how a participatory notion of incarnation offers a new and unified view of not only Jesus but all of creation. We do not know, on the basis of historical analysis, why it was possible for Jesus to participate so completely with fellow humanity and God as to bring about a new understanding of God's presence in the world. But we do understand, on the basis of faith, that he did. The self as given by God, who we are by nature, is a set of potentialities that finds fulfillment in deep relation. The self, shaped by the conditions of finite existence, seeks always to find its place within creation. The tragedy of this life is bound up with its glory: created with a "sense and taste for the infinite," we refuse to accept the constraints of finite existence. Instead of understanding that the deep longing for union is fulfilled within the very confines of finitude, we seek to break the barriers of time and space through self-absorption and the misuse of relational power.

This is the core of the Christian message. Bound as we are by the conditions of finitude, the barriers to the infinite are nonetheless transcended within finitude. Jesus, in living a fully receptive human life, illumines the path toward deification. In his life of full participation with creation and creator, we are shown that even the finality of death is overcome. It is only through fully accepting the reality of our embodied relational existence that the possibility of a future union with God is ours. Christianity teaches that Jesus, the God-receiving man, died, as do we all. But the Christian hope does not end with termination of the finite reality. Through a life of full participatory relation within the confines of embodied existence, Jesus experienced resurrection into God. And so, says the Christian tradition, this is a promise and a possibility for us all.

Selfhood has been defined as a result of achieving clarity in the midst of the complexity of relational living.[50] This clarity is a kind of self-knowledge that allows one to enter into participatory relation fully cognizant of one's own emotions as distinct from another's, and comes about as a result of the multiphasic process of development described in chapter 5. The divine *logoi*, God's plan for creation, is constitutive of the core human self. Embedded within all of creation is the ordering principle, the repository of divine possibility that comes to fruition within humanity in the development of a healthy self. Receptivity and revelation ensure interrelation with the world, but each individual comes about through a process of

> creative improvisation with the materials at hand. . . .
> Thus, the self is a manifestation of limited freedom or
> contextual creativity; things like role expectations and
> material resources place contextual limitations on our
> creative possibilities . . . the blending of multiple influ-
> ences into a particular identity is always a creative
> expression of individual personhood.[51]

All of creation is endowed with the *potential* to incarnate the divine, as revealed through our understanding of cosmic *sympatheia*. But given the randomness inherent in the matrix of infinite possibilities, only rarely in history has it happened that individual expressiveness, creativity, and life events coincide as they did in the event of Jesus Christ. We saw how there can be a radical openness to the divine that results in the ability to speak as the mouthpiece of God, exemplified in the lives of the prophets. But in the life of Jesus, there was the ability so to open self to God that something unique occurred—in the openness to God and revelation of self came a true transcendence into God. In Jesus we see the self-realization of humanity in God and of God in humanity. God always already ventures forth from the original divine unity in the process of executing the divine aims within creation. In Jesus God's aims have been carried out such that both the human and the divine experience a constitutive, essential transformation into plural union. In him, as absolute symbol, God has been rendered present to humankind.

God is available eternally as the capacity for participatory relation, having ventured forth from the divine unity in the creation of the universe. Embedded in creation are the seeds of possibility for the deification of all. Jesus exercised his personal freedom, creativity, and choice so as to become the symbol of God. Jesus, in radically going out from himself toward God "crossed over" into deification, becoming the link between time and eternity, God and humankind. Jesus was so completely able to enter into the lifeworld of his fellow human beings through horizontal transcendence that his very self was transformed. He was so completely capable of fully participatory encounter with his fellow humans that in the living out of this life, something new was created, a human life within which the self-fruition of God found completion.

Abraham Heschel said that the prophetic response of sympathy results in an opening to transcendence. Dietrich Bonhoeffer wrote that in Jesus, "the man for others," transcendence is experienced by virtue of his "being there for others." This being there for others is the ground of his power: "Our relation to God is a new life in existence for others, through participation in the being of Jesus. The transcendental is . . . the neighbor who is within reach."[52] God's empathic living care for the world continues to be made manifest in the world through the participatory life of the community of believers.

To understand Jesus within this framework allows reflection on how his relation to God and humanity transcends time and space, and why so short a life has changed the world. Entrainment, the ability to synchronize oneself with others, is an essential aspect of intersubjective participation. For Judaism, the divine *pathos* was the "unity of the eternal and temporal, of meaning and mystery, of the metaphysical and the historical."[53] For the Christian, Jesus as Christ embodies the *pathos* of God, and he becomes the unity of time and eternity. Jesus was uniquely—but not necessarily exclusively—capable of participation with both God and humankind, and in the process completed that which remains asymptotic for humanity, namely, deification. It is possible that Jesus' disciples experienced something of the capacity to transcend time, saw moving out before them the back of God (Exod. 33:23) in their encounter with his harmonized soul.

There is in this revision an implicit doctrine of grace united with action. The grace of God, cosmic *sympatheia*, is present in and through all of creation, experienced at the human level through participatory encounter. Infinite love forms the bridge across the gap between time and eternity, and is experienced as movement or *kinesis*, Rahner's idea of *Vorgriff*. Jesus is Christ and symbol of God in that his ability to attune to and entrain with both the divine and human enable him uniquely to reveal God in time. Jesus, the Word, mediates between God and humanity. Time—the manifestation of the never-beginning, never-ending circle of eternity—mediates between the possible and the actual. God's own self has entered into time in the incarnation, opening us to infinite possibility.

Time and temporality, so long understood to be constitutive of that which differentiates humanity from God, may in truth constitute that which makes it possible for us to know anything of God at all. It is clearly constitutive of our ability to know self and other. The awareness of temporally synchronous events in the human infant is intimately tied to development of the sense of self. Virtually from birth we have our own temporal rhythm "of self-synchronous behavior [that] is like an orchestra, in which the body is the conductor and the voice is the music."[54] Each of us comes into the world endowed with her own life rhythm and is also aware of and able to attune to the temporal rhythm of the world into which we have come. Temporal attunement and entrainment are vital to intersubjectivity. Without them, empathy, and by extension human compassion—the urge to relieve the suffering of others—would not occur. We have been created with an innate ability to attune to and entrain with our fellow creatures that makes possible an actual temporal synergy among living beings. Time truly is a moment within eternity. Embedded in our very beings is the capacity to hear and respond to the evocative rhythms of divine love.

Time is a mystery, just as is the incarnation understood as God's participation in time. Our own participation in the mystery of time may be the most basic datum of the "asymptotic longing" for God. Gregory of Nyssa understood divine infinity as exemplified by our endlessly following God, in our seeing only God's back. Time and God, always and everywhere, escape our grasp. Infinite desire signifies a "quasi-space" and a "quasi-time" between God and creation.[55]

Therefore a christology of divinely empathetic and humanly sympathetic participation is clearly open to the possibility that the Christ, the paradigmatic image of God in history, has been and will be made manifest in other human beings, in other times. To vision God's interaction with creation as *pathos* is to underscore God's intimate relationality. This God who allows creation to have an impact on God's own self is a God who requires that we be responsible for what has been created. Undoubtedly, Jesus is affirmed as most fully human, and his special relation to God and awareness of God's presence within him is underscored.

Creation has its reality in relationship to God and cannot be conceived of apart from "the matrix of the living God."[56] Each of us is endowed with two natures or ways of being in the world, the finite humanity that exists within space and time, and the inherent capacity for divinization through participatory relation—what we might call the *imago dei* or image of God in us. Jesus became the Christ in that he found his true reality in the very being of God and so entered into the divine perichoretic process of self-fruition. In him, the finite humanity united with full participatory relation to God and world, and in so doing, his human nature found its essential reality in the divine *pathos*. Jesus attained *de facto* synergy with the divine aims. He thereby achieved true self-transcendence and came to manifest within the spatiotemporal realm the one divine *hypostasis*, an actual, tangible manifestation of God's own self.

Far from being a sentimental christology of emotion, interpreting the incarnation as participation locates God in the intersubjective realm of dispositions and tendencies. It locates incarnation in the quasi-space of human reality where the impetus toward loving, ethical response to world and others arises. To locate incarnation in the quasi-time of participation is to insist that relation to all others, indeed to all of creation, is holy ground. The ethically immutable God participates fully in the cosmos as creator and companion, advocate and judge, Pathos and Sovereign. We are thereby indicted most personally for our individual roles in sustaining the tragic nature of human existence. To "become participants of the divine nature" (2 Pet. 1:4) is to be called to healthy, liberative action in relation to self and others. It is to live a life of "subject-subjects" rather than "subject-object" relation.[57]

Jesus is for us today the *archēgos* of our salvation, "the pioneer and perfecter of our faith."[58] In his fully participatory life, Jesus mapped out new territory. He provided "a living example of actual personal unity in a tumultuous field of shaping and directing energies," thereby making it possible for each of us to give birth to a "unifying passion" which "collects, informs, and unifies the elements of [the] mind, inspires the voluntary motions of [the] body, and forms [the] chief bond of interest with [the] world."[59] For the Christian, Jesus as Christ exhibits a kind of causal efficacy through the evocative power of participatory relation. God acted in Jesus in the same way God acts in all of us: "basically the active influence of the Logos on the human 'nature' in Jesus in a physical sense may not be understood in any way except the way this influence is exercised by God on free creatures elsewhere."[60] In following Jesus, the Christian travels the path toward deification. Divine love, expressed as the promise and possibility of participation in God, evokes within creation the longing for union with the divine.

This ontological understanding of incarnation as participation shows how the presence of God is made known to us. God is present as offer and possibility throughout creation, known to us in the capacity to recognize the sufferings and joys of others, and to be moved to action on the other's behalf. All of creation is potentially revelatory of the divine, since grace is loose in the world. Nature in all its wonder and awesome power is the most basic realm of potential encounter with the divine. The experience of God is always mediated through symbol, and nature itself is a symbol of divine creativity.

We remember Jesus' injunction that "whoever does not receive the kingdom of God as a little child will never enter it" (Mark 13:15). It may be that the child's sense of wonder is one of the many facets of meaning embedded in this statement. Children seem inherently to entrain with and attune to the rhythms of nature. Perhaps this reflects an uncorrupted awareness of cosmic *sympatheia*, a way of being-in-the-world that sadly tends to be extinguished or suppressed as we become adults. A revised understanding of incarnation as indicative of God's presence to all of creation from eternity, not just to the human and not just to the Christian, encourages renewal of this vital honoring of our status as one among many of God's creations. The experience of participation leads us to speak symbolically as Paul did: "it is no longer I who live, but it is Christ who lives in me" (Gal. 2:20).

7

Participation in Good and Evil

A yeshiva boy—a young man studying in a rabbinical college—took instruction from three rabbis. A friend asked him his reactions.

"The first I found very difficult, disorganized, and poorly explained . . . the second was a lot clearer. . . . "

"And the third? They say he is very good."

"Oh, he was brilliant! . . . I was transported to realms beyond my imagining! . . . and I didn't understand a word."

The Collapse of Chaos

Revisioning incarnation through the lens of participation is enormously helpful for thinking about Jesus' identity, God's intentions, and the interrelatedness of all creation. But two other important questions call for attention, however briefly. First, how might we translate a doctrine of incarnation as participation into real-world living? Second, what does it contribute to understanding the problem of evil and suffering? A theology that does not address the questions of practicality and theodicy should not itself be taken seriously. Theology must meet head-on the challenges of everyday life as well as the depths of inhumanity and depravity that confront us.

CREATING COMPASSIONATE COMMUNITY

> Religion that is pure and undefiled before God is this: to care
> for orphans and widows in their distress.
>
> JAMES 1:27

During a presentation of an earlier form of these ideas, a colleague
asked what I now know to be a crucial question: How does one
teach sympathy or compassion to others?[1] The questioner is an
active volunteer for Habitat for Humanity, and the volunteers in his
area had recently encountered a puzzling situation. They had built
several homes on the same street. As the latest qualifying family
prepared for move-in day, the neighboring residents—who had
only recently qualified for a Habitat home and moved in themselves—objected vociferously to having to live next door to "those
people." The Habitat volunteers found themselves in a very difficult
position: recipients of compassion were apparently unable to
extend compassion to the new neighbors. Beyond stressing the
power of modeled compassion, obviously already so much a part of
these people's lives, there was not much that I could suggest at the
time. Yet this problem is vital, since it underscores the truth that
unless theological reflection translates into action it is no more
than rhetoric.

A good place to start is with recognition that all human beings
have a great deal in common: each of us has a physical body, emotions, and some sort of intellectual capacity. We are born, we will
die, and none of us wants to suffer meaninglessly. These are not
insignificant points of commonality. They are the materials out of
which our life stories grow.

Sharing those stories can be a powerful tool in the development
of empathy. This is so because "the formal quality of experience
through time is inherently narrative."[2] The self is to some degree
narrative, in that we are historical beings. We understand ourselves
in terms of the narrative character of our lives. Since this is so, story
becomes a most effective means to develop understanding of others.[3] In the Habitat situation, this may have been the most effective

tool available. Inviting the families to sit together as part of a program for new homeowners, with the focus on getting to know the need that brought them all together might help to defuse some of the prejudice that was operative in the situation.

True empathy is a mental and emotional getting into the other's experience, not re-entering one's own. Another example can help here: in my interaction with a troubled teenager, a good starting point is to remember who I was at the same age and attempt to put that remembered self into the teen's experience. But if I stop there, I have not empathized. I have only re-entered my own experience and projected it onto the teen. To truly participate with the other, I must move beyond that projection into my own past. I transcend my own experience in moving toward comprehension of what it means to be *this* individual.

Failure of empathy is destructive to self and others. Purely cognitive identification without affective sharing becomes manipulation.[4] Sympathy without the corrective transcendence of empathy can lead to over-identification with others, to the detriment of both parties. Likewise, empathy can be hampered by the inclination to put self before all others. Perhaps this is the error sensed by Susan Brooks Thistlethwaite in her criticism of feminist relational theologies: white, middle-class feminist theologians, in their eagerness to help heal the oppressive experience of less fortunate women have tended to fuse with rather than empathize, assuming a sameness that minimizes rather than empowers the other.[5]

As I have shown, empathy is a possibility, at least to some degree, for us all. It can be improved with practice. Education and training for psychotherapists and counselors involve guidance in developing the innate capacity for empathy. For those of us without the time or inclination to undergo such training, quite powerful methods can enhance these skills. In a sense learning increased empathy is akin to learning to be unselfish—difficult, but not impossible.[6]

LEARNED COMPASSION IN BUDDHISM

For the Christian interested in learning to "practice incarnation" in everyday life, Buddhism has much to teach. The Buddha taught extensively on compassion. He understood how difficult it is to live a deeply compassionate life and also understood the power for healing that compassion brings. He offered meditations to aid in learning compassion for ourselves, family, friends, and our enemies. *Anukampā*, to be moved in accord with or in response to others, is the central concept of the Buddha's teachings.[7] This emphasis is present in the earliest and most austere form of Buddhism but has been especially developed within the Mahayana tradition.

While the definitive goal of all Buddhist practice is *nirvana*, the *bodhisattva* is the most highly revered of all living beings. The *bodhisattva* has achieved enlightenment but is so filled with compassion that he or she postpones attainment of *nirvana* in order to work for the salvation of all. The greatest of all the *bodhisattvas* is the embodiment of compassion, variously known in Asia as Avaloketeshvara, Guanyin, or Kannon. For Tibetan Buddhists, His Holiness the Dalai Lama is compassion itself, Avaloketeshvara reborn. Westerners have tended to misinterpret this key point due to a widespread misunderstanding of the Buddha's teachings on detachment.

The Buddha taught that all of life is suffering, caused by the human inclination to attempt to make permanent that which is everchanging—most particularly the ego or self. In the late twentieth century Christian and Jewish theologians began to speak of this reality in exploring the tragic nature of existence. This is the First Noble Truth of Buddhism, recognized by the Buddha many centuries ago.[8] Given that to live is to suffer, the highest expression of holiness for the Buddhist is to work for the relief of suffering. In order to be effective in relief of suffering, the Buddhist must cultivate compassion for all sentient beings.

There are four Sublime Attitudes or Immeasurable Minds: love, compassion, sympathetic joy, and equanimity. The Buddha taught his disciples to cultivate these attitudes in meditation, since they form the basis for all social action. The Ultimate Light Sutra, from the most ancient of Buddhist writings, defines the attitudes:

> Love is the state of desiring to offer happiness and welfare with the thought "May they be liberated from their sufferings." . . . Compassion is the state of desiring to

remove suffering and misfortune, with the thought "May
they be liberated from these sufferings." . . . Sympathetic
joy is the state of desiring the continuity of [other's] happiness and welfare with the thought "You beings are
rejoicing; it is good." . . . Equanimity is the state of observ-
ing [another's] suffering or happiness and thinking "These
appear because of that individual's own past activities.⁹

In this teaching, the Buddha offers a kind of anatomy of participatory experience not entirely unlike my own. The Attitudes are
complementary and must be refined concomitantly—enlightenment
comes about only when the practitioner can live all four.¹⁰

Thich Nhat Hanh points out that the root of the Pali word translated "love" means friendship, which has the goal of offering
happiness.¹¹ Sympathetic joy is a deep rejoicing and sharing in the
well-being of others. The third of the Attitudes, *karuna*, is translated into English as compassion, but this is somewhat misleading.
The word compassion implies that one must "suffer with" another
in order to alleviate suffering. But the Buddha taught that the only
emotion we should seek to share with others is joy. We are to cultivate compassion, equanimity, and love in regard to suffering, but
not sympathy—the Buddha understood the problematic character
of sympathy many centuries before Western philosophers and psychologists began to explore the concept. Since sympathy is a state of
confusion, wherein it is not always possible to differentiate my
experience from yours, the Buddha insisted that we sympathize
only with the most positive of emotions. For the Buddhist, joy, as
positive, can be a symbiotic emotion. We can share in the joy of
another, experience it as if it were our own, so long as we acknowledge that it belongs to the other. In this way, we can avoid negative
"follow-on" emotions like envy or "giddiness," since we recognize
the joy within the context of a larger goal. Over-involvement in
another's success is unhealthy.

The distinction made here, that we seek to share in the joy of
others but not to share the emotions of suffering, is an important
one. *Karuna* is desiring that others be free from suffering, "care
without grief."¹² The Buddha understood that emotional immersion

in the suffering of others interferes with our ability to act effectively. According to Buddhagosa, the fifth-century C.E. Buddhist scholar, if we experience sadness during our practice in cultivation of compassion, it means that the mind has turned away from the beneficial state (contemplation of the other as free from suffering) and fallen into the detrimental state of feeling aversion toward suffering.[13] Aversion toward suffering is incompatible with full acceptance of the First Noble Truth of Buddhism—that life itself is suffering. Effective action to relieve suffering requires that we not turn away from it, that we face it head-on, but without wallowing in it.

Equanimity is the most misunderstood of the Attitudes. It is not neutrality devoid of ethical incentive. In spite of claims to the contrary by some Western interpreters, unbiased concern is the ethical norm of Buddhism even in its most ancient form. *Upeksha*, equanimity, comes from *upa*, meaning "over," and *iksh*, meaning "to look." Since this concept has been so grossly misinterpreted, it is best to allow a Buddhist practitioner and teacher, Thich Nhat Hanh, to interpret:

> You climb the mountain to be able to look over the whole situation, not bound by one side or the other. If your love has attachment, discrimination, prejudice, or clinging in it, it is not true love. People who do not understand Buddhism sometimes think upeksha means indifference, but true equanimity is neither cold nor indifferent. . . . Upeksha has the mark called samatajnana, "the wisdom of equality," the ability to see everyone as equal, not discriminating between ourselves and others.[14]

Cultivation of the four Sublime Attitudes is so essential to enlightenment that many teachings focus on meditative techniques designed to enhance our capacity for it. The Buddha recommended a sequential meditation practice, moving from easiest to most difficult. He knew that for selfish humanity the easiest form of love is self-love, so this is where we begin. Once the Attitudes can be practiced toward ourselves, we move to meditation on loved ones, then for someone or something about which one is neutral, until the ultimate challenge is reached—practice toward someone about whom we feel hostility or hatred. Observed over time, this approach results in a greater capacity to enter into and be moved to relieve the sufferings of others.[15]

There are, then, tried and true methods for teaching participatory relation. This means that a theology of incarnation as participation has practical application in everyday life. Incarnation can be a lived reality as each of us strives to encounter the other in deeply compassionate relation.

SIN AND EVIL IN PARTICIPATORY CREATION

> Listen! Even if we assume that every person must suffer because his suffering is necessary to pay for eternal harmony, still do tell me, for God's sake, where the children come in.
>
> IVAN'S PROTEST, *The Brothers Karamazov*

Although achieved by Jesus within the confines of finitude, deification remains asymptotic for humanity. The divine offer and possibility are embedded in the very matrix of creation, but this is a bittersweet reality, given the tragic nature of human existence. There is within us a tendency toward self-absorption that perverts the capacity for participation. Christians express this in the myth of the fall of Adam and Eve. What follows is not a thoroughly developed doctrine of suffering and evil. It is only a few words to answer possible criticism that emphasis on relation in theology undercuts the seriousness of evil.[16]

Some have argued that the human is innately solipsistic, but this is not entirely accurate.[17] The healthy human self is formed in going out from the self, and we are constituted by relationality. Sin, understood as self-absorption, interferes with the capacity for participation. The tragic is deeply embedded in finite existence. That this is so is revealed in the reality that true empathic relation is rarely achieved in human encounter. It is so rare that those individuals who do achieve it tend to be celebrated in history—the rescuers of Jews in Nazi Europe, Gautama Buddha, Mohandas K. Gandhi, Mother Teresa.

The pull toward self-absorption is deeply embedded in human experience, so much so that it has been wrongly interpreted by some to be the primary constituent of human nature. The self-absorption of the mythic first man and woman is passed on in inadequate human relation, not through some sort of perversion of human nature as such. Human nature, created by God with the ability to respond to the participatory rhythms of creation, is good. The infant's nascent self reaches outward for growth through the innate entraining and attuning process. If these early efforts repeatedly fail to be received and mirrored by the child's environment, the fragile self turns inward. Thus begins the destructive tendency toward self-absorption that haunts humanity. Created to seek out relationship—indeed, unable to survive without it—the human infant quickly learns whether his or her environment is hostile or nurturing.

An infant whose early experience is of an environment devoid of healthy participants in the dialectic of receptivity and revelation will develop overconcern for the self to a greater or lesser degree. Narcissism is not so much psychopathology as it is an adaptive developmental response to the tragedy of humanity.[18] Born in an originary expectation of fully participatory encounter in which needs are adequately met, the infant quickly adapts to an inadequate environment by substituting care of self for that not received. Self-idolatry is the result. "If we set ourselves, our goods and interests, up as gods in place of God, our tendency is to draw everything into our domain and make it subservient to our desires," says Peter Hodgson.[19] In this way, the social structures of sin pervert the very process through which the human lives in relation.

While criticism has been leveled at relational christologies for failure to take oppressive sociopolitical power structures seriously enough, this understanding of incarnation as participation makes clear that power structures do indeed "situate the self but also shape and define it."[20] To speak of incarnation as occurring in the realm of intersubjectivity is to insist that each of us plays a role in the situating and shaping of selves. In this framework, power structures are understood to have their origin in the interpersonal region of daily interaction with other living beings. Empowerment for liberative change can thereby become a part of the way in which each of us exists in relation to all others.

As the Buddha intimated and Hannah Arendt cautioned, global critiques of sociopolitical ills can lead to paralysis.[21] Change at any level comes about as a result of individual acts. A man made aware of his participation in the subjugation of women can do no more than influence his local world. A woman can only do the same. Kyriarchal structures of oppression can only be overturned by empowerment of the individual to action. Tell me I am responsible for the transformation of all of society, and I am overwhelmed. Tell me I am responsible for my own relationships, and I can envisage a way forward. Empower me to begin living in right relation to each individual I meet, and my reach can eventually be broadened to include the groups of which I am a member.

This is a more modest proposal than is implicit in some recent theologies. Few can manage the burden of a call to change the entire social or cultural or political system. The final goal ought most certainly to be a restructured society free from oppressive influences. We should most certainly "think globally," but in truth few can do more than "act locally." Even Jesus, empowered as he was by the deepest of all possible relationships with God, acted—and probably even thought—locally. He taught fellow Jews, after all. Jesus' example teaches us that we can dream of global transformation, but it will only come about through individual acts. Understanding God and Christ in relational terms empowers the individual act and places it within the fullest context of love's purposes.

Empathy is a powerful and potentially injurious tool for influencing others. Empathic projection carries with it intensely ethical considerations. Its power for healing is indicative of its theological importance. Used inappropriately, it can result in manipulation and domination.

In psychoanalysis, the therapist learns to project himself or herself into the lifeworld of the patient to provide a space of acceptance: this then leads to healing. But this encounter can and unfortunately does result in abuse. For example, the natural activity of attunement can be deliberately manipulated in a kind of hypnotic technique.

Neurolinguistic Programming (NLP) is a method for influencing human behavior through mirroring of posture, facial expression, tone of voice, and other aspects of body language. It has enjoyed popularity within sales and marketing circles as a means of influencing decision-making. One book that offers a popularized version of the technique proclaims that if you purchase it you will "Maximize your charisma with . . . the NLP program that creates intimacy, persuasiveness, power!"[22] The ethical implications of this are astounding—perverting a God-given ability to share in the life-world of others into a technique for making money, winning friends, and getting one's own way is a gross evil.

Empathy can be misused in therapy through the natural evolution of transference between therapist and client. In all successful therapy, at some point feelings that actually have to do with significant others out of the client's past are displaced onto the therapist. In other words, the client often believes himself to have "fallen in love with" the therapist for a time—this is a natural result of the experience of true empathy offered in a controlled setting. Therapists who have not achieved high levels of maturity themselves or who desire to exert power over others have at times taken advantage of this emotional vulnerability for personal gratification of egotistical, sexual, or even financial longings.

Sin and evil are radically communal in nature. The sinful act is an individual choice, and the accumulation of sinful acts within a community gives rise to evil. Sin is never purely and simply the sole purview of an individual person: sin is always relational, either against God and self or against God and another person. Sin becomes corporate action, and evil, corporate suffering.[23]

Perhaps the greatest sin, and therefore most powerful source of evil, is self-absorption. Putting one's own concerns, needs, and desires before all else results in a kind of self-deification, or narcissistic idolatry. Putting oneself at the center of one's universe displaces God and creation. When the world is viewed exclusively in terms my experience, I overlay my own desires onto the other. Giving becomes presenting not what the other needs but what I want to give. The world and others live in the shadow of my own idolatrous relationship to myself.

"Evil mimics the good, the demonic mimics the divine, destructive spirits mimic the Holy Spirit. Human beings strive to be 'like God,' and they are remarkably successful at this deception," says Peter Hodgson.[24] There have been occasions in human history when the power to understand the deepest needs of others has been perverted on a grand scale. It is heartrending to admit that the twentieth century alone provided us with numerous examples to illustrate this point: I will use the now classic case of Adolf Hitler.

Those who knew him depict Hitler as an intense and unusually charismatic man. It is said that he knew the hearts of the German people and this explains his ability to inflame crowds with zeal for his program. It may well be that Hitler was a master at empathic manipulation—discerning that which others most wanted to hear and offering it as a agenda for political control.

There has been a tendency to speak of the Holocaust as the work of a few evil men—Hitler and his assistants—but this is not the whole story. Daniel Jonah Goldhagen incited tremendous controversy in Germany a few years ago with the publication of his book *Hitler's Willing Executioners: Ordinary Germans and the Holocaust.* His thesis is that without the cooperation of thousands of German citizens, the Holocaust could not have happened. Goldhagen shows that it was not economics or totalitarianism alone that made the Holocaust possible. It was, he says, "ideas about Jews that were pervasive in Germany and had been for decades." These ideas—of the Jews as different—"induced ordinary Germans to kill unarmed, defenseless Jewish men, women, and children by the thousands, systematically and without pity."[25]

These beliefs about the Jews were the direct antithesis of the Christian message, yet it was German Christians who accepted and acted on them.[26] Nazi Germany underscores the truth that all power is relational and social—Hitler only had the power to accomplish his aims because of the willing contributions of individual power by people just like you and me. He was not a "Svengali" hypnotizing crowds into performing acts against their wills. He was, perhaps, a master at conscious empathic projection devoid of sympathy. In the case of Jesus the inverse is true: without the willing contribution of each individual's personal power, the presence of the divine made incarnate in him would not have given birth to the continuing presence of his reality through the church.

To speak of incarnation as participation goes a long way toward hampering the kinds of thinking and responding that make genocidal programs possible. It is true that love of neighbor is a basic tenet of Christianity. But without emphasis on the cosmic nature of divine incarnation, it is all too easy to decide that I am to love *only* my neighbor, not those different from me. The Holocaust was a massive enactment of evil made possible by the additive effects of individual decisions and acts.

We are sinful individuals, yet capable by virtue of God's participation in creation of doing righteous acts. God's deciding center is ethically immutable, always for-the-other. Our deciding center is not, but altruism shows us what ought to be. The capacity to participate compassionately in the lives of others is ours by grace. Through it we are facilitated in the healing of our infected natures.

Salvation comes through the healing that results from breaking out of self-centeredness and grasping, not through the mere performance of compassionate acts. We carry out deeds of compassion and the infection of self-centered existence begins to heal. The healing that comes to us in participatory being, incarnating the divine, is a gift of grace and the mode of salvation.

This revisioning of the incarnation as participation is a radically communal vision of life. In it, individuality is preserved as constituted within the divine matrix of relationality. It is a hopeful and optimistic vision, as is required by the Christian message itself. It is not, however, naïve or soft: in this understanding of incarnation as participation lies recognition that alongside the possibility of making present the very being of God in the encounter with others also lies the possibility of incarnating evil. Human existence carries with it a tragic character. While God is always already present in creation as offer, possibility, gift, and grace, freedom of the will always includes the possibility of refusal. The moral tragedy of human existence lies in the frequency with which humans choose to ignore the gift. It is in the places where we are closest to God that the greatest potential for evil also resides. Because we can decide for or against God's gift, it is when we stand in the presence of others that we possess the power to do the greatest good or the most horrendous evil. The choice is ours.

NOTES

Preface

1. See R. P. C. Hanson, *The Search for the Christian Doctrine of God: The Arian Controversy, 318–381 A.D.* (Edinburgh: T. & T. Clark, 1988); Christopher Haas, "The Alexandrian Riots of 356 and George of Cappadocia," *Greek, Roman, and Byzantine Studies* 32:3 (1991), 281–93; Timothy Barnes, *Constantine and Eusebius* (Cambridge: Harvard Univ. Press, 1981); and idem, *Athanasius and Constantius: Theology and Politics in the Constantinian Empire* (Cambridge: Harvard Univ. Press, 1993).

2. John Hick, *The Metaphor of God Incarnate: Christology in a Pluralistic Age* (Louisville: Westminster John Knox, 1993), xi.

3. Edward T. Hall, *The Dance of Life: The Other Dimension of Time* (New York: Anchor Doubleday, 1983). Back cover.

4. Max Scheler, *The Nature of Sympathy,* trans. Peter Heath (Hamden, Conn.: Archon, 1973).

1. Was Jesus God?

1. David Friedrich Strauss, *The Life of Jesus Critically Examined*, ed. Peter Hodgson, trans. George Eliot (Philadelphia: Fortress Press, 1973). See chapter 2 for current scholarship on this question.

2. Albert Schweitzer, *The Quest of the Historical Jesus,* ed. John Bowden, trans. Donald Nineham (Minneapolis: Fortress Press, 2001 [1910]).

3. Josephus, *Jewish Antiquities,* 20.5.1, 20.8.6, 17.10.7, and *The Jewish*

War, 2.13.5, 2.4.3, 7.29, in *The New Complete Works of Josephus.* trans. William Whiston (Grand Rapids, Mich.: Kragel, 1999).

4. Although this is not widely accepted among scholars, at least one member of the Jesus Seminar publicly supports this thesis that the Dead Sea Scrolls are contemporary with the Gospels and that they refer to Jesus. See Barbara Theiring, *Jesus the Man: New Interpretations of the Dead Sea Scrolls* (Trenton, Mich.: Corgi/Transworld, 1993).

5. Michael O. Wise, *The First Messiah: Investigating the Savior before Jesus* (San Francisco: Harper SanFrancisco, 1999).

6. Other disputed topics in New Testament studies include the meaning of and extent to which Jesus used apocalyptic language and the character of messianic expectations among the Jews generally during this period.

7. "Historical evidence for Jesus' divinity or the absolutist principle—formerly thought to be plentiful—has been reduced almost to nothing by historical criticism." This assertion is from Wesley J. Wildman, *Fidelity with Plausibility: Modest Christologies in the Twentieth Century* (Albany, N.Y.: SUNY, 1998), 274.

8. Schubert Ogden, *The Point of Christology* (San Francisco: Harper and Row, 1982), 18–19, 23.

9. A. M. Allchin, Foreword to *Man and the Cosmos: The Vision of St. Maximus the Confessor*, by Lars Thunberg (Crestwood, N.Y.: St. Vladimir's, 1985), 8.

10. Marcus J. Borg and N. T. Wright, *The Meaning of Jesus: Two Visions* (San Francisco: Harper SanFrancisco, 1999), 270 n.6.

11. Roger Haight, *Jesus, Symbol of God* (Maryknoll, N.Y.: Orbis Books, 1999), 424. Also, Wildman's *Fidelity with Plausibility.*

12. Haight, *Jesus, Symbol of God*, 399–410.

13. For a recent theological interpretation of this issue, see Sallie McFague, *Super, Natural Christians: How We Should Love Nature* (Minneapolis: Fortress Press, 1997). Also, her most recent book, *Life Abundant: Rethinking Theology and Economy for a Planet in Peril* (Minneapolis: Fortress Press, 2000).

14. McFague's *Life Abundant* explores (in part) an "ecological economic Christology" that is both prophetic in its call to action and sacramental in its affirmation of life. It is a functional and descriptive christology that attends to the meaning of Christ for how we should interact with the environment. My own thesis is an attempt to explore the "mechanism" of incarnation itself.

15. Scripture quotations are taken from the New Revised Standard Version.

16. Object Relations Theory, and especially D. W. Winnicott's work, particularly comes to mind with regard to infant-caregiver fusion. Theories of this type focus on development of self in relation to external "objects" or

others. Freudian interpretations of human development are representative of those that view development as a contest of differentiation, focused on the internal development of self.

17. Quoted in Matt Ridley, *The Origins of Virtue: Human Instincts and the Evolution of Cooperation* (New York: Penguin, 1996), 1.

18. Ridley tells of the tragic response one individual had to the revolutionary concept of the "selfish gene": After reading the conclusions of one of the early proponents of this theory, George Price studied genetics in order to disprove the theory that altruism was nothing more than a byproduct of selfish genes. In the process of trying to disprove the theory, he made corrections to the original mathematics and ended up substantiating it instead. He entered into collaboration with the originator of the theory, but over time showed signs of mental deterioration, became intensely concerned with religion, donated everything to the poor, and committed suicide, apparently in part due to the conflict between his religious beliefs and scientific discoveries (19).

19. Further support for this line of thought is found in medical research regarding the role that intimacy plays in survival after serious physical illness among humans. Just as we seem to have been encoded with the ability to feel another's suffering so as to motivate us to act, we are encoded with the need for intimate relationship. Extensive study comparing people who have a close relationship as opposed to those who do not has found that those with intimate partners consistently show increased immune response, lower serum cholesterol, lower death rates generally and from cancer specifically. A Duke University study of 1,000 cardiac patients found that those without spouse or close friends had triple the death rate within five years of diagnosis. The theological datum of the absolutely relational character of humanity is well-supported by medical research. Janice Kiecolt-Glaser and Ronald Glaser, *The Fourth International Congress of Behavioral Medicine*, Washington, D.C., 1996; idem, *Psychosomatic Medicine* 55 (1993): 395–409; P. Moen, D. Dempster-McClain, and R. Williams, "Successful Aging," *American Journal of Sociology* 97 (1993): 1612–38; J. S. House, K. R. Landis, and D. Umberson, "Social Relationships and Health," *Science* 241 (1988): 540–45.

20. Daniel N. Stern, *The Interpersonal World of the Infant: A View from Psychoanalysis and Developmental Psychology* (New York: Basic, 1985).

21. Cf. Philem. 6; 1 Cor. 1:7-9; 10:16-17; 2 Cor. 1:7; 8:23; 13:14; 1 Peter 4:13; Phil. 3:10-11, where the term appears translated as *participation, communion, association, fellowship, contribution.*

22. Ian Barbour, *Religion in an Age of Science,* the Gifford Lectures 1989–1991, vol.1 (San Francisco: Harper SanFrancisco, 1990), 3–30.

23. Haight, *Jesus, Symbol of God*, xi.

2. The Question of Incarnation

1. John J. O'Donnell, *Trinity and Temporality: The Christian Doctrine of God in the Light of Process Theology and the Theology of Hope* (New York: Oxford Univ. Press, 1983), 1–24.

2. Gordon D. Kaufman, *God, Mystery, Diversity: Christian Theology in a Pluralistic World* (Minneapolis: Fortress Press, 1996), 42–53, 110–24.

3. Maurice Wiles, "Christianity without Incarnation?" in *The Myth of God Incarnate*, ed. John Hick (Philadelphia: Westminster Press, 1977), 5.

4. Manabu Waida, "Incarnation," in *The Encyclopedia of Religion*, vol. 7, ed. Mircea Eliade (New York: Macmillan, 1987), 156–61.

5. Geoffrey Parrinder, *Avatar and Incarnation* (New York: Oxford Univ. Press, 1982), 17, 29–30.

6. From the *Bhagavad Gita*, quoted in *The Ways of Religion*, ed. Roger Eastman (Oxford: Oxford Univ. Press, 1995), 36.

7. Richard A. Gard, *Buddhism*, Great Religions of Modern Man (New York: Washington Square Press, 1963).

8. Waida, "Incarnation," 159.

9. Richard C. Martin, *Islamic Studies: A History of Religions Approach*, 2nd ed. (Upper Saddle River, N.J.: Prentice Hall, 1982). Also Waidu, "Incarnation," 159; Parrinder, *Avatar*, 192–205.

10. Jacob Neusner, *The Incarnation of God: The Character of God in Formative Judaism* (Philadelphia: Fortress Press, 1988), 6. Another Jewish scholar, Michael Wyschogrod, argues a similar point for different reasons in "A Jewish Perspective on Incarnation," *Modern Theology* 12 (April 1996): 195–209.

11. Neusner, *The Incarnation of God*, xi, 220.

12. Ibid., 166. This brief survey of incarnational motifs in religious traditions is not intended as an exercise in comparative religion nor as an effort to support or refute the validity of themes found in other faiths. I have made no attempt to examine the variations in incarnational themes found among the world's religions, nor have I addressed the issue of inter-religious influence. Nor do I mean to gloss over the important differences among the interpretations offered by these traditions.

13. Cf. Mary Daly, *Beyond God the Father: Towards a Philosophy of Women's Liberation* (Boston: Beacon Press, 1973), 69–97; Naomi Goldenberg, *Changing of the Gods: Feminism and the End of Traditional Religion* (Boston: Beacon Press, 1979), 22.

14. Frances Young, "Two Roots or a Tangled Mass?" *The Myth of God Incarnate*, ed. John Hick (Philadelphia: Westminster Press, 1977), 87–124.

15. John Hick, "Jesus and the World Religions," *Myth of God Incarnate*, 169.

16. John Hick, *The Metaphor of God Incarnate* (Louisville: Westminster John Knox, 1993).

17. Hick, *Myth of God Incarnate*, 180.

18. Hick, *Metaphor of God Incarnate*, 103.

19. Michael Green, "Jesus in the New Testament," *The Truth of God Incarnate*, ed. Michael Green (Grand Rapids, Mich.: Eerdmans, 1977), 40.

20. Neusner, *The Incarnation of God*, 7.

21. Brian Hebblethwaite, *The Incarnation: Collected Essays in Christology* (New York: Cambridge Univ. Press, 1987), 50–51.

22. Brian Hebblethwaite, "The Uniqueness of the Incarnation," *Incarnation and Myth. The Debate Continued*, ed. Michael Goulder (Grand Rapids, Mich.: Eerdmans, 1979), 191.

23. Philipp Melanchthon, *Loci communes* 19:21–22, in *The Loci Communes of Philipp Melanchthon, with a Critical Introduction*, trans. Charles Leander Hill (Boston: Meador, 1944).

24. John Macquarrie, *Jesus Christ in Modern Thought* (Philadelphia: Trinity, 1991), 171.

25. J. N. D. Kelly, *Early Christian Creeds*, 3rd ed. (Essex, U.K.: Longman House, 1972), 296.

26. Ibid., 297–98.

27. Not only were theologians and philosophers of the early church at home in the language of Nicea and Chalcedon, but apparently the average believer was as well. Speaking of Constantinople, Gregory of Nyssa, the fourth-century bishop, once wrote: "For all the districts of the city are full of such things—the alleyways, the marketplaces, the streets, the roads, the clothing dealers, the bankers, the food-merchants. If you ask about the weights, someone philosophizes to you about the Begotten and Unbegotten. If you inquire about the price of bread, someone adjudges the Father to be greater, and the Son subject to Him. And if you should say that the bath is pleasant, someone determines that the Son exists out of non-being." *Oratio de deitate Filii et Spiritus Sancti*, PG 46: 557 B-C. Translation from the Greek by Thomas Smith.

28. J. N. D. Kelly, *Early Christian Doctrines*, 2nd ed. (New York: Harper & Row, 1978) 339–40.

29. See discussion later in this chapter.

30. Hebblethwaite, *The Incarnation*, 74.

31. E. P. Sanders, *The Historical Figure of Jesus* (London: Penguin Books, 1993), 10–11.

32. Cf. John 3:17; 6:38; 8:23, 38, 42, 58; 10:30, 36; 14:7,10; 16:28; 17:5, 18, 24. See below for further development of this question. Martin Hengel notes that the main theme of Johannine theology is not the deification of Jesus but the incarnation of the love of God—"its goal is the salvation of humankind"—and reference to God the Father occurs more frequently in John than to all the christological titles combined. *Studies in Early Christology* (Edinburgh: T. & T. Clark, 1995), 368. Be that as it may, the Gospel clearly portrays divine *relational* (not substantial) unity with Jesus. And so critiques of the language of the creeds are correct in advocating revision of the language of substance metaphysics.

33. James D. G. Dunn, *Christology in the Making: A New Testament Inquiry into the Origins of the Doctrine of the Incarnation,* 2nd ed. (Grand Rapids, Mich.: Eerdmans, 1989), 265. Also Macquarrie, *Jesus Christ in Modern Thought,* 100.

34. A. T. Hanson and R. P. C. Hanson, *Reasonable Belief: A Survey of the Christian Faith* (Oxford: Oxford Univ. Press, 1980), 59. Compare also Marcus Borg's portrait of Jesus as a Jewish mystic or "spirit person" in *Meeting Jesus Again for the First Time: The Historical Jesus and the Heart of Contemporary Faith* (Harper SanFrancisco: San Francisco, 1995); idem, *Jesus in Contemporary Scholarship* (Valley Forge, Penn.: Trinity, 1994).

35. Dunn, *Christology in the Making,* 251–53. Also Macquarrie, *Jesus Christ in Modern Thought,* 36–47.

36. Martin Hengel, *The Son of God: The Origin of Christology and the History of Jewish-Hellenistic Religion* (Philadelphia: Fortress Press, 1976), 21–22.

37. Dunn, *Christology in the Making,* 22. Also Macquarrie, *Jesus Christ in Modern Thought,* 42–43. I am dealing here with the issue of titles in relation to the question of incarnation. Another important issue for christology centers on the question of whether Jesus thought he was the long-awaited Jewish messiah. The Jewish messiah and the incarnation of God are not the same thing at all. Jesus could well have believed himself to be the messiah and had no thought of himself as God incarnate. The same is true of his followers. This is a point that sometimes gets lost in these discussions. Scholars are divided here, as on most of these questions. See Marcus J. Borg and N. T. Wright, *The Meaning of Jesus: Two Visions* (San Francisco: Harper SanFrancisco, 1999), especially 47–52, 54–58, 96–100, 146–47, 225–28.

38. Borg and Wright, *The Meaning of Jesus,* 166.

39. Hanson and Hanson, *Reasonable Belief,* 63.

40. Geza Vermes, *The Religion of Jesus the Jew* (Minneapolis: Fortress Press, 1993), 152–183. Although it is striking that Jesus did not appear to

have used the concomitant appellation "Our King," there is no philologi-
cal evidence to support claims that "Abba" as a form of address to God
originated with Jesus. See also Vermes's *Jesus the Jew* (Philadelphia:
Fortress Press, 1973), 210.

41. Cf. Hengel, *Son of God;* Macquarrie, *Jesus Christ in Modern
Thought,* 27–47; Dunn, *Christology in the Making;* Reginald Fuller, *The
Foundations of New Testament Christology* (New York: Scribner, 1965).

42. John Knox, *The Humanity and Divinity of Christ* (Cambridge:
Cambridge Univ. Press, 1967), 95. Although Knox's delineation of these
stages is somewhat confusing, it is still helpful as a mode of presentation
of the issues at stake. Macquarrie, *Jesus Christ in Modern Thought,* 144–46,
notes that Knox passes quickly over something like a fourth stage, which
he calls "incarnationism." This "incarnationism" seems to be an interme-
diate point between *kenosis* and docetism. It is the belief that a divine
pre-existent *hypostasis* took a truly human life; this has come to be the
classical understanding of the doctrine of Jesus as God-Incarnate. At one
point, Knox uses the term to refer to a time during which adoptionism
was being conformed to ideas of pre-existence. At another it refers to
Paul's combination of adoptionist and pre-existence themes. Later he uses
the term to refer to the christology of John's Gospel. For Knox pre-
existence is understood in terms of God's foreknowledge. He assumes it
requires only small steps to move from the idea that God foreknew the
identity of Jesus as messiah to belief in his ontological pre-existence, and
then to the idea that Jesus, as a divine being, emptied himself of divinity
for a time in order to become human. So he offers three stages but speaks
of four and does not clearly define his terms at the outset. All christologies
must necessarily be considered "incarnational," in that they attempt to
explain how it is that God has been revealed in the flesh-and-blood
human life of Jesus of Nazareth. Be that as it may, his stages are useful for
a concise presentation of the main issues.

43. John Knox, *Humanity and Divinity,* 9–10.

44. Ibid., 11.

45. Paula Fredriksen, *From Jesus to Christ: The Origins of the New
Testament Images of Christ,* 2nd ed. (New Haven, Conn.: Yale Univ. Press,
1988), 174.

46. Ibid., 162. The quote refers to Paul's rejection of Judaizing, but it applies
equally well to all attempts at interpreting what he intended to communicate.

47. Carey C. Newman, James R. Davila, and Gladys S. Lewis, eds., *The
Jewish Roots of Christological Monotheism: Papers from the St. Andrews
Conference on the Historical Origins of the Worship of Jesus,* Supplements to
the Journal for the Study of Judaism, vol. 63 (Boston: Brill, 1999); Larry

Hurtado, *One God, One Lord: Early Christian Devotion and Ancient Jewish Monotheism* (Philadelphia: Fortress Press, 1988); A. P. Segal, "Pre-existence and Incarnation: A Response to Dunn and Holladay," *Semeia* 30 (1985) 83–95; idem, *The Other Judaisms of Late Antiquity* (Atlanta: Scholars Press, 1987); Jarl E. Fossum, *The Name of God and the Angel of the Lord: Samaritan and Jewish Concepts of Intermediation and the Origin of Gnosticism* (Tübingen: Mohr-Siebeck, 1985).

48. Brendan Byrne, "Christ's Pre-Existence in Pauline Soteriology," *Theological Studies* 58 (1997), 308–31.

49. Bart D. Erhman, *The Orthodox Corruption of Scripture: The Effect of Early Christological Controversies on the Text of the New Testament* (New York: Oxford Univ. Press, 1993), 97.

50. Ibid., 27. We have about 5,366 "copies of the copies of the copies" of the New Testament texts in the Greek language alone, dating from the second to the sixteenth centuries, and no two of them are exactly alike (27). There are more than 8,000 copies of the Latin Vulgate (43 n.107). No one knows how many differences there are in surviving texts, but "best guess" estimates place the number in the hundreds of thousands. Many of the variants are clearly unintentional errors on the part of scribes, but there are easily five or six dozen surviving alterations that indicate a theological motive (276). It was common knowledge in the early church that theologians might alter texts. Rev. 22:18–19, for example, ends with a curse on anyone who might alter the text. We find accusations of text-tampering in Irenaeus and Origen, among others (26).

3. A Short History of Christology

1. James D. G. Dunn, *Christology in the Making: A New Testament Inquiry into the Origins of the Doctrine of the Incarnation.* 2nd ed. (Grand Rapids, Mich.: Eerdmans, 1989), xxx.

2. Origen, *Against Celsus*, in *The Fathers of the Third Century*, vol. 3: The Ante-Nicene Fathers: Writings of the Fathers down to A.D. 325, eds. Alexander Roberts and James Donaldson (Grand Rapids, Mich.: Eerdmans, 1978). Also, Gregory of Nyssa, *On Not Three Gods*, in *Gregory of Nyssa: Dogmatic Treatises: Select Writings and Letters*, A Select Library of Nicene and Post-Nicene Fathers of the Christian Church, vol. 5, ed. Philip Schaff and Henry Wace (Grand Rapids, Mich.: Eerdmans, 1978).

3. Edwin Hatch, *The Influence of Greek Ideas and Usages upon the Christian Church*, ed. A. M. Fairbairn (London: Williams and Norgate, 1891), 1–24. While Dead Sea Scrolls scholarship helps clarify the deeply Jewish roots

of Christian eschatological thinking and perhaps even of the Last Supper tradition, it is true that the doctrinal formation of the early church took place within a Greco-Roman arena. See Lawrence H. Schiffman, *Reclaiming the Dead Sea Scrolls: Their True Meaning for Judaism and Christianity* (New York: Doubleday, 1995).

4. The conflict actually seems to have broken out over scriptural exegesis of Prov. 8:22-31. There Wisdom speaks prophetically of herself not as divine and pre-existent but as an act of God or an aspect of divinity that was "poured out" like the Holy Spirit, as the first of God's acts in creation. Jaroslav Pelikan, *The Christian Tradition: A History of the Development of Doctrine*, vol. 1: *The Emergence of the Catholic Tradition (100–600)* (Chicago: Univ. of Chicago Press, 1971), 186.

5. J. N. D. Kelly, *Early Christian Doctrines*, 2nd ed. (San Francisco: Harper and Row, 1978), 226–31.

6. Catherine Mowry LaCugna, *God for Us: The Trinity and Christian Life* (San Francisco: Harper Collins, 1991), 21–52.

7. Athanasius, *On the Incarnation of the Word* in *St. Athanasius: Selected Works and Letters*. A Select Library of Nicene and Post-Nicene Fathers of the Christian Church, vol. 4, ed. Philip Schaff and Henry Wace (Grand Rapids, Mich.: Eerdmans, 1978).

8. Athanasius, *Four Discourses against the Arians*, II. 70, in ibid.

9. See Christopher Stead, *Divine Substance* (Oxford: Clarendon, 1977). Second-century gnostic writers introduced *homoousios* into Christian language. Irenaeus used it to refute gnostic emanationist theories of creation, and Origen first used it in reference to the Trinity. At the time of Nicea, there was no "orthodox" or "heretical" use of the term, because it had not been important to theological reflection. Stead says the issue was and has been problematic for theology because "answers were sought before the question [of God's substance] was adequately defined" (158). Most Christian writers assumed the Platonic maxim that God is beyond being/substance. So it is probable that their use of *ousia* did not refer to the question of God's existence. To refer to God's existence, they most often used *hypostasis*. In the Nicene documents, *hypostasis* and *ousia* are used as synonyms. The nuances became very important in subsequent christological discussions at Chalcedon (160–61). It is likely that the framers of the Nicene Creed did not intend *homoousios* in an ontological sense, to say that the Son is of the same status as the Father. They seem to have meant that the Son was not "made" like things but given birth to out of the Father's reality. Unfortunately, the term's fluidity (which made it attractive in the first place) made it possible to attach the very ontological meanings to it that it was designed to avoid (233).

10. LaCugna, *God for Us*, 36.

11. Pelikan, *Emergence*, 210.

12. Tertullian, *Against Praxeas*, 27, in *Latin Christianity: Its Founder, Tertullian*, The Ante-Nicene Fathers: Writings of the Fathers down to A.D. 325, vol. 3, eds. Alexander Roberts and James Donaldson (Grand Rapids, Mich.: Eerdmans, 1978).

13. Augustine, Sermon 186, I, *Sermons III/6 (184–229Z) on the Liturgical Seasons*, trans. Edmund Hill, ed. John Rotelle, The Works of St. Augustine: A Translation for the 21st Century (New Rochelle, N.Y.: New City, 1993).

14. Harry A. Wolfson, *The Philosophy of the Church Fathers: Faith, Trinity, Incarnation*, 3rd ed. (Cambridge, Mass.: Harvard Univ. Press, 1970), 372–86. Wolfson notes other types: (1) *Aristotelian mixture:* Like a union of composition, the things united in a mixture retain their individual natures, and the mixture is resolvable into its constituents. However, the result of the union is a *tertium quid*—a mixture of wine and water, for example. (2) *Stoic mixture:* The things united are imperceptible in union, but still capable of being separated out. (3) *Union of confusion:* The result is a *tertium quid* that cannot be resolved into its parts.

15. Ibid.

16. Kelly, *Early Christian Doctrines*, 280–309.

17. Jaroslav Pelikan, *The Christian Tradition: A History of the Development of Doctrine*, vol. 2: *The Spirit of Eastern Christendom (600–1700)* (Chicago: Univ. of Chicago Press, 1974), 81.

18. Maurice Wiles, *The Christian Fathers*, 2nd ed. (London: SCM, 1977), 74.

19. Kelly, *Early Christian Doctrines*, 292.

20. Apollinaris, quoted in ibid., 293.

21. Gregory Nazianzen, *Letter 101* in *Socrates: Church History from A.D. 305–438; Sozemus: Church History from A.D. 323–425*, A Select Library of Nicene and Post-Nicene Fathers of the Christian Church, vol. 2, ed. Philip Schaff and Henry Wace (Grand Rapids: Eerdmans, 1978).

22. Gregory of Nyssa, *Against Eunomius, Book XII* in *Gregory of Nyssa: Dogmatic Treatises; Select Writings and Letters*, vol. 5: A Select Library of Nicene and Post-Nicene Fathers of the Christian Church, ed. Philip Schaff and Henry Wace (Grand Rapids: Eerdmans, 1978).

23. Theodore of Mopsuestia quoted in Kelly, *Early Christian Doctrines*, 304.

24. Ibid., 304–8.

25. John Meyendorff, *Christ in Eastern Christian Thought* (Washington, D.C.: Corpus, 1969), 51.

26. E. Amann, "Theopaschite Controverse" in *Dictionnaire de Theologie Catholique* (Paris, 1946), vol. 15, coll. 505–12.

27. Kelly, *Early Christian Doctrines,* 310–13.

28. See the next chapter for a more detailed look at the role *apatheia* has played in Christian theology.

29. Quoted in D. M. Baillie, *God Was in Christ: An Essay on Incarnation and Atonement* (London: Faber & Faber, 1948), 83.

30. Ibid., 83. Some at Chalcedon thought the solution was to be found in Latin terminology. Two centuries before Chalcedon, a North African Christian lawyer named Tertullian had introduced a juridical understanding of Christ as mediator. In the Eastern churches, redemption was conceived as deification: God became human in order that we might become God. But for Tertullian and the West redemption came through sacrifice and reconciliation, so to say that Jesus Christ is both God and human is essential. Tertullian was the first to make use of the terms substance and person (*substantia, persona* in Latin) in explaining Christ's makeup. Although there is some dispute among scholars as to what extent Tertullian used these terms in their Roman legal sense, their introduction provided the West with a less controversial christological language.

31. Cf. John 10:30, "The Father and I are one," to Luke 22:42-44, where Jesus prays in the garden at Gethsemane, displaying anguish, sweating profusely, and needing consolation from an angel of God.

32. LaCugna, *God for Us,* 21–44.

33. A recent article published in *Newsweek* documents current lay and pastoral confusion about the doctrine of the Trinity, of which the incarnation obviously is an integral part. Marguerite Schuster's study of 3,000 sermons written by predominantly non-Pentecostal ministers reports "considerable confusion" among "the preachers' understanding of the Father, Son, and Holy Spirit." Many ministers equate the work of the Spirit with that of Christ, while others commonly collapse trinitarian theology into modalism. "In one sermon, Billy Graham himself confesses that while he believes in the Trinity, 'Don't ask me to explain it. I can't.'" Personal experience is reported to be the primary criterion used by the average American Christian in assessing the truth value of theological doctrines. Kenneth L. Woodward, "Living in the Holy Spirit," *Newsweek* (April 13, 1998), 54–60.

34. Pelikan, *Spirit of Eastern Christendom,* 76–77.

35. Lars Thunberg, *Microcosm and Mediator: The Theological Anthropology of Maximus the Confessor,* 2nd ed. (Chicago: Open Court, 1995), 21–32.

36. Maximus the Confessor, *Book of Ambiguities,* 41, *Patrologia Graeca* (PG) 91:1308. Quoted in Pelikan, *Spirit of Eastern Christendom,* 267.

37. Ibid., 20; PG 91:1237; and *Questions to Thalassius on the Scripture*, 22; PG 90:321. Quoted in Pelikan, *Spirit of Eastern Christendom*, 11.

38. Thunberg, *Microcosm*, 28–31.

39. Maximus, *Questiones ad Thalassium*, 60; PG 90:621. Quoted in Meyendorff, *Christ*, 102.

40. Maximus, *Dialogue with Pyrrhus*, PG 91: 324d. Quoted in Meyendorff, *Christ*, 104.

41. Meyendorff, *Christ*, 99–105.

42. Ibid., 106–15.

43. Andrew Louth, *Wisdom of the Byzantine Church: Evagrios of Pontos and Maximos the Confessor* (Columbia: Univ. of Missouri Press, 1997), 12–13.

44. Heiko Augustinus Oberman, *The Harvest of Medieval Theology: Gabriel Biel and Late Medieval Nominalism* (Cambridge: Harvard Univ. Press, 1963), 250–53.

45. Martin Luther, quoted in Douglas Ottati, *Jesus Christ and Christian Vision* (Louisville: Westminster John Knox, 1996), 35–38.

46. Friedrich Schleiermacher, *The Christian Faith*, ed. H. R. Mackintosh and J. S. Stewart (Edinburgh: T. & T. Clark, 1989), §13.

47. Ibid., §97.

48. Ibid., §94.

49. Claude Welch, *Protestant Thought in the Nineteenth Century, volume I: 1799–1870* (New Haven: Yale Univ. Press, 1972), 104–5.

50. Peter C. Hodgson, *God in History: Shapes of Freedom* (Nashville: Abingdon, 1989), 60–62.

51. G. W. F. Hegel, *Lectures on the Philosophy of Religion: The Lectures of 1827*, ed. Peter C. Hodgson (Berkeley: Univ. of California Press, 1988), 455.

52. Ibid., 456 n.173, from the 1831 lectures. Cf. Hegel's statement regarding the preconditions of faith: "Faith in the divine is only possible if in believers themselves there is a divine element which rediscovers itself, its own nature, in that on which it believes, even if it be unconscious that what it has found is its own nature . . . only a modification of the Godhead can know the Godhead." *G. W. F. Hegel: Theologian of the Spirit*, ed. Peter C. Hodgson (Minneapolis: Fortress Press, 1997), 65.

53. Hegel, *Lectures*, 457, 462.

54. Hegel, in *Theologian of the Spirit*, 58.

55. Welch, *Protestant Thought*, 278–81.

56. Isaak August Dorner, *System of Christian Doctrine*, §100, in Claude Welch, ed. and trans., *God and Incarnation in Mid-Nineteenth Century German Theology* (New York: Oxford Univ. Press, 1965).

57. Ibid., §104.

58. Ibid., §100.

59. Dorner, *The Dogmatic Concept of the Immutability of God*, in Welch, *God and Incarnation*, 150–55.

60. Welch, *Protestant Thought*, 277.

61. Karl Rahner, *Foundations of Christian Faith*, trans. William V. Dych (New York: Seabury, 1978), 430.

62. Linell Cady, "Relational Love: A Feminist Christian Vision," *Embodied Love: Sensuality and Relationship as Feminist Values*, ed. Paula M. Cooey, Sharon A. Farmer, Mary Ellen Ross (San Francisco: Harper & Row, 1987), 147.

63. The following owes much to Stephen J. Duffy, *The Dynamics of Grace: Perspectives in Theological Anthropology* (Collegeville, Minn.: Liturgical, 1993).

64. Karl Rahner, *Hearer of the Word: Laying the Foundation for a Philosophy of Religion*, trans. Joseph Donceel, ed. Andrew Tallon (New York: Continuum, 1994), 16.

65. Andrew Tallon, Editor's Introduction, *Hearer of the Word*, xiv. *Vorgriff* has been misunderstood, in part due to its having been rendered "pre-concept" or "pre-apprehension" when first translated into English. It is not "an act of knowledge. It is a moment of such an act . . . the condition of the possibility of knowledge" not of a single object, but of "the totality of the possible objects of human knowledge" (48). For Martin Heidegger, human transcendence is toward nothingness, since finitude cannot grasp the infinite. But for Rahner, although anticipation does not "put God as an object before the mind . . . the *Vorgriff* aims at God." We know this only after the fact, since it is in anticipation that we know the finite as limited. Thus this could be said to be an *a posteriori* demonstration of God (50–51).

66. Ibid., 39–41; 53–54.

67. Ibid., 120.

68. Karl Rahner, *The Love of Jesus and the Love of Neighbor*, trans. Robert Barr (New York: Crossroad, 1983), 71.

69. Duffy, *Dynamics*, 287.

70. Karl Rahner, *Theological Investigations*, vol. 1: *God, Christ, Mary, and Grace*, trans. Cornelius Ernst (Baltimore: Helicon, 1961), 300–15.

71. Rahner, *Hearer of the Word*, 53–54.

72. Duffy, *Dynamics*, 269.

73. Karl Rahner, *Theological Investigations*, vol. 4: *More Recent Writings*, trans. Kevin Smyth (Baltimore: Helicon, 1966), 110.

74. Ibid., 116.

75. Rahner sometimes refers to the incarnation as God's "self-empty-ing." I deliberately avoid reference to *kenosis* because (1) Rahner does not intend the traditional meaning of the term, and (2) the word has been

misunderstood in Christian history. Feminist thinkers have argued—and I agree—that there has been far too much emphasis in the Christian tradition on the giving up of self, and this has played a part in the subjugation or marginalization of women and others (cf. Valerie Saiving, "The Human Situation: A Feminine View," *Journal of Religion* 40 [1960]: 100–12; Elizabeth Johnson, *She Who Is: The Mystery of God in Feminist Theological Discourse* (New York: Crossroad, 1996), 61–65, and others.) What Rahner is speaking of here is the going out from, but not abandonment of, self into full encounter with another. For him there is always an original unity out of which the plurality of being arises and to which it returns—for all being. In succeeding chapters I will demonstrate that full encounter with others requires a healthy sense of self that is never abandoned or fused with the other but is shaped by and supported in relationship. The language of *kenosis,* while poetic and aesthetically pleasing, has proven dangerous to adequate understandings of selfhood and played a part in the confusion of sympathetic fusing with empathetic relation.

76. Rahner, *Theological Investigations,* vol. 4, 114; Duffy, *Dynamics,* 309–10.

77. Ibid., 225, 244. On the basis of his trinitarian thought, Rahner explicates his ontology of the symbol in the context of multiplicity. If we claim that God is a plural unity of one God known in three persons, we must take this into account when attempting a theological anthropology. This ontology of the symbol plays an important role in my constructive argument below.

78. Rahner, *Theological Investigations,* vol. 1, 158–63, 180–82.

79. Karl Rahner, *Theological Investigations,* vol. 5: *Later Writings,* trans. Karl Kruger (Baltimore: Helicon, 1966), 171–73.

80. Ibid., 178.

81. Ibid., 176–78.

82. Ibid., 177–84. Rahner's insistence on the once-and-only-once incarnation in Christ results in some inconsistency. He says that the offer of God is available to all creation but in trying to hold on to absolute uniqueness and finality ends up having to say that Jesus is not really like us in all respects. See Roger Haight, *Jesus, Symbol of God* (Maryknoll, N.Y.: Orbis Books, 1999), 432–35.

83. Johnson, *She Who Is,* 270.

84. Ibid., 234–40, 270.

85. See Bernard McGinn, "God as Eros: Metaphysical Foundations of Christian Mysticism," in *New Perspectives on Historical Theology. Essays in Memory of John Meyendorff,* ed. Bradley Nassif (Grand Rapids, Mich.:

Eerdmans, 1996), 189–209, for discussion of theological notions of God's love as *agape* and *eros* throughout Christian history.

86. Rita Nakashima Brock, *Journeys by Heart: A Christology of Erotic Power* (New York: Crossroad, 1988), 26.

87. Ibid., 11.

88. Ibid., 52, 105.

89. What precisely she means by metaphors of heart and erotic power is not clear. At times, these metaphors are interchanged, at others not. Heart can mean the self, or God's grace, or Winnicott's realm of potential space between selves. See her use of the terms on pages 17, 25, 35–37, 45, 52, 76.

90. Elisabeth Schüssler Fiorenza, *Jesus: Miriam's Child, Sophia's Prophet: Critical Issues in Feminist Christology* (New York: Continuum, 1995), 54.

91. Ibid., 51.

92. Susan Brooks Thistlethwaite, *Sex, Race and God. Christian Feminism in Black and White* (New York: Crossroad, 1989), 89–97, 107.

93. Hannah Arendt, *On Violence* (New York: Harcourt, Brace, & World, 1969), 64–65.

4. The Empathic, Relational God

1. In the late nineteenth century, see Edwin Hatch, *The Influence of Greek Ideas and Usages upon the Christian Church,* ed. A. M. Fairbairn (London: Williams and Norgate, 1891); in the late twentieth century, see, e.g., Richard A. Norris, *God and World in Early Christian Thought* (London: Adam & Charles Black, 1966); John J. O'Donnell, *Trinity and Temporality: The Christian Doctrine of God in the Light of Process Theology and the Theology of Hope* (New York: Oxford Univ. Press, 1983).

2. Norris, *God and World,* 32.

3. See Friedrich Schleiermacher, *The Christian Faith,* ed. H. R. Mackintosh and J. S. Stewart (Edinburgh: T. & T. Clark, 1989), § 52. The concept of unchangeability functions to ensure that "no religious emotion shall be so interpreted, and no statement about God so understood, as to make it necessary to assume an alteration in God of any kind."

4. Aristotle, *Metaphysics,* book XII, chap. 7, in *Introduction to Aristotle,* ed. Richard McKeon (New York: Random House, 1947).

5. Frederick Copleston, *A History of Philosophy,* vol. 1 (New York: Image, 1993), 209.

6. Ibid., 329–30.

7. Abraham Heschel, *The Prophets: An Introduction,* vol. 2 (New York:

Harper Torchbooks, 1962), 27–47.

8. John M. Rist, *Stoic Philosophy* (London: Cambridge Univ. Press, 1969), 25–26; also Rist, "The Stoic Concept of Detachment," in *The Stoics*, ed. J. M. Rist (Berkeley: Univ. of California Press, 1978), 259–68.

9. Heschel, *The Prophets*, vol. 2, 35, citing Wilhelm Dilthey *Gesammelte Schriften*, vol. 2 (Leipzig: B. G. Teubner, 1914), 47. The Stoic legacy lives on in Clement of Alexandria, Origen, Gregory of Nyssa, Tertullian, Ambrose, Jerome, and Augustine.

10. Clement of Alexandria, *The Stromata, or Miscellanies*, The Ante-Nicene Fathers: Writings of the Fathers down to A.D. 325, vol. 2, ed. Alexander Roberts and James Donaldson (Grand Rapids, Mich.: Eerdmans, 1978).

11. Heschel, *The Prophets*, vol. 2, 35. Immanuel Kant, *Critique of Judgment*, trans. Werner Pluhar (Indianapolis: Hackett, 1987), par. 29.

12. Heschel, *The Prophets*, vol. 2, 38–39.

13. This and the immediately following insights are those of Peter C. Hodgson, *Jesus—Word and Presence* (Philadelphia: Fortress Press, 1971), 168–69, 196–99. Emphasis in scriptural quotations is mine.

14. Karl Barth, *Church Dogmatics*, vol. 4, "The Doctrine of Reconciliation," Part 2, ed. G. W. Bromiley and T. F. Torrance (Edinburgh: T. & T. Clark, 1958), 185–87.

15. Heschel, *The Prophets*, vol. 2, 28–29.

16. Anselm, *Proslogium*, 6, 7 (1945), *Monologion and Proslogium with the Replies of Gaunilo and Anselm*, trans. Thomas Williams (Indianapolis: Hackett, 1995), 11, 13.

17. Thomas Aquinas, *Summa Theologiae* Ia, q. 20, art. 1, obj. 1, Blackfriars ed. (New York: McGraw-Hill, 1964).

18. Ibid., art. 2, Answer.

19. Ibid., q. 21, art. 3, Answer.

20. Marcel Sarot, *God, Possibility and Corporeality: Studies in Philosophical Theology*, ed. Adriaanse and Vincent Brümmer (Kampen, the Netherlands: Kok Pharos, 1992), 12–16.

21. See ibid., for an excellent overview of the issues.

22. Jürgen Moltmann, *The Crucified God: The Cross of Christ as the Foundation and Criticism of Christian Theology*, trans. R. A. Wilson and John Bowden (New York: Harper & Row, 1973), 222, 230. Also idem, "The Crucified God and the Apathetic Man," *The Experiment Hope*, ed. and trans. Douglas Meeks (Philadelphia: Fortress Press, 1975).

23. Alfred North Whitehead, *Process and Reality: An Essay in Cosmology* (New York: Macmillan, 1929), 532.

24. David Ray Griffin, *A Process Christology* (Philadelphia: Westminster, 1973), 189.

25. Charles Hartshorne, *The Divine Relativity: A Social Conception of God* (New Haven: Yale Univ. Press,1948), 1–50.

26. Griffin, *Process Christology*, 174.

27. Ibid., 191.

28. This is true perhaps because, in the original system of process philosophy as developed by Whitehead, the concept of God was an "add-on" to the cosmology. This aspect of the system has received criticism in theological circles, since it appears that God was a necessary addition, inserted into the system to make it work.

29. Marjorie H. Suchocki, *God-Christ-Church: A Practical Guide to Process Theology* (New York: Crossroad, 1995), 90–93.

30. Griffin, *Process Christology*, 216–18.

31. Paul Knitter also questions whether uniqueness is a necessary aspect of process christology. See *No Other Name? A Critical Survey of Christian Attitudes toward the World Religions,* American Society of Missiology 7 (Maryknoll, N.Y.: Orbis Books, 1985), 189–92.

32. Griffin, *Process Christology*, 222.

33. David Ray Griffin, "Creation Out of Chaos and the Problem of Evil," *Encountering Evil: Live Options in Theodicy,* ed. Stephen T. Davis (Atlanta: John Knox, 1981), 112–13.

34. *Adv. Her.* 3:18-19 and *Adv. Her.* 5:1.1. in *The Apostolic Fathers with Justin Martyr and Irenaeus,* The Ante-Nicene Fathers: Writings of the Church to A.D. 325, vol. 1, ed. Alexander Roberts and James Donaldson. (Grand Rapids: Eerdmans, 1978).

35. "The Christic," in *The Heart of the Matter,* trans. Rene Hague (New York: Harcourt Brace Jovanovich, 1976), 90.

36. William M. Thompson, *Jesus, Lord and Savior: A Theopathic Christology and Soteriology* (New York: Paulist, 1980), 134.

37. Heschel, *Man Is Not Alone* (New York: Noonday, 1979 [1951]), 244.

38. Heschel, *The Prophets,* vol. 1, ix–xv.

39. Ibid., 144–50.

40. Heschel, *God in Search of Man* (New York: Noonday, 1983 [1955]), 259.

41. Heschel, *The Prophets,* vol. 2, 219; vol. 1, 9.

42. Ibid., vol. 2, 226–29.

43. Ibid., 89.

44. Ibid., 231, 99.

45. Ibid., 308–9.

46. Jürgen Moltmann, "The Crucified God and the Apathetic Man," 76.

47. Moltmann, *The Crucified God*, 270–71.

48. Thompson, *Jesus, Lord and Savior*, 136–38.

49. David S. Ariel, *What Do Jews Believe? The Spiritual Foundations of Judaism* (New York: Schocken, 1995), 34–37. It was primarily through Moses Maimonides that Judaism incorporated the Platonic and Aristotelian divine *apatheia*. Maimonides taught that the human idea of God is made up of projections of our own ideal qualities, a theme that was to reappear in Ludwig Feuerbach and Sigmund Freud. Maimonides' God was Absolute Transcendence, in contrast to the rabbinic God, who is both immanent and transcendent.

50. See E. P. Sanders, *Jesus and Judaism* (Philadelphia: Fortress Press, 1985).

51. The claim that the "Jews killed Jesus" has fueled Christian self-righteous justification of church- and government-sanctioned murder more than once in history. Marking the "Christ killers" for easy identification was not an innovation of Adolf Hitler's Nazi regime. It was first instituted by papal decree during the Middle Ages. Pope Innocent III in 1215 ordered Jews to wear yellow badges on their chests and cone-shaped hats (to symbolize their allegiance to the devil). Pogroms began not with Hitler but many centuries before, with the Christian crusaders' zeal to eradicate "heresy" in Europe. So it matters very much how we interpret the order to execute Jesus. See John Dominic Crossan, *Who Killed Jesus? Exploring the Roots of Anti-Semitism in the Gospel Story of the Death of Jesus* (San Francisco: Harper San Francisco, 1995).

52. Thompson, *Jesus, Lord and Savior*, 146.

53. Ibid., 140. Thompson describes God as "Pathos and Lord." I replace "Lord" with "Sovereignty," meaning supremacy of authority, to avoid as far as possible the negative implications of "lordship" language in relation to the divine. Sallie McFague, Elisabeth Schüssler Fiorenza, and others have shown that this kind of prose operates to re-inscribe kyriarchal structures of oppression that have operated throughout Christian history in ways antithetical to the message of Jesus Christ. See Sallie McFague, *Models of God: Theology for an Ecological, Nuclear Age* (Philadelphia: Fortress Press, 1987); and Elisabeth Schüssler Fiorenza, *Rhetoric and Ethic: The Politics of Biblical Studies* (Minneapolis: Fortress Press, 1999).

54. Edward Farley, *Divine Empathy: A Theology of God* (Minneapolis: Fortress Press, 1996). J. E. Barnhart ("Incarnation and Process Philosophy," *Religious Studies* 2 [1967] 225–32) offered an interpretation of incarnation as empathy. He described the empathic relation between Jesus and God as a "mutual adoption." In God there exists a "primordial will-to-experience-humanity," which accounts for this event. The thesis is

helpful, but Barnhart does not define empathy, nor does he explore how the interrelation occurs. The "belief that the everlasting God empathizes with lowly, creaturely man is what the disciples caught from the lowly Nazarene (230)." Apparently Barnhart did not see the significance of the Jewish tradition and scriptural record regarding God's intensely empathic involvement with humanity. He saw empathic involvement as a kind of contagion "caught from" Jesus through the incarnation. Like Farley, Barnhart passed over the finer points of empathic and other structures of participation and so offered a promising but undeveloped means for reinterpretation of the incarnation.

55. Farley, *Divine Empathy*, 295.
56. Ibid., xvi, 282, 283.
57. Ibid., 281–82.
58. Ibid., 256, 260.
59. Ibid., 282.
60. Ibid., 305 n.1.
61. Ibid., 296, 304–5.
62. Ibid., 311–12.
63. Elizabeth Johnson, *She Who Is: The Mystery of God in Feminist Theological Discourse* (New York: Crossroad, 1996), 232.

5. The Empathic, Relational Human

1. Daniel Stern, The *Interpersonal World of the Infant: A View from Psychoanalysis and Developmental Psychology* (New York: Basic Books, 1985), 4–11. Subsequent citations to this work will appear parenthetically in the text. Also idem, "The Infant's Subjective Experience of its Objects," in *Zeitschrift für Psychoanalytische Theorie und Praxis* 1997 (12): 8–21; idem, "The Relevance of Empirical Infant Research to Psychoanalytic Theory and Practice," *Clinical and Observational Psychoanalytic Research: Roots of a Controversy,* ed. Joseph Sandler and Anne-Marie Sandler, Psychoanalytic Monographs 5 (Madison, Conn.: International Universities, 2000), 73–90.

2. Alan Fogel, "Relational Narratives of the Prelinguistic Self," *The Self in Infancy: Theory and Research.* ed. Phillipe Rochat (Amsterdam, Netherlands: Elsevier Science, 1995), 117. Theorists advocating a fusion/separation model include Freudian thinkers and advocates of the Object Relations school of psychoanalysis.

3. Neurobiologist Antonio Damasio now describes the self in quite similar language. He speaks of the neurobiology of selfhood as a multiphasic reality, made up of a proto-self, emergent core conscious self, and

an autobiographical self. Antonio Damasio, *The Feeling of What Happens: Body and Emotion in the Making of Consciousness* (New York: Harcourt Brace, 1999).

4. Psychologist Robert Kegan appeals to Zen in explaining how it is that a noun or entity can also be a process: This is a "magic trick we can perform together right now. Make a fist. Now we shall make your fist disappear. Ready? Okay—open your hand. You see?—or rather you don't see—your fist is gone! . . . The so-called thing (a fist) can be made to 'disappear' because it is not only a thing; disguised as a noun, it is as much a process (the act of closing the hand)." *The Evolving Self. Problems and Process in Human Development* (Cambridge: Harvard Univ. Press, 1982), 8. This exercise is helpful in illuminating how it is that the "self" can be sensed as having a core structure and at the same time understood to be fluid.

5. Fogel, "Relational Narratives,"117.

6. Dale F. Hay, Alison Nash, Jan Pederson, "Responses of Six-Month Olds to the Distress of Their Peers," *Child Development* 52 (1981): 1071–75.

7. Nancy Eisenberg, *The Caring Child* (Cambridge, Mass.: Harvard Univ. Press, 1992), 143.

8. Nancey Murphy and George Ellis, *On The Moral Nature of the Universe: Theology, Cosmology, and Ethics* (Minneapolis: Fortress Press, 1996), 22–24.

9. See also Daniel Stern, Lynne Hofer, Wendy Haft, and John Dore, "Affect Attunement: The Sharing of Feeling States between Mother and Infant by Means of Inter-Modal Fluency," *Social Perception in Infants,* ed. Tiffany M. Field and Nathan A. Fox (Norwood, N.J.: Ablex, 1985), 249–68. This research explored how mental states are knowable between people. Here again, the unconscious nature of attunement is emphasized, in distinction from the cognitive steps involved in empathy. Both begin with a "feeling-what-has-been-perceived-in-the-other," but with "affect attunement, it is as if the route to empathy has been departed from" (263). The experience is of a fluid nature, unbroken but varied in intensity. It is not always a perfect process, being subject to over-, under-, and non-attunement. It functions as a mode of sharing, participation, joining-in that implies more a "communing with" than "communication of" (263–65).

10. Eisenberg, *The Caring Child,* 8–16.

11. See Fraser Reid and Susan Reed, "Cognitive Entrainment in Engineering Design Teams," *Small Group Research* 31 (2000): 354–82; Deborah Ancona and Chee Leong Chong, "Cycles and Synchrony: The Temporal Role of Context in Team Behavior," *Research on Managing Groups and Teams: Groups in Context,* vol. 2, ed. Ruth Wageman (Stamford, Conn.:

JAI, 1999) 33–48; Joseph E. McGrath, ed., *Time and Human Interaction: Toward a Social Psychology of Time* (New York; Guilford, 1986); and idem, *The Social Psychology of Time* (Newbury Park, Calif.: SAGE, 1988).

12. William S. Condon, "Communication and Empathy," *Empathy II*, ed. Joseph Lichtenberg, Melvin Bornstein, and Donald Silver (Hillsdale, N.J.: Analytic, 1984), 35–58.

13. William S. Condon and L. S. Sander, "Neonate Movement Is Synchronized with Adult Speech," *Science* 183 (1974): 99–101. One example of research will suffice to support the validity of Condon's argument. Harvard University researchers in a 1988 article reported that synchrony between mothers and their children can be observed and reliably rated. Using videotaped interactions, synchronous behaviors were examined. The study observed mothers with their own and with unfamiliar infants. Perceptible differences in interaction were noted between mother-child as opposed to mother-unrelated-child situations. Synchrony between mothers and their own children was significantly higher than in unrelated pairs. Frank J. Bernieri, J. Steven Reznick, and Robert Rosenthal, "Synchrony, Pseudosynchrony, and Dissynchrony: Measuring the Entrainment Process in Mother-Infant Interactions," *Journal of Personality and Social Psychology* 54 (1988): 243–53. See also Beatrice Beebe, Stanley Feldstein, Joseph Jaffe, Kathleen Mays, and Diane Alson, "Interpersonal Timing: The Application of an Adult Dialogue Model to Mother-Infant Vocal and Kinesic Interactions," *Social Perception in Infants*, 217–47.

Also, in his own research into how change occurs in psychotherapy, Stern has studied events that seem very like entrainment and attunement as I have described them. He calls these events "moments of meeting"—involving implicit knowing through intersubjective understandings of relationships—and "communicational alliances"—behaviors involving posture and gaze that signal rapport and therapeutic involvement. See Daniel Stern, "The Process of Therapeutic Change Involving Implicit Knowledge: Some Implications of Developmental Observations for Adult Psychotherapy," *Infant Mental Health Journal* 19 (1998): 300–308; Yves de Roten, Elisabeth Fivaz Despeursinge, Daniel Stern, Joeelle Darwish, and Antoinette Corboz Warnery, "Body and Gaze Formations and the Communicational Alliance in Couple-Therapist Triads," *Psychotherapy Research* 10 (2000): 30–46.

14. Condon, "Communication and Empathy," 46.

15. Additional evidence for entrainment comes from psychologists interested in hypnosis. Neurolinguistic Programming, or NLP, a technique of "enhanced communication" sometimes called hypnosis, is heavily dependent upon behavioral entrainment and attunement. Practitioners

are taught, among other techniques, smoothly to mirror posture, facial expression, tone of voice, etc. The approach has become quite popular among salespersons, for example, and is said to enhance rapport. This approach has grown out of the work of psychologists Richard Bandler and John Grinder. See chapter 6 for specific references.

16. Neil Agnew and John Brown, "The Rhythms of Reality: Entrainment Theory," *Canadian Psychology* 30 (1989): 198. Attribution in the text is to "Ayensu & Whitfield 1981, p.153" but unfortunately the full reference was omitted from the article's bibliography.

17. Condon, "Communication and Empathy," 37. Emphasis mine.

18. Lauren Wispé, "The Distinction between Sympathy and Empathy: To Call Forth a Concept, a Word Is Needed," *Journal of Personality and Social Psychology* 50 (1986): 316.

19. Edward Bradford Titchener, *A Beginner's Psychology* (New York: Macmillan, 1915), 198.

20. Changming Duan and Clara E. Hill, "The Current State of Empathy Research," *Journal of Counseling Psychology* 43 (1996): 261–74; Wispé, "The Distinction between Sympathy and Empathy," 314–316.

21. Gail S. Reed, "The Antithetical Meaning of the Term 'Empathy' in Psychoanalytic Discourse," *Empathy I*, eds. Joseph Lichtenberg, Melvin Bornstein, and Donald Silver (Hillsdale, N.J.: Analytic, 1984), 137–166.

22. Carl Rogers, "Empathic: An Unappreciated Way of Being," *The Counseling Psychologist* 5 (1975): 2–10. Heinz Kohut, *How Does Analysis Cure?* (Chicago: Univ. of Chicago Press, 1984), 66, 77.

23. Stanley Olinick, "A Critique of Empathy and Sympathy," *Empathy I*, 139.

24. Martin Hoffman, "Empathy, Its Development and Prosocial Implications," *Nebraska Symposium on Motivation, 1977*, vol. 25 (Lincoln, Neb.: Univ. of Nebraska Press, 1977), 169–217.

25. See, for example, Nancy Eisenberg and Paul Mussen, *The Roots of Prosocial Behavior in Children* (Cambridge: Cambridge Univ. Press, 1989), 130.

26. A. R. Hornblow, "The Study of Empathy," *New Zealand Psychologist* 9 (1980): 19–28.

27. Steven Levy, "Empathy and Psychoanalytic Technique," *Journal of the American Psychoanalytic Association* 33 (1986): 363–78.

28. Richard Restak, "Possible Neurophysiological Correlates of Empathy," *Empathy I*, 63–75.

29. Ross Buck and Benson Ginsburg, "Communicative Genes and the Evolution of Empathy," *Empathic Accuracy*, ed. William Ickes (New York: Guilford, 1997), 17.

30. Max Scheler, *The Nature of Sympathy*, trans. Peter Heath (Camden, Conn.: Archon Books, 1973), 246. Scheler's work was an attempt to do

something very like what I have done here. The philosopher was limited by the times in which he wrote, living as he did when Freud still reigned supreme in the world of psychoanalysis and developmental psychology was itself in its infancy.

31. See chap. 1 n.18.

32. M. Basch, "Developmental Psychology and Explanatory Theory in Psychoanalysis," *Annals of Psychoanalysis,* vol. 5 (New York: International Universities Press, 1977): 229–66.

33. Condon, "Communication and Empathy," 48, 52.

34. Agnew and Brown, "Rhythms of Reality," 198. In ancient times, Egyptian and Greek thinkers considered rhythm to be a dominant aspect of aesthetics, metaphysics, and psychology. The biological rhythm has been noted at least since Aristotle's time; and recently a new discipline has arisen, chronobiology, which studies these phenomena. Rhythmicity is basic to human perception, and is somehow tied to some speech impediments, reading difficulties, memory, even the neural activity of the human brain and life at the level of the atom. See Charles Elliott, "Rhythmic Phenomena—Why the Fascination?" James Evans and Manfred Clynes, eds., *Rhythm in Psychological, Linguistic, and Musical Processes* (Springfield, Ill.: Charles Thomas, 1986), 3–12.

35. Edward T. Hall, *The Dance of Life: The Other Dimension of Time* (New York: Doubleday, 1983), 178.

36. See Evans and Clynes, eds., *Rhythm;* also Robert W. Levenson and Anna M. Ruef, "Physiological Aspects of Emotional Knowledge and Rapport," Ickes, ed., *Empathic Accuracy,* 44–72.

37. M. Mirmiran, J. Kok, K. Boer, H. Wolf, "Perinatal Development of Human Circadian Rhythms: Role of the Foetal Biological Clock," *Neuroscience and Biobehavioral Reviews* 16 (1992): 371–78; David R. Weaver and Steven M. Reppert, "Direct in Utero Perception of Light by the Mammalian Fetus," *Developmental Brain Research* 47 (1989): 151–55.

38. David Abrams eloquently explores this reality from a philosophical standpoint in *The Spell of the Sensuous: Perception and Language in a More-than-Human World* (New York: Vintage Books, 1996). On the basis of phenomenology and Maurice Merleau-Ponty's philosophical speculation, Abrams seeks to demonstrate that humanity suffers from a loss of "our carnal, sensorial empathy with the living land" (69).

39. Nancy Eisenberg, *Altruistic Emotion, Cognition, and Behavior* (Hillside, N.J.: Lawrence Erlbaum, 1986).

40. Scott A. Boorman and Paul R. Levitt, *The Genetics of Altruism* (New York: Academic, 1980), glossary. I do not mean to imply that there is no

difference between altruism displayed by humans and the kinds of altruistic behavior found among other forms of life. It is clear that as we move from the realm of nonhuman nature to the human community, altruism becomes a larger, more sweeping concept with undeniably moral implications. See chapter 6.

41. Gerald S. Wilkinson, "Reciprocal Food Sharing in the Vampire Bat," *Nature* 308 (1984): 181–84. See also L. K. Denault and D. A. McFarlane, "Reciprocal Altruism between Male Vampire Bats, *Desmodus Rotundus*," *Animal Behavior* 49 (1995): 855–56.

42. This explanation is based on a construct borrowed from game theory, called "Tit-for-Tat." See Robert Wright, *The Moral Animal: Evolutionary Psychology and Everyday Life* (New York: Vintage Books, 1994), 191–209. See also Holmes Rolston III, *Genes, Genesis and God. Values and Their Origins in Natural and Human History* (Cambridge: Cambridge Univ. Press, 1999); Lyall Watson, *Dark Nature: A Natural History of Evil* (New York: Harper Perennial, 1995); and Matt Ridley, *The Origins of Virtue: Human Instincts and the Evolution of Cooperation* (New York: Penguin, 1996).

43. Ridley, *The Origins of Virtue*, 62–63.

44. Richard Dawkins, *The Selfish Gene* (Oxford: Oxford Univ. Press, 1976).

45. Watson, *Dark Nature*, 84–85; also J. W. Porter, "*Pseudorca* Stranding," *Oceans* 10 (1977): 8.

46. Watson, *Dark Nature*, 85.

47. Richard Dawkins, introduction to *The Evolution of Cooperation* by Robert Axelrod (New York: Basic Books, 1984). Richard Alexander also acknowledges the existence of true altruism and self-sacrificial behavior but insists that when it appears, it is always "an evolutionary mistake for the individual showing it." See Richard D. Alexander, *The Biology of Moral Systems* (New York: Aldine de Gruyter, 1987), 191. While insisting that altruism is purely a product of the genes, Alexander and others at the same time advocate that humans find ways to upend the selfish genetic imperative and strive to "expand the circle of sympathy for others" (George C. Williams, quoted in Rolston, *Genes, Genesis and God,* 264). Holmes Rolston, a philosopher of biology and religion, argues that the very fact that these advocates of genetic and biological reductionism insist on concern for others taking precedence over genetically programmed selfishness demonstrates a something-more at work in humanity: "Far from a killjoy reduction of ethics to nothing but biology, we have discovered that ethics is naturalized only at the start . . . afterward it is conceived and socialized

in culture. As it matures, we are left wondering whether it does not even move beyond, glimpsing universals. The genesis of ethics, especially in the genesis of generosity, distinctive to the human genius, continuing but exceeding the genesis in the genes, reveals transcendent powers come to expression point on Earth" (ibid., 291).

48. Marjorie H. Suchocki, *The Fall to Violence: Original Sin in Relational Theology* (New York: Continuum, 1995), 24–26.

49. Ibid., 36, 147.

50. Ibid., 41.

51. Karl Rahner, *Theological Investigations*, vol. 13: *Theology, Anthropology, Christology*, trans. David Bourke (New York: Seabury, 1975), 127. Translation from Mark Lloyd Taylor, *God Is Love: A Study in the Theology of Karl Rahner*, American Academy of Religion series 50 (Atlanta: Scholars, 1986), 67.

52. Phyllis Trible, *God and the Rhetoric of Sexuality*, Overtures to Biblical Theology 2 (Philadelphia: Fortress Press, 1978), 33.

53. Elizabeth A. Johnson, *She Who Is: The Mystery of God in Feminist Theological Discourse* (New York: Crossroad: 1992), 101–102; idem, *Consider Jesus: Waves of Renewal in Christology* (New York: Crossroad, 1997), 117.

54. N. Joseph Torchia, "*Sympatheia* in Basil of Caesarea's *Hexameron*: A Plotinian Hypothesis," *Journal of Early Christian Studies* 4 (1996), 359–78. Basil's notion of *sympatheia* was a teleological understanding of God's providence in ordering the universe and did not hold the deterministic inference of Stoic thought. The Stoics believed that the connection of all things through *sympatheia* meant it was possible to predict the future. Abraham Heschel distinguishes between the cosmic sympathy of Greek philosophy, particularly in Plotinus, and the Hebrew prophets. His major point is that Plotinian cosmic sympathy implies a passivity and moral neutrality that is unlike the prophets' response to God. Prophetic sympathy is an act of will, "a moral act, motivated by considerations for right and wrong." Abraham Heschel, *The Prophets*, vol. 2 (New York: Harper Torchbooks, 1962), 98. The prophets emphasized the transcendence of God and so, says Heschel, "sympathy is not inherent in [the human]" (98). We have seen in this chapter that this interpretation is in error. Sympathy is, in truth, constitutive of humanity.

6. The Incarnation of Participation

1.   The statement is Stephen Jay Gould's. I unfortunately cannot locate the exact source.

2. Douglas E. Ottati, *Jesus Christ and Christian Vision* (Louisville: Westminster John Knox, 1996 [1989]).

3. Ibid., 55–61. Much has been written on the role of narrative in theology and Scripture. Ottati relies heavily on Robert Alter's *The Art of Biblical Narrative* (New York: Basic, 1981).

4. Ibid., 66. Emphasis mine. Ottati quotes Schubert Ogden to show that what we have in the Gospels is not what Jesus said and did, but what he was heard to have said and seen to have done.

5. See chapter 4 for detailed discussion of these portions of the Gospel stories.

6. Kristen Renwick Monroe, *The Heart of Altruism: Perceptions of a Common Humanity* (Princeton: Princeton Univ. Press, 1996), 217. Parenthetical page referencing will be used to simplify notations.

7. This wonderful phrase is from a book by Thomas O'Meara on grace: *Loose in the World* (New York: Paulist, 1974).

8. Research documenting the impact of relationship on physical health has been published in a variety of journals. Interpersonal conflict has been shown to decrease the effectiveness of the immune system, increase blood pressure, and affect health in other negative ways. The positive impact of helping others has been found to be particularly important. In one Cornell University research project, 427 married women were followed for thirty years, and it was found that women who belonged to a volunteer organization were significantly less likely to suffer a major illness (36 percent, as opposed to 52 percent of those who did not perform some sort of volunteer service for others), and more likely to live longer. A 1988 study of about 3,000 people found that those who gave volunteer time at least once a week to help others were two and one-half times less likely to die during the 9–12 years of the study than those who never volunteered. See Janice Kiecolt-Glaser and Ronald Glaser, The Fourth International Congress of Behavioral Medicine, 1996; *Psychosomatic Medicine* 55 (1993): 395–409. Also P. Moen, D. Dempster-McClain, and R. Williams, "Successful Aging," in *American Journal of Sociology* 97 (1993): 1612–38; J. S. House, K. R. Landis, and D. Umberson, "Social Relationships and Health," *Science* 241 (1988): 540–545.

9. Karl Rahner, *Hearer of the Word: Laying the Foundation for a Philosophy of Religion,* trans. Joseph Donceel (New York: Continuum, 1994), 28.

10. Ibid., 120.

11. The masculine pronoun is used throughout in reference to the Hebrew prophets, since the tradition has it that the major prophets were men. Judges 4 (Deborah), 2 Kings 22 (Huldah), Nehemiah 6 (Noadiah), Isaiah 8 (Isaiah's wife) make reference to women as "prophetesses."

12. Heschel, *The Prophets*, vol. 1 (New York: Harper Torchbooks, 1962), 187.

13. Ibid., 126.

14. Ibid., 126–28.

15. The so-called "Little Apocalypse" of Matthew 25 is an obvious exception.

16. Heschel, *The Prophets*, vol. 1, 6–7.

17. Ibid., 5.

18. It is important to remember that sympathy is affective fusion, not a "becoming like" or taking on actual attributes of the other. It is inability to differentiate between one's own emotions and the other's, believing the other's to be one's own.

19. Justin Martyr, *Second Apology,* chap. 6 in Ante-Nicene Fathers: Writings of the Fathers Down to A.D. 325, ed. Alexander Roberts and James Donaldson (Grand Rapids, Mich.: Eerdmans, 1978).

20. See Origen, *Commentary on the Gospel according to John, Books 1–10*, The Fathers of the Church: A New Translation, vol. 80, trans. Ronald E. Heine (Washington, D.C.: Catholic Univ. of America Press, 1989); Thomas Aquinas, *Summa Theologiæ* Ia, Quest. 13, Blackfriars ed. (New York: McGraw-Hill, 1964).

21. Paul Tillich, *Theology of Culture* (London: Oxford Univ. Press, 1959), 53–67.

22. Karl Rahner, "The Theology of the Symbol," *Theological Investigations*, vol. 4, trans. Kevin Smyth (Baltimore: Helicon, 1966), 221–52; idem, "Behold This Heart! Preliminaries to a Theology of Devotion to the Sacred Heart," *Theological Investigations,* vol. 3, trans. Karl Kruger and Boniface Kruger (Baltimore: Helicon, 1967), 321–52. There is a distinct similarity between Rahner's reflections of the concept of "heart" and those of Douglas Ottati and Rita Nakashima Brock. In the essay "Behold this Heart!" Rahner speaks of what he called primordial words, those that make a reality present to us (322). A primordial word is one that cannot be defined through using better-known words or phrases, understood by Rahner as what he will in a later essay refer to as the symbol. With his interest being explication of the Roman Catholic devotion to the Sacred Heart of Jesus, he explains that "heart" is an archetypal concept that appears in many cultures, to describe the innermost core of the human: the "heart-centre" is the place where body, soul, and spirit are anchored, so to speak (332). The physiological referent of the word is derivative, but in this sense the word is an "Ursymbol" (327). Rahner says that the human person is composed of attitudes as well as attributes. Within the plurality of attitudes there is "a unity of form which merges the attitudes . . . into one structured, meaningful whole." Others react to our attributes insofar as the attributes have under-

gone "a quite definite existential characterization" in the attitudes (335). In other words, like Ottati, Rahner is saying that you know who I am primarily through my actions, which are formed by my attitudes and symbolized as my heart (336). Extending this to reflect Rahner's understanding of symbols, my "heart" is the means by which who-I-am is made present to the world. And so to practice devotion to the Sacred Heart of Jesus is to reflect upon the attitudes and attributes that made Jesus who he was and is.

Brock's conception of heart in *Journeys by Heart: A Christology of Erotic Power* (New York: Crossroad, 1988) has several meanings. When she interprets "heart" in terms of Object Relations theorist D. W. Winnicott's "Third Space," and as equivalent to the self, she is closest to Rahner's thought. However, the Third Space of potentiality is not equivalent to the self for Winnicott, and so there is some confusion of terms in her work. Theological caution is in order, as Winnicott's thesis is somewhat problematic, in part because he sees the transition from undifferentiation into selfhood as a kind of fall out of the garden of perfect existence into the reality of life. As one reads his work, one is left with the sense that the becoming of a self is a tragedy. For Winnicott, the Third Space between "me" and "not-me" is about potentiality, and is an illusion. It functions to buffer the True Self from the real world, providing a sort of portable Garden of Eden to which we periodically retreat. It is at the same time the *illusory* space within which we encounter others, and out of which creativity emerges. See my "Theology and Winnicott's Object Relations Theory: A Conversation," *Journal of Psychology and Theology* 27 (1999): 3–19, for a more complete assessment of this theme's place within theological reflection. When Brock speaks of heart as God's grace, there is an implicit tendency to equate the human self with divine grace.

23. The best attempt to explore the power of symbol in Rahner's christology is a work that he himself gave high praise, *Logos-Symbol in the Christology of Karl Rahner* by Joseph H. P. Wong (Rome: Libreria Ateneo Salesiano, 1984). In the foreword to this work, Rahner said, "he arrives at an appreciation of my christology which is original on the one hand and which on the other synthesizes many of the insights which I myself up to this time have left unconnected. . . .Thus Fr. Wong also allows the presuppositions of my christology to become more clearly recognizable than they are in my own explicitly dogmatic christological essays in *Theological Investigations*."

Wong argues that Rahner's christological reflections involve both a "from above" and "from below" approach that can be harmonized through the concept of Logos-Symbol. Rahner's own short article on the ontology of the symbol in theology is, he says, a compendium of Rahner's philo-sophical writings. According to Wong, understandings of Rahner's theolo-gy of incarnation have been deficient, a problem that stems from the fail-ure to take into account Rahner's Ignatian background. As a Jesuit priest, Rahner was first and foremost a mystic: he was steeped in the tradition of meditation on the earthly life and death of Jesus as prescribed in *The Spiritual Exercises of St. Ignatius*. A brief example from this sixteenth-cen-tury work suffices to underscore the influence these meditations had on Rahner. From the meditations for the fourth week of practice, on "Contemplation to Attain Divine Love," Ignatius wrote: "Consider how God dwells in His creatures: in the elements, giving them being; in the plants, giving them life; in the animals, giving them sensation; in men, giv-ing them understanding. So He dwells in me . . . consider how God works and labors for me in all created things." *The Spiritual Exercises of St, Ignatius*, trans. Anthony Mottola (Garden City, N.Y.: Image, 1964), 104.

24. Rahner, "Theology of the Symbol," 225.

25. Tillich, *Theology of Culture*, 53–67. For Tillich, it is only in and through symbols that humanity encounters the divine ground of all that is. Even "God" and "Christ" are symbols of the truths revealed in Christianity. Language is the means by which we humans are able to tran-scend our environment, and the symbolic character of language gives us access to the divine in a unique way. Theology's task is not to speak of God; it is rather to interpret religious symbols. This means indicating pos-sibilities inherent in the use of symbols, pointing out dangerous errors or healing possibilities embedded within the symbols of a religious tradition. The truth of symbols is tied to the truth of that which they purport to reveal: a symbol is true when that which it reveals is true revelation. All symbols function to open us up to some greater reality and meaning, are an outgrowth of the cultural or religious unconscious, and can cease to function as symbols when they are not responsive to changing society. Religious symbols perform a mediating role between humanity and God. Through symbols, and only through them, we are able to participate in the divine ground. God is revealed to us, and we are healed via this par-ticipation. This understanding of *symbol* is very close to the word *sacra-ment*, as an "outward and visible sign of inward and spiritual grace." Anything can function as a religious symbol, and so all of creation is potentially sacramental means of revelation. Jesus as the Christ functions as a symbol in Christianity. Through his suffering and death, Jesus of Nazareth became the ultimate symbol, transparent to the divine ground from which he, unlike the rest of humanity, was not estranged.

26. Rahner, "Theology of the Symbol," 244; also Wong, *Logos-Symbol*, 32.

27. Taylor, *God Is Love: A Study in the Theology of Karl Rahner* (Atlanta, Ga.: Scholars, 1986), 172–74. James J. Buckley argues that the ontology of symbol is incomplete because Rahner's concept of the self is incomplete, having adequacy as a synchronic concept but not as a diachronic one. Filtered through the lens used here, I believe that Rahner's notion of the self as symbolic succeeds not only descriptively but across time in terms of human development as well. See Buckley's "On Being a Symbol: An Appraisal of Karl Rahner," *Theological Studies* 40 (1979): 453–73.

28. Rahner, *Theological Investigations*, vol. 4, 70.

29. S.v.*Webster's II New Riverside University Dictionary.*

30. Rahner uses this phrase in his explanatory footnotes for the essay on theology of symbols, where he says that moments of a being are expressions of it. *Theology of the Symbol*, 226. See Wong, *Logos-Symbol*, 76.

31. Rahner, *T"Theology of the Symbol,"* 226.

32. Ibid., 234.

33. Alfred Margulies, *The Empathic Imagination* (New York: W. W. Norton, 1989), xii.

34. Rahner, "Theology of the Symbol," 230.

35. Rahner, *Theological Investigations,* vol. 5, trans. Karl Kruger (Baltimore: Helicon, 1966), 173.

36. Rahner, *Foundations of Christian Faith*, trans. William Dych (New York: Seabury, 1978), 304.

37. Rahner, "Theology of the Symbol," 238.

38. Ibid., 115, 244.

39. Rahner, "Theology of the Symbol," 239.

40. See, for example, Roger Haight, *Jesus, Symbol of God* (Maryknoll, N.Y.: Orbis Books, 1999), 432–33. Haight does not grapple with the implications of Rahner's theology of symbol for a doctrine of incarnation, even though he understands his work to be in the tradition of Rahner, among others. His own understanding of symbol is more like Tillich's than Rahner's, from an anthropological standpoint. See his pp. 196–212.

41. Rahner's term for the direction toward which human love is pulled is *Woraufhin,* sometimes translated as horizon or goal. I think the intent is more kinetic. The human is always in motion toward the divine, and so God is that toward which we are inclined, ever moving upward in transcending the self through participation. Regarding love, Rahner argues that God is love, and the most fundamental of human acts is the act of love. For him, love is the giving of self and is, I think, not too divergent in meaning from what I have identified here as participation. But what I am speaking of here is something prior to love, the innate human capacity for relating to others that makes possible the

development of love. Further, the word love has unfortunately lost meaning as a powerful symbol for divine-human relation. This is so in large part due to the American cultural equation of love with sexual intercourse and infatuation. For these reasons I find it beneficial to understand Rahner's concept of love in terms of the capacity for participation.

42. Taylor, *God Is Love*,177.

43. Farley, see chapter 4 above.

44. Lucinda Stark Huffaker, *Creative Dwelling: Empathy and Clarity in God and Self* (Atlanta: Scholars, 1998), 45–46.

45. Ibid., 148.

46. See Meyendorff's *Christ in Eastern Christian Thought* (Washington, D.C.: Corpus, 1969) on *synergeía* in Gregory Palamas.

47. Rahner, "Theology of the Symbol," 239.

48. Haight, *Jesus, Symbol of God,* 440.

49. J. N. D. Kelly, *Early Christian Doctrines,* 2nd ed. (San Francisco: Harper and Row, 1978), 298.

50. Huffaker, *Creative Dwelling,* 85.

51. Ibid., 101.

52. Dietrich Bonhoeffer, *A Testament to Freedom: The Essential Writings of Dietrich Bonhoeffer,* ed. by Geffrey B. Kelly and F. Burton Nelson (San Francisco: Harper Collins, 1995), 511.

53. Heschel, *The Prophets,* vol. 2, 11.

54. Daniel Stern, *The Interpersonal World of the Infant: A View from Psychoanalysis and Developmental Psychology* (New York: Basic, 1985), 83.

55. Paul Plass, "Transcendent Time and Eternity in Gregory of Nyssa," *Vigiliae Christianae* 34 (1980), 186.

56. Elizabeth A. Johnson, *She Who Is: The Mystery of God in Feminist Theological Discourse* (New York: Crossroad, 1996), 232.

57. See Sallie McFague, *Super, Natural Christians: How We Should Love Nature* (Minneapolis: Fortress Press, 1997), for an exploration of this distinction.

58. Hebrews 2:10; 12:2.

59. Richard R. Niebuhr, "Archēgos: An Essay on the Relation between the Biblical Jesus Christ and the Present-Day Reader," in *Christian History and Interpretation: Studies Presented to John Knox,* ed. W. R. Farmer, C. F. D. Moule, R. R. Niebuhr (Cambridge: Cambridge Univ. Press, 1967), 96, 93.

60. Rahner, *Foundations of Christian Faith,* 287.

7. Participation in Good and Evil

1. "Conversation as Sacrament: Toward a Hermeneutic of Sympathy," Paper presented to Philosophy and Religion Section, American Academy

of Religion, Southeastern Region, Knoxville, Tenn.: March 21, 1998.

2. Stephen Crites, "The Narrative Quality of Experience," in *Journal of the American Academy of Religion* 39 (1971), 291.

3. Alistair McIntyre, *After Virtue: A Study in Moral Theory*, 2nd ed. (Notre Dame: Univ. of Notre Dame Press, 1984), 211–12.

4. Samuel P. Oliner and Pearl Oliner, *The Altruistic Personality: Rescuers of Jews in Nazi Europe* (New York: Free Press, 1988), 376 n.11.

5. Susan Brooks Thistlethwaite, *Sex, Race and God: Christian Feminism in Black and White* (New York: Crossroad, 1989).

6. See my "Teaching and Self-Formation: Why the Ignoble 'Intro to World Religions' Really Matters," *Teaching Theology and Religion* 4 (2001): 15–22, for methods of modeling and teaching empathy in the classroom.

7. Harry B. Aronson, *Love and Sympathy in Theravada Buddhism* (Delhi, India: Motilal Banarsidass, 1980), 3. Etymologically, the term derives from one meaning "to vibrate towards" (98 n.1).

8. The Four Noble Truths are: all of life is suffering; suffering is caused by grasping after permanence; suffering stops when grasping ceases; grasping is overcome by following the Eightfold Path of right outlook, right resolve or intent, right speech, right action, right livelihood, right effort, right mindfulness, right meditation. See Peter Harvey, *An Introduction to Buddhism: Teachings, History and Practices* (Cambridge: Cambridge Univ. Press, 1990).

9. From the Pali Canon quoted in Aronson, *Love and Sympathy*, 63–64. See Thich Nhat Hanh's *Teachings on Love* (Berkeley, Calif.: Parallax Press, 1998) for an excellent interpretation of the Four Immeasurable Minds for the Western lay practitioner.

10. Aronson, *Love and Sympathy*, 88.

11. Thich Nhat Hanh, *Teachings on Love*, 4–5.

12. Aronson, *Love and Sympathy*, 65.

13. Buddhagosa's *The Path of Purification* was the first summary of Theravada doctrine. Aronson, *Love and Sympathy*, 106, n.10.

14. Thich Nhat Hanh, *Teachings on Love*, 8–9.

15. A cursory look at the burgeoning corpus of popular literature on Buddhism revealed that instruction in the so-called "Loving Kindness" meditation can quite easily be found. See, for example, *The Art of Happiness: A Handbook for Living* by His Holiness the Dalai Lama and Howard C. Cutler (San Francisco: Riverhead Books, 1999); also Christine Longaker, *Facing Death and Finding Hope: A Guide to the Emotional and Spiritual Care of the Dying* (New York: Doubleday, 1998). The best and most complete treatment that I have found is Thich Nhat Hanh's *Teachings on Love*.

16. See Wendy Farley, *Tragic Vision and Divine Compassion: A Contemporary Theodicy* (Louisville: Westminster John Knox, 1990), for a theodicy of God as compassionate love.

17. This idea appears in psychoanalytic, philosophical, and theological speculation. The Freudian paradigm with its emphasis on drives and sexuality is one example. Edward Farley, *Divine Empathy: A Theology of God* (Minneapolis: Fortress Press, 1996), describes the human in these terms as well. It is possible to argue philosophically and biologically that the core self can never be *directly* experienced by another self. But in speaking of human development this argument has little or no practical value. It has contributed to erroneous ideas of human interpersonal experience. For current theories of selfhood from the neurobiological perspective, see Antonio Damasio, *The Feeling of What Happens: Body and Emotion in the Making of Consciousness* (New York: Harcourt, Brace, 1999).

18. Heinz Kohut, "Narcissism and Narcissistic Rage," *The Psychoanalytic Study of the Child* 27 (New York: Quadrangle, 1972).

19. Peter C. Hodgson, *Winds of the Spirit: A Constructive Christian Theology* (Louisville: Westminster John Knox, 1994), 217.

20. Elisabeth Schüssler Fiorenza, *Jesus: Miriam's Child, Sophia's Prophet: Critical Issues in Feminist Christology* (New York: Continuum, 1995), 51.

21. Hannah Arendt, *On Violence* (New York: Harcourt, Brace, and World, 1969).

22. See works by Richard Bandler and John Grinder, *Trance-Formations: Neurolinguistic Programming and the Structure of Hypnosis* (Moab, Utah: Real People Press, 1981); and idem, *The Structure of Magic: A Book about Language and Therapy* (Science and Behavior Books, 1990). Also by Richard Bandler, *Reframing: Neurolinguistic Programming and the Transformation of Meaning* (Moab, Utah: Real People Press, 1989). One popularized version of NLP is Michael Brooks, *Instant Rapport* (New York: Warner Books, 1989). This is the book jacket referred to in the text.

23. Friedrich Schleiermacher, *The Christian Faith*, ed. H. R. Mackintosh and J. S. Stewart (Edinburgh: T.&T. Clark, 1989), § 82.

24. Hodgson, *Winds of the Spirit*, 290.

25. Daniel Goldhagen, *Hitler's Willing Executioners: Ordinary Germans and the Holocaust* (New York: Vintage Books, 1997), 8–9.

26. Robert P. Ericksen and Susannah Heschel, eds., *Betrayal: German Churches and the Holocaust* (Minneapolis: Fortress Press, 1999). See also the controversial book by John Cornwell, *Hitler's Pope: The Secret History of Pius XII* (New York: Penguin Books, 1999).

INDEX

193